BEYOND THE MARKET AND STATE

For my sisters Sandy, Elene and their children who never knew the benefits of a universal welfare state.

Beyond the Market and State

Social enterprises and civil democracy in a welfare society

VICTOR A. PESTOFF
The Program on Politics, Economics and Organization
Södertörns högskola
Stockholm, Sweden

Ashgate

Aldershot • Brookfield USA • Singapore • Sydney

Published by
Ashgate Publishing Company
Gower House
Croft Road
Aldershot, Hants
GU11 3HR
England

Ashgate Publishing Company
Old Post Road
Brookfield
Vermont 05036
USA

Ashgate website:http://www.ashgate.com

Reprinted 1999

British Library Cataloguing in Publication Data
Pestoff, Victor A.
Beyond the market and state:social enterprises and civil democracy in a welfare state
1. Welfare State
I. Title
361.6'5

Library of Congress Catalog Card Number: 98-72797

ISBN 1 84014 575 7

Printed in Great Britain by Biddles Limited,
Guildford and King's Lynn

Summary Table of Contents

Table of Contents

List of Figures and Tables

Acknowledgments

A great many people have helped me formulate the arguments in this book both through their writings and discussion, but unfortunately only a few can be mentioned here. In particular, I would like to thank my Swedish colleagues Drs Yohanan Stryjan, Brigitta Wadell, Ingela Wahlgren and Professor Solveig Wikström, as well as Professors Carlo Borzaga, John Campbell, Jerzy Hausner, Lev Jakobson, Hans Keman, Ove-Kai Pedersen, John D. Stephens and Isabel Vidal.

The Swedish Work Environment Fund (AMFO), now the Swedish Council for Research on Work Life (SCRWL) generously supported the field work of the Swedish Project on Work Environment and Cooperative Social Services (WECSS) during 1992 - 1996. Without this support most of the arguments presented herein would lack a systematic factual base.

I was assisted in the planning and field work of the WECSS Project by *fil.lic.* Liliana Gullström (Anna Holm) and *fil.kand.* Gustav Onn, and by Ms. Rebecka Pestoff in the preparation of the manuscript.

My colleagues at *Södertörns högskola*, Stockholm's newly established Baltic Sea university, granted me a leave of absence in the Spring of 1998, which made possible the completion of it. I am also grateful for the Japanese interest in this topic and in particular to Professor Akio Fujita at the Faculty of Economics, Kanazawa University, for providing a congenial environment for revising the book.

1. Social Enterprises and Civil Democracy

In March of 1998 Mr. Frank Field, the Minister for Welfare Reform, and the Prime Minister, Tony Blair, presented the British Labour Government's Green Paper on the "New Contract for Welfare" (Minister of Welfare Reform, 1998). It proposes comprehensive reforms of the British universal welfare state and outlines the principles for revamping it completely by the year 2020. The new system will be built around work and security. These sweeping reforms are motivated by profound economic, political and social changes in British society since Sir Beveridge first initiated a universal welfare state 50 years ago. The welfare system has been reformed repeatedly since then, but it has not kept pace with changes in society. Britain needs a system designed to meet the changing needs of each generation, and solve today's problems, not yesterday's.

These proposals neither intend to dismantle the welfare state, leaving only a low-grade safety-net for the destitute; nor to keep it in tact and increasingly out of tune with changing needs. Rather, a third way is proposed for re-building and modernizing the welfare state in the next century. The "contract" proposed between the citizens and state is based on the idea of "stakeholder democracy", where rights are matched by responsibilities, which means work for those who can and security for those who cannot work. The Green Paper identifies four stages of development in welfare in Britain: the poor laws to stop outright destitution; the beginning of the welfare state to alleviate poverty, the current proposals for preventing poverty and a future stage of promoting opportunity and developing potential. In a similar vein, Mr. T. Blair also proposed a "New Way for the Left in Europe" (*Dagens Nyheter* & *The Independent*, 9 April, 1998).

The Swedish welfare state is nearly 50 years old and it has also been subject to growing criticism for many years, permitting both its critics and adherents speak of the crisis of the welfare state. The origins of this crisis include ideological, political, financial, economic and demographic trends. Each of these five trends challenges the future of the welfare state as we know it in Sweden; and contributes to the urgency of finding new collective solutions to and developing new models for providing personal social services. Moreover, both political and financial constraints on the welfare state in the final decade of the 20th Century, have rapidly changed the relationship between the state and Swedish citizens. Privatization, the "Freedom of Choice Revolution", brought about by radical reorientation of politics during the neo-liberal Bildt coalition government (1991-94); and the subsequent austerity policy pursued by the social democratic governments (1994-?) have already resulted in sweeping changes in the Swedish welfare state.

Demographic changes alone, both in Sweden and most other European Union countries, pose an urgent challenge to the welfare state. The growing ranks of pensioners who live longer and make more demands for social and medical services as they age and become frail have been called a "ticking financial bomb". The baby-boom generation of the 1940s poses a particular problem; their approaching retirement will sharply decrease the ratio of active persons on the labor market to those not active. Reductions in public spending combined with increasing demand for services mean that citizens are beginning to look for other, often private for-profit, solutions to their needs of today and tomorrow, including private health insurance to supplement the amount not covered by public insurance. This further undermines the legitimacy of the universal welfare state based on tax financing.

Given this crisis plus Sweden's recent membership in the European Union and eventual membership in the European Monitory Union, we are led to ask whether the welfare state can survive, and whether it is possible any longer to have a universal welfare state in a single country? The "New Contract for Welfare" argues that it is both possible to reform and develop the welfare state in Britain. The evidence and arguments provided in this book also suggest that the answer to both these questions can be affirmative, if ways and means can be found for transforming the Swedish welfare state into a welfare society in the New Millennium. However, rather than the British emphasis on work and security, we propose the development of an organizational model for promoting greater worker participation in the provision of social services and greater citizen participation in the production of the social services they demand, i.e., social enterprises and civil democracy.

The model proposed here for transforming welfare state into a welfare society has several benefits over a residual model and/or the current universal welfare state. The principal benefits of the proposed model are that it can: improve the work environment of the women who provide social services, while at the same time increasing their level of co-determination;

empower citizens in their capacity as co-producers; and thus help to transform the welfare state into a welfare society. Such changes will guarantee that all or most citizens have a viable stake in the survival of publicly financed welfare services and the development of a welfare society in the New Millennium.

This chapter examines the politics of the welfare state and various models or types of welfare states, including a voluntary welfare state first introduced by Titmuss in 1958, but largely forgotten since then. We also discuss the two central concepts of the Swedish project on Work Environment and Cooperative Social Services, (WECSS)[1], social enterprises and civil democracy. It is necessary to understand these concepts in order to appreciate their contribution to the enrichment of work life, the improvement of the work environment, the empowerment of citizens as co-producers; and their joint contribution to the rejuvenation of the welfare state and its transformation into a welfare society. Social enterprises are discussed at greater length in Section 1.C, while civil democracy is defined in Section 1.D.

The introductory chapter is followed by several chapters which discuss other concepts related to social enterprises and civil democracy, including such topics as civil society, the third sector, shifts in the welfare mix, a participatory state, enduring social services, citizens as co-producers, multi-stakeholder organizations, social accounting, the psychosocial work environment, etc. It is necessary to discuss all these concepts at greater length as we propose to introduce a new model for providing personal social welfare services in Sweden, one primarily based on cooperative self-management and citizens as co-producers. This new model is, however, not presented as an alternative that can or will replace the public or municipal provision of personal social services in the short run, but rather a complement to the existing public provision within a greatly reformed universal welfare society. Thus, we do not want to replace the universal welfare state nor tax financed social services with a residual welfare state nor minimal "social safety net" normally promoted by neo-liberals. Rather we propose that it should be transformed into a welfare society based on greater citizen participation.

---

[1] Called *Arvbetsmiljö och social service i kooperativ* regi in Swedish. The WECSS Project was financed by the Swedish Work Environment Fund between 1992 - 1996. The SWEF has now changed its name to the Swedish Council for Research on Work Life.

Our model gains inspiration from the Scandinavian negotiated economy, which comprises an alternative both to the neo-liberal and the planned economy models for organizing society (Nielsen & Pedersen, 1989b). We also want to examine our ideas in light of hard facts, thus extensive empirical materials have been collected about work environment in social enterprises and citizens as co-producers. Some of the main empirical materials of the WECSS Project are presented briefly in the second part of this book. They permits us to test our ideas about the development of a voluntary based welfare state and see whether they comprise a coherent model for a new participatory welfare society in the New Millennium. We maintain, of course, that our results show that they do.

1.A The Politics of the Welfare State

Aside from the need for change to meet the changing needs of citizens and generations and its own shortcomings, one additional reason for the debate on the welfare state is the growing internationalization of Sweden, the Swedish economy and society. Swedish membership in the European Union, not only serves to accentuate this process, but also to dramatize it. A loss in power for the nation-state and a transfer of power upwards and downwards changes one of the main parameters of the welfare state, namely being able to decide about the welfare of those persons or citizens living within the national boundaries of a given country (Hirsh & Thompson, 1996).

Internationalization, however, has quite different implications for the major social actors. In spite of worker and trade union internationalism, the nation-state remains the most significant level for the promotion of labor's interests (Streeck, 1991; Giddens, 1994 & 1996). The universal welfare state is/was primarily a national project, as well as a social democratic project (Esping-Andersen, 1990). The importance of the nation-state is decreasing more rapidly for capital than labor. The globalization of commerce has proceeded farther than in most other areas or segments of society. Given the nature of the European Community, European Union and the European Monetary Union, it comes as no surprise that business has taken the forefront of internationalization. Swedish business is clearly a major actor in the trend toward internationalization. Swedish business is the most concentrated and probably one of the most internationally integrated in all of Europe.

One measure of economic concentration and internationalization is found in the number of firms each country has among the 500 largest firms in Europe. In absolute terms Sweden ranks fourth (after the United Kingdom, W. Germany and France), while in *per capita* terms she come second, just after Switzerland (Pestoff, 1990; Pestoff, 1995b). In 1965 two-thirds of the staff of Swedish multi-national companies was employed at home, while one-third was employed abroad. In the late 1980s more than half of the employees of Sweden's 30 largest manufactures were employed outside Swedish borders (Porter, *et al.*, 1991). Today, Swedish multi-national firms employ 39 per cent of their staff in Sweden and 61 per cent abroad (Ben Habib, H. & F. Andersson, *Dagens Nyheter,* 22 May, 1997). Eleven of the 25 firms with the greatest sales on the Stockholm Stock Market had more than two-thirds of their employees abroad and seventeen of them had three-fourths or more of their sales abroad (Selander, *Svenska Dagbladet,* 17 May, 1997, p. NL 1). Thus, Swedish business is truly on the cutting edge of international integration.

Swedish business also began to play a much more active role in domestic politics in the 1970s and participated energetically in the Swedish political debate in recent decades (Pestoff, 1995b). Business interest associations spent twice as much annually as all the parliamentary parties taken together on the formation of opinion in the recent election years of 1988, 1991 (Pestoff, 1995b) and again in 1994. Later, during the 1994 referendum on membership in the European Union Swedish business interests spent more than ten times as much in favor of EU membership as all the groups opposing it (Premfors, *Dagens Nyheter*, 17/11-94).

In the 1980s and 1990s the Confederation of Swedish Employers, SAF, vigorously debated the future of the welfare state. Its campaigns were designed to delegitimize the universal welfare state, by calling into question its efficiency, fairness and financing. Moreover, Swedish firms' growing concentration and internationalization, together with Swedish membership in the European Union, provided new fuel to their criticism of "too high wages, too high taxes and too lavish welfare provisions". Many Swedish firms could compare these with lower wages, taxes and levels of welfare provision in other countries where they operated.

Thus, the future of the welfare state is again the focus of one of the major social discourses of the 20th Century. The welfare state is not, or should not, however, be conceived, as a final destination or the ultimate goal in civilizing the market. Like all human projects it changes, and must change with time. Old solutions are often ill equipped to resolve new problems, but they nevertheless somehow become institutionalized. As the shortcomings of current solutions are discovered and debated, new reforms are naturally proposed. Numerous solutions have been put forward for resolving the crisis of the welfare state in the final decade of this century.

By far the most well known is the neo-liberal receipt for drastically lower taxes and a minimal night-watchman state, combined with a dramatically increased reliance on market solutions to meet the needs of citizens. However, this proposal is rejected here since it solves many problems of the welfare state by introducing price mechanisms and pricing public services out of reach for ordinary citizens, while only retaining a minimal safety net and charity that would cater mainly to the "deserving poor". This would surely increase the legitimacy of public financed services in the eyes of many of the well-to-do and many persons with well-paid jobs. But, it would exclude the less well-off, unemployed, single parent families, etc., and further undermine the legitimacy of such a regime in their eyes. Thus, we need to look beyond the market for solutions to the crisis of the welfare state.

There is a growing political and fiscal urgency in Sweden to find models for renewing the public sector and rejuvenating the welfare state. However, similar to the Labour Government in Britain, we do not believe it is possible to reform the welfare state with a Big Bang nor by a Shock Therapy policy. Rather, we prefer to explore and present social enterprises and civil democracy, as an alternative that we claim is both more and less radical at the same time. It is more radical, because we want to consider a major shift in the provision of welfare in terms of facilitating greater citizen participation both by greater co-determination at work and by greater citizens' involvement as co-producers of the services they demand. But it is also less radical since we propose the maintenance of the present levels of public financing for social services, while developing a more participatory welfare society on the foundation of the present universal welfare state.

Changes in the welfare state are, of course, highly controversial topics in Sweden, as elsewhere in Europe, and quite naturally, it has many adherents. Among them are both those who see the need for reforms and those who reject any change. Those who want to keep the welfare state intact and think that all services should continue to be provided by the state are often called "étatists". For example, a recent government study compared child and elderly care in Germany and Sweden. The "Welfare Project" was initiated and financed by the Swedish Ministry of Social Affairs and published a report series known as "*Facts/Knowledge*". However, it misrepresented alternative or non-municipal day care services as a marginal phenomenon in Sweden (Antman, 1996). Nothing could be farther from the *facts*. In 1995 alternative day care services enrolled one of eight pre-school children attending publicly financed day care facilities in Sweden. In urban areas it approaches one of four children enrolled in day care facilities. Furthermore this report failed to distinguish between private for-profit firms, social enterprises and cooperative providers. It also ignored the main values promoted by social enterprises that provide social services, e.g., an improved work environment, greater consumer empowerment, the transformation of the welfare state into a welfare society, etc. Rather, according to étatists, the main attraction of cooperative day care services is/was for persons wishing to jump the municipal queue or to crowd in on the waiting line.

Most of the information gathered by the Work Environment and Cooperative Social Services and presented in this book and in a subsequent empirical report (Pestoff, forthcoming) contradicts this negative image of the development of new social enterprises. Detailed information about the growth and development of this social phenomenon are presented in the WECSS report and summarized briefly in Chapter 8 below in order to set the facts straight. The materials found in the chapters on work environment (Chapter 9) and parental participation (Chapter 10) clearly refute this negative image of social enterprises providing social services. They document how social enterprises enrich work life of the women employed there, improve their psychosocial work environment, increase their co-determination; so much so that the overwhelming majority of the women with experience from both forms clearly prefer working for social enterprises, rather than for municipal day care facilities. (See Chapter 9 for more details). They also show how social enterprises empower citizens as co-producers of the services they use. In addition to the work obligation found in most social enterprises, many clients hold an elective or honorary office in them. Parents with experience from both forms also clearly prefer social enterprises to municipal day care services. (See Chapter 10 for more details). Thus, we also need to look beyond the state for solutions to the crisis of the welfare state.

Interest in the potential of the social economy and an appreciation for the contribution of social enterprises and the third sector to the provision of social services appears greater elsewhere in Europe and America (Salamon & Anheier, 1996). For example, in 1994 a conference was organized in Valencia to explore social enterprises and cooperatives as "New Models for Governing the Public Sector". However, in Sweden, any interest in the potential contribution of social enterprises and cooperative alternatives for rejuvenating the public sector seems remote. Rather a black/white debate tries to force all alternatives into one of two categories: public or private, state or market, socialist or conservative, and *laissez-faire* or planned economy. The constraints of this narrow black/white perspective leave little room for voluntary, mutual and cooperative solutions. At best, they are begrudgingly granted a marginal role or called into focus when all other alternatives fail, as now in terms of long-term unemployment among immigrants and other disadvantaged groups. Previously, they were mainly discussed in terms of reducing the costs of public services. Social enterprises providing social services in Sweden probably do both these things, and do them reasonably well; but so what? What other values do they promote in addition to the politically motivated goals of job creation and cost reduction?

The current debate about public vs. private social services is highly ideological. Few of the protagonists take third sector alternatives and their potential seriously. This niggardly treatment of such important social phenomena ignores the present and future contribution of the voluntary, mutual and cooperative sector to the welfare state (Esping-Andersen & Korpi, 1987; Esping-Andersen, 1996), both in terms of what it does today and of what it could contribute to transforming the welfare state into a welfare society. Social engineering solutions to the problems now facing the Swedish welfare state, whether the neo-liberal type of tearing it down and replacing it by market mechanisms or the centralized/étatist solutions of leaving it unchanged both miss the mark. Both neo-liberalism and étatism perspectives fail to understand the true potential of the third sector to create social capital and trust by bringing citizens together in small horizontal groups to achieve the goals they decide upon or to produce the services they demand. The third sector and social enterprises, however, provide a possibility for breaking this ideological dead-lock and for finding a common ground for proposing alternative solutions that neither fit neatly into the square nor round holes, proposed by neo-liberals or étatists. Thus, we need to move beyond the market and state.

We would like to consider this book as a contribution to a greater understanding and development of mutual or cooperative welfare provision and of a mutual or cooperative welfare model. Hopefully, it can make a small contribution to removing the blinders of this black/white perspective and to recognizing such solutions as legitimate alternatives in their own right. We firmly believe that this model, although still underdeveloped and poorly understood, can be clearly distinguished both from the existing welfare state in Britain or Sweden and from the privatized residual welfare state so often depicted as the *only* alternative in the British or Swedish debate. Furthermore, we maintain that a mutual and cooperative model could clearly contribute to renewing the Swedish welfare state from within, while transforming it into a welfare society at the same time.

1.B From the Welfare State to a Welfare Society

There are still major differences today in the structure of social insurance and welfare states in Europe (Olsson Hort, 1993; Palme, 1990). Differences in cultural tradition and history are inherent in the basic strategies behind the construction, regulation, financing and administration of the social welfare or insurance systems. Some systems focus on basic security others on income security; some are work-related while others are universal for all citizens; some are based on individual contributions while others are tax financed; and finally, some are mainly redistributive over the life-cycle and others show greater equity in redistributing between better-off and worse-off groups of citizens (*ibid.*). Such differences are related to variations in the forms of organizing the provision of welfare and to types of welfare states in Europe. Numerous dimensions are relevant for distinguishing between welfare states. As the focus of our efforts is related to social enterprises and civil democracy, we will only address those dimensions that are relevant to these efforts. Other dimensions will, of course, be stressed by other authors with different purposes.

Titmuss (1958, as presented by Olsson Hort, 1993) distinguished between four forms for providing welfare, they are: a) social, b) fiscal, c) occupational and d) voluntary. The *social* form of organizing welfare is based on the statutory social provision, often cash and in-kind benefits, as illustrated by the modern universal welfare state. The *fiscal* form of organizing welfare is through tax credits and deductions instead of cash benefits. The *occupational* form of organizing welfare is via employment and fringe benefits from the enterprise level of provision to the nation-wide level through contracts negotiated by the employers and workers, usually via trade unions. The *voluntary* form of organizing welfare relies on spontaneous solidarity or voluntary assistance, charitable activities, mutual-aid associations, etc.

All four of these forms for providing basic social services can coexists in the same welfare system, and normally several of them are found in most countries. Each of them has certain administrative and/or limiting characteristics. Thus, statutory social welfare is normally universal and once established politically difficult to curtail. Fiscal welfare is limited to persons paying taxes and their families; thus, excluding many poor persons.

Occupational welfare is only available to persons active in the work-force and their families; thus, subject to economic cycles or the supply and demand for labor (Perrow, 1988), and also often dependent on the bargaining power of workers or trade unions. Voluntary welfare is often based on private and/or charitable activities and thus, patchwork or fragmented in nature (Kramer, 1981), and it is nevertheless largely dependent on public grants for financing (*ibid.*; Salomon, 1987).

There are of course gray zones in between these four forms of organizing basic social services. Most countries normally employ all four forms of providing basic social services to their citizens simultaneously, with emphasis on one or the other to a greater or lesser degree. Titmuss (1974, as presented by Olsson Hort, 1993), however, distinguished between three types or models of basic social services, i.e. a) a residual, b) an industrial achievement-performance and c) an institutional model. This trichotomy is widely used; but following American usage, it is usually condensed into a dichotomy of residual vs. institutional welfare. We will briefly examine each of them a bit closer below.

The *residual* model of social policy is normally associated with the lack of comprehensive coverage as manifest in postwar America. There we find a commitment to market sovereignty, limited government involvement in the distribution of welfare, based on the assumption that most people can/should plan for and contract their own welfare and that state intervention is needed only when the normal channels of distribution fail. Individual heads-of-household should normally be able to sustain themselves and their families through their participation in the labor market. Residual welfare is therefore means-tested and targeted towards the marginal segments of society lacking a personal safety-net, e.g. the "deserving poor" and destitute who are incapable of self-help. The demarcation between the deserving and undeserving poor becomes a major political, economic and administrative concern of residual welfare systems.

The *industrial achievement* or performance model comes closest to a modern version of the original Bismarck model and is widely found in Western Europe. Social welfare institutions and policies are secondary to economic performance and productivity. Social needs are met on the basis of merit, participation in the work-force and economic performance. Universal coverage is never developed here to the same extent as in the UK or Scandinavia. The system was/is fragmented, with separate schemes for different groups in the labor-market. Such welfare schemes are compulsory, but usually administered jointly by employers and employees or their representatives, with the state sometimes acting as a third party. Benefits are pegged to income and the normal wage-earner becomes the standard. Those outside the labor market are, however, absent and therefore not measured by the same standards.

The *institutional* model was first developed in postwar Britain, under the Beveridge plan of welfare after W.W.II. It does not accept a clear division between the market and the state in terms of welfare commitments and sees individual welfare as the responsibility of society as a whole. The institutional welfare model promotes the principle of"social citizenship" or a "social minimum", where all citizens are equally and unconditionally entitled to a decent standard of living. Benefits are paid by the state at fixed-rate, rather than income related, and they partially replace the market as the primary distributive network of welfare, i.e. they aim at redistributing welfare between groups. Sweden attempted to bridge the gap between the industrial achievement and the institutional model through an active labor market policy and a policy of full employment, until the early 1990s.

Notably absent in this trichotomy from the mid-1970s is a system or model related to *voluntary* or mutual welfare provision (introduced by Titmuss, 1958). Nonprofit organizations, NPOs, or non-governmental organizations, NGOs, however, are normally a feature of the other three models. This book is an attempt to stake out the limits and some of the content of mutual or cooperative welfare provision, a model designed to empower citizens as co-producers.

More recently, in a similar vein Leibfried (1991, as presented in Olsson Hort, 1993) distinguishes between four types of welfare states in Europe: a) the modern universalistic system, found in the Scandinavian or Nordic countries; b) the liberal free-market based system, found in the United Kingdom and Ireland; c) the continental labor-market participation or workfare system, found in Germany, France, Austria, the Netherlands and Belgium; and finally d) the Latin-rim or rudimentary system, found in Italy, Spain and Portugal, and perhaps also in Greece.

However, Habermas (1989, as presented by Olsson Hort, 1993) suggests the emergence of a fifth type, a communitarian or participatory model, based on the alternative culture, self-help and ecology movements of Western Europe, i.e., one similar to the type introduced, but then forgotten by Titmuss. Moreover, a new type of welfare state is emerging on the ruins of the Central and Eastern European compulsory enterprise-focused welfare state. It is comprised of a minimal safety-net accompanied by social insurance, but with some of the institutions of the old system still intact (Pestoff, 1995a; Pestoff, 1996a).

There are numerous efforts to reform welfare systems and social insurance in Western Europe. However, according to Hansen (1993), systems that are based on market insurance principles, on the one hand, normally have problems with market failure. Here reforms tend to introduce more features of public systems. Public insurance systems that are universal and tax-financed, on the other hand, tend to suffer from problems of lack of effectiveness, unbalanced budgets, incentive problems, etc. Here solutions are posed in terms of the introduction of market mechanisms. Occupational insurance systems, so prominent in Western Europe, face problems typical both of market and public social systems, and solutions are often framed in terms of introducing both more market and public features.

By a welfare society we refer to Titmuss' (1974) "unfinished" or voluntary model for organizing social welfare, or what Habermas (1989) calls a communitarian or participatory model of social welfare. We are also referring to the emergence of new forms for greater citizen participation in the provision of social services they demand themselves. This often takes the form of social enterprises based on cooperative self-governance forms for providing these social services. In a welfare society the public sector is no longer the sole, nor even necessarily the main provider of such services, but it retains full responsibility for financing social services and regulating their quality. Thus, the financing and provision of social services are separated from each other. (See Section 3.E for further discussion.)

1.C Social Enterprises: the Social Values of Cooperatives and Voluntary Organizations

A variety of alternative models for providing social services are being tried in various parts of Sweden. Contracting out to the third sector, purchaser-provider models, cooperative social services, volunteering and third party provision are but a few of the models now being tried in order to resolve the acute ideological and financial problems currently facing the Swedish welfare state. Privatization and contracting out has led to the growth of many new social enterprises, which have become an important alternative to the public provision of such social services.

Taking day care services as the main illustration, the number of "private" or non-municipal day care centers more than tripled between 1988 and 1995, going from 538 to 1,900 facilities, while the number of children attending them more than quadrupled during the same period, increasing from 8,500 to 39,100 (Pestoff, 1996a; Stryjan, 1995). Nearly two-thirds of these "private" day care centers are either parent or worker cooperatives, or voluntary organizations (Pestoff, *op. cit.*). As mentioned earlier, non-municipal day care now accounts for more than ten per cent of all children enrolled in day care facilities, and include more than one-fourth of the children in the major urban areas of Sweden. Social enterprises have also been established in other areas such as elderly care Wahlgren (1996), health care, handicap care, etc.

1.C.1 SOCIAL ENTERPRISES

Social enterprises are firms that try to fulfill several goals simultaneously, recognizing that no single goal can constantly be maximized, but rather that several of them can be satisfactorily fulfilled, at the same time. Social enterprises do not exist to maximize the return on capital nor the revenues over expenses, but rather are willing to accept a lower, but nevertheless satisfactory, economic return on their efforts. They do this in order to combine the necessary economic goal with other important social goals, that can also be achieved or satisfied. Therefore, they provide a more rewarding occupation for the employees, or greater citizen participation, and socially meaningful goals for the firm. This may lead to a positive selection of the staff, since employees are not one-dimensional utility maximizers seeking the highest possible wages or the shortest working hours. Rather they wish to maximize several goals simultaneously, like satisfying financial rewards, a meaningful occupation, stimulating and flexible working conditions, care giving, etc. It may also lead to a positive selection of parents, who are not merely interested in the closest facility, the longest opening hours, the lowest fees. Rather they see value in the work obligation and holding an honorary office, and they want to promote greater parental influence and democratic forms of decision-making.

The main competitive advantage of social enterprises is that they generate trust between their staff and clients/consumers, since they clearly have more than one goal, including one or more major social goals. They simultaneously try to fulfill these diverse and multiple goals, while accepting a satisfactory rather than a maximal return on capital or of income over expenses. This clearly indicates a policy of not exploiting the information asymmetries related to the provision of their services/products for their own personal and private benefit; i.e., they will not behave opportunistically vis-à-vis their clients (Enjolras, 1995; Borzaga & Mittone, 1997). This provides a minimal guarantee of trust to their clients/customers and to the local community in which they operate (Pestoff, 1998c). Such trust could be greatly enhanced by the development of multi-stakeholder models of organization and the employment of annual social audits. (See Chapters. 5 & 6 for more details.)

In Sweden social enterprises normally take the legal form of a voluntary organization or a cooperative or economic association. In principle they may even incorporate as a private firm. However, while the latter is normally the privileged and preferentially treated business form in national legislation in most European countries, it can undermine one of the main competitive advantage of social enterprises, i.e., trust. The latter type of organizations, are, therefore, normally excluded from our study. But they are nevertheless frequently found in France, Italy and Spain.

Our main theoretical consideration now shifts to the social values promoted by cooperatives and voluntary organizations. Various actors have different interests in complex organizations and they also have different social relations with each other. The interest model of the firm has been criticized for being static, for assuming a harmony of interests between the actors and for failing to take differences in power between various actors into account (Mabon, 1977 & 1992). Thus, the social relations between various actors are determined in part by whether they are the dominant actor in a firm. What is important for our discussion of the social dimension of social enterprises are the implications of the dominance of one of these interests. If we assume that a dominant actor pursues its own interest, then variations in social relation have different implications for a firm's social dimension and for society at large. Later we will discuss the implications of replacing this dominance with representation of all significant stakeholders in multi-stakeholder organizations. (See Chapter 5 for more details).

Private firms are noted for their contribution to efficiency in production and the allocation of resources. Their activities are geared towards maximizing returns on invested capital. Public bureaucracy and public enterprise are more often associated with equity than efficiency, and they also assure the availability of various goods and services to the general public, without extensive consideration to prices. Third sector and cooperative organizations are often seen as an alternative, or at least a compliment to both the public and private sectors. They are associated with innovation, advocacy and the promotion of civic values (Kramer, 1981).

1.C.2 The Social Values of Cooperatives and Voluntary Organizations

In this section we will discuss how differences in the social dimensions of the firm are related to differences in the internal social relations of their main actors. It is argued that differences in these social relationships have clear social and political implications at both the micro and macro levels. Thus, preferences in favor of one or the other form of production should take into account differences in the type of social enterprises.

Three main potential contributions of social enterprises are the renewal and enrichment of working life, the empowerment of consumers or clients and the enhancement of other social values and/or of goal fulfillment in the public sector. Each of these contributions is more closely related to one type of social enterprise than another, and they are in turn related to differences in the social relations within each social enterprises. It is important to keep these differences in mind when discussing their social dimension and comparing cooperatives with private firms or public bureaucracies.

The provision of social services by social enterprises is local and small scale in nature. Social enterprises can provide the producers of social services, the consumers or clients of such services and the resource-poor or risk groups who depend upon such services with greater influence in their operation. This results in greater citizen control over the social services they demand and depend on and it also promotes local grass-root democracy. Moreover, greater employee influence and client empowerment not only result in greater involvement as producers and/or consumers of social services, but normally will also result in better service quality.

What are the implications of the changes brought about by reforms in the provision of social services in Sweden? What and how can the social dimension of social enterprises contribute to the renewal and enrichment of working life, the empowerment of citizens as co-producers and the transformation of the welfare state? We want to consider what the most likely impact would be on relations between employees and clients of such services of a change from the public provision of social services to provision by social enterprises. Financial and strictly economic aspects are of course one main difference, but also quite different work and customer relations are implied by each form of provision. Public provision often implies standardization of welfare services according to some publicly agreed upon and politically approved norms. These norms are usually determined by relevant experts and applied through political decisions to all providing units within a given territorial jurisdiction. Uniform higher education, particularly for social workers and civil servants, insures good professional standards and a standardized application of such norms (William-Olsson, 1988 and *Dagens Nyheter* 18/1-90). However, such standardization has been criticized for resulting in the application of Fordist principles of mass production to the provision of personal social services (Christensen, 23/1-90 and Tarschys, 29/1-90 in *Dagens Nyheter*), which often alienates both the employees and clients. The post-Fordist and post-modern emphasis on decentralization, flexible specialization and mass-customization rejects the Taylorist and Fordist model of production (Nielsen, 1989; Nielsen & Pedersen, 1989b; Pedersen, 1992; Giddens, 1994 & 1996; Firat, 1990; Firat, *et al.*, 1995; see also Chapter 7 below).

Competitive, private for-profit provision of welfare services, it is often argued, results in greater flexibility, and hence greater differences between providing units. Standard or uniform norms applied from above are no longer allowed to determine all or even most aspects of service, but only a few basic or strategic ones. Efficiency and profit in providing services are not determined by standardization, but rather by market expectations and flexible local solutions. Nor are private providers always subject to the same public scrutiny and debate as public providers, as much of their operations will be covered by "trade secrets". Private social services will be relatively small scale, at least at the outset. The greater flexibility and specialization of the services provided may welcome by both the workers and clients.

There are, however, limits to the renewal of social services via private commercial provision. The flexibility and innovation expected by clients will be limited by the economic constraints of private for-profit firms. Many employees will also face equal or perhaps even stronger economic constraints in the private sector than in the public sector (Szulkin, 1989). Thus, except for the owners and/or managers of these private firms providing social welfare services, possibilities for the renewal and enrichment of working life may be limited to the greater flexibility provided by smaller bureaucratic units. This may, however, provide some psycho-social improvement for the employees. Social enterprises could provide other benefits to society and its citizens than private commercial providers.

1.C.3 The Renewal and Enrichment of Working-Life

The first major potential contribution of social enterprises concerns the renewal and enrichment of working-life associated with changes in providing welfare services. Quite different work relations are, however, implied by different forms of social enterprise. But, there are three basic forms or models of social enterprises providing social services in Sweden. One is the worker cooperative model, where all or most of the providers of a social service are also members of the service cooperative, but where the clients only have a formal customer relation with the providers. The second is the consumer cooperative model, which is primarily associated with consumer empowerment and is discussed in greater detail below. Here workers remain employees. The third are voluntary organizations, but they imply as clear changes of relations between the employees and clients. Here employees and clients share common social values related to the purpose of the voluntary organization. Thus, voluntary organizations appear to comprise a more diffuse category in terms of renewing work life.

The worker cooperative model suggests the greatest potential for the renewal and enrichment of working life, since it combines the roles of owning a firm with that of being an employee. Hirschman (1982a) argues that greater participation in working life and the discussions concerning it can help to bridge the gap between the instrumental and the expressive attitudes of employees. This should render work less instrumental and introduce more expressive aspects, something which would in turn make work more satisfying and rewarding to most employees. Employee satisfaction and engagement it is assumed, will be positively related to service quality.

There are, however, certain problems associated with worker ownership. The risk of under- or over-consumption of work environment and/or co-determination is one such problem. The members of social service co-ops of the worker type might ignore some of their own interests as employees, for example, in making investments to improve their work environment. They might be inclined to do this in a highly competitive situation, in order to save their jobs. But, a good work environment could also provide an advantage, like more engaged personnel, and clients would also share in many of its benefits. The member/workers of this type of social service cooperative might, however, make improvements in their work environment at the expense of their clients and/or financiers of these social services, thus, leading to an over-consumption. The staff of worker cooperative social services would also be expected to give greater priority to co-determination than employees in the other two alternative forms of social services.

There is also a risk that members of worker co-ops social services would give preference to their own interests, rather than those of their clients in other ways. Their preferences for increased salaries may outweigh those of their clients for better service environment or for high quality services at reasonable prices. In short, the worker cooperative model primarily promotes worker power.

1.C.4 Empowerment of Clients and Consumers

A second major potential contribution of cooperative social services is found in the area of consumer empowerment. Consumer influence in social welfare services is governed by one of two principles, i.e. either by exit or voice (Hirschman, 1970; see also Section 4.C below). Private provision of social welfare services is undertaken on a commercial basis, while public provision depends upon political decisions. The former is primarily subject to consumer exit, the latter to the political voice of the citizens. As such, the political voice operates at infrequent intervals, e.g. every 2nd, 3rd, 4th or 5th year or more infrequently, depending on election periods and the saliency of issues related to welfare services in election campaigns. Not only private providers of social welfare services, but also social service cooperatives run on a worker cooperative basis and perhaps to a lesser extent, voluntary organizations operating under commercial constraints are primarily subject to exit or market responses, if the market is competitive, but they are subject to little or no voice reactions.

Local consumer cooperatives providing social welfare services to members as consumers of these services can, however, readily combine both exit and voice options among their guiding principles at the level of production. It is their ability to combine both of these guiding principles that makes it possible to discuss the empowerment of clients as consumers, since consumer cooperatives make clients directly responsible for the service produced, thus turning them into co-producers. By involving members in the day-to-day operations of their cooperatives, in addition to giving them a voice in the running of the cooperative as a whole, clients-cum-members obtain an institutionalized voice in the provision of social welfare services. This voice can be employed to determine the standards of quality of the services and the level of production. This institutionalized voice is not normally found in other forms of welfare service provision. Thus, clients/customers become empowered with rights and responsibilities by virtue of an institutionalized voice made available to them through membership in the social service cooperative.

There are, however, some problems associated with member ownership. Some employees may resent having to deal with clients as members and employers. Certain employees may even consider it an infringement upon their professional prerogatives. Under- and over-consumption of work environment may also pose a serious problem. Members may not always understand the necessity of making investments to improve the work environment. However, it should be kept in mind that the work environment is shared both by the producers and consumers of these services, as both groups spend anywhere from six to eight or more hours per day on the same premises. So, on the contrary, their investments in work environment may even be to the detriment of the economic well-being or survival of their social service cooperative. Moreover, it is the clients not the staff who determine the activities of consumer cooperatives, so employees may see little difference in terms of co-determination between consumer cooperatives and public services. In short, the consumer cooperative model primarily promotes consumer power.

1.C.5 The Advantages of Voluntary Organizations

The final form of social enterprises providing social welfare services involves voluntary organizations. It bears some of the features of cooperatives, but also has some unique characteristics of its own. Great variation is found between countries in terms of the characteristics of voluntary organizations and their role in the provision of personal social services (Kramer, 1990a). Seen from a Nordic perspective, voluntary organizations often rely on idea-based or purposive groups, which usually provide welfare services to members. Voluntary organizations do not, however, normally attempt to cater to the public-at-large, but only to persons subscribing to, or at least not rejecting, certain of the NPO's basic values. Such shared values can facilitate a dialogue between the employees and clients of personal social services. Voluntary organizations will therefore provide uncertain benefits in terms of enriching working life and empowering the consumers. Thus, they will serve as a neutral or half-way category in our empirical study.

In his seminal work on voluntary agencies and the welfare state, Kramer (1981) compares the role of voluntary organizations in the USA, UK, Netherlands and Israel in providing services to the handicapped. He argues that voluntary handicap agencies combine three unique functions not normally associated with service provision by either public or for-profit agencies in most welfare states; i.e., pioneering or innovation through specialization, advocacy, and the preservation of specific civic values of participation by clients or consumerism. However, voluntary organizations can also make a significant contribution to the ability of the public sector to reach out to clients with special characteristics (Pestoff, 1992; & Walden Laing & Pestoff, 1997). For example, without voluntary organizations it would be impossible for the public authorities to come into contact with most HIV/AIDS risk groups, or to inform them, test them, and provide them with counseling and services. Nor would it be possible to provide them with humane conditions and treatment once their HIV-positive situation becomes more acute.

The relationship between governmental and voluntary organizations varies from country to country, over time and according to the issue or problem at hand. Kramer discusses five major strategies for relating government to voluntary agencies in the delivery of personal social services (*ibid.*). They range from nationalization, government dominance, and "pragmatic partnership", to "empowerment" and "reprivatization". He characterizes developments between governments of the four countries in his study with one or the other of these strategies.

In a more general sense, if clients are organized in self-help groups, then they can play a more active role in articulating and promoting the interests of their members in designing and delivering social services. This gives them greater influence in the provision of such social services. Their participation may initially promote some disagreement between such self-help groups and public sector agencies over the quality and quantity of such services. However, in the long-run it should promote a greater dialogue between these groups. In short, voluntary organizations primarily promote other kinds of social values than worker or consumer empowerment, but they may also include them.

1.C.6 Summary of the Social Values of Various Social Enterprises

The social dimensions both of consumer and worker cooperatives as well as voluntary organizations can make unique contributions to renewing the public sector and enriching the welfare state, if their role is increased in the provision of personal social services. Worker co-ops can enrich and renew the working life of the women providing such services, as well as improve their work environment; consumer co-ops can empower the clients and consumers of such services; while other types of voluntary organizations can contribute to greater user influence and greater effectiveness in achieving the goals of special groups and thereby of the welfare state. Thus, rather than simply privatizing the welfare state, there are strong theoretical arguments for democratizing and cooperativizing it by letting various types of social enterprises provide social services.

Figure 1.1 summarizes the advantages of the various organizational alternatives in relation to the enrichment of working-life, the renewal of the public sector and the welfare state; to market and political reactions characterized as exit and voice; to the enhancement of the effectively of the public sector, as well as to the equal access of all citizens to personal social services. One "X" indicates the expectation of a weak relationship with an alternative form of providing social welfare service, while two "XX"s indicate a medium relationship and three "XXX"s indicate a strong relationship. The existence of an "X" in parentheses indicates that the potential influence of a given alternative depends on certain circumstances.

Thus, the influence of exit on private providers of social welfare services is highly dependent on the existence of market competition. Clearly, this not only varies from country to country and from branch to branch in any given country, but also from one locality to another.

In this chapter, our intention has been to consider three often ignored alternatives to public and private social services. The public and private provision of social services, which are extensively discussed and debated, have only been summarily dealt with herein. Our main focus is on social enterprises, and they are compared and contrasted with each other in the figure below. The main contribution of worker cooperatives to renewing the public sector and enriching the welfare state is in terms of directly enriching working life, improving work environment and increasing co-determination. In short, they promote worker power. They also indirectly contribute, under certain circumstances to revitalizing the market or exit alternatives and to greater public goal fulfillment.

Figure 1.1 Strength of Social Values of Various Organizations Providing Social Services

Social Values/ Organizational Alternatives:	**Work Environment**	**Exit**	**Voice**	**Effectivity in Public Programs**	**Equal Access**
Worker Co-ops	XXX	XX(X)	X(X)	X(X)	XX
Cons Co-ops	X(X)	X(XX)	XXX	X(X)	XX
Vol. Orgs	X(X)	X(X)	X(X)	XXX	XX
Private Firms	X	X(XX)	(X)	X	X
Public Bodies	X(X)	(X)	X(X)	XX	XXX

Source: modified from V. Pestoff, 1992. X=low, XX=medium, XXX=High and (X)=potential.

The main contribution of consumer cooperatives to renewing the public sector and enriching the welfare state comes in terms of directly empowering the clients or consumers of such services, and providing them with an institutionalized voice. This also indirectly contributes to enriching working life and enhancing public goal fulfillment. In short, they promote consumer power. The main contribution of voluntary organizations to renewing the public sector and enriching the welfare state is in terms of directly enhancing the social goals of such organizations and also promoting the effectiveness and goal fulfillment of the public sector. In short, they promote greater power for other social values. They can also make an indirect contribution under certain circumstances to client empowerment and enriching working life.

1.D Civil Democracy

We will now turn our attention to a discussion of the concept of civil democracy. It is indirectly related to the idea of social capital found in R. Putnam's seminal book, *Making Democracy Work - Civil Traditions in Modern Italy* (1993). Here he discusses the historical and contemporary importance of voluntary organizations and their contribution to economic and social development in Italy. Elsewhere he explores the disappearance of "social capital" in the USA (Putnam, 1995). In the first work, he notes that success in overcoming the dilemmas of collective action depends on the broader social context in which human interaction takes place. "Voluntary cooperation is easier in a community that has inherited a substantial stock of social capital, in the form of reciprocity and networks of civic engagement" (Putnam, 1993, 167). He proceeds to define social capital with reference to:

> ...features of social organization, such as trust, norms and networks, that can improve the efficiency of society by facilitating coordinated action.... Like other forms of capital, social capital is productive, making possible the achievement of certain ends that would not be attainable in its absence. (*ibid.*)

Most forms of social capital, such as trust, are what A. Hirschman (1970) has called "moral resources", i.e., resources whose supply increases rather than decreases with use, but which also become depleted if not used. Moreover, social capital is ordinarily a public good, and like all public goods it tends to be undervalued and undersupplied by private agents. This means that social capital, unlike other forms of capital, must be produced as a by-product of other social activities. The greater the level of trust within a community, the greater the likelihood of cooperation, where as cooperation in turn breads trust (Putnam, 1993, 169-71).

If horizontal networks of civic engagement help participants solve dilemmas of collective action, then the more horizontally structured an organization, the more it should foster institutional success in the broader community. Thus, membership in horizontally ordered groups, like sports clubs, choirs, and cooperatives, should be positively associated with good government, while membership in hierarchical ordered organizations, like the Mafia or Catholic Church, should be negatively associated with good government. These expectations are consistent with the evidence found in his study of Italy (*ibid.*, 176).

One current political challenge to the legitimacy of the welfare state stems from the growing "democratic deficit" in Sweden. This deficit is most acutely felt at the level of local governmental, where the number of municipalities was reduced from nearly 2,500 in 1950 to just over one-tenth, or 280 after the municipal reforms in the 1970s (SOU 1996:162; Jönsson, *et al.*, 1997). This resulted in much larger local government units, but also eliminated many non-professional and part-time politicians. More recently, the growing use of market models for providing local services increases this democracy deficit. Public accountability is circumvented by the provision of public financed services by municipally owned limited companies. During the past decade an additional 9,000 non-professional or free-time politicians have been relieved of their responsibilities; decisions have been delegated to local bureaucrats; buy-sell models have taken over a growing part of public services and contracting-out to private for-profit suppliers has increased dramatically; municipal limited companies have restricted both public accountability and their employees possibilities of informing the public about their operations. Criticism of this development gained new fuel from the excessively generous "golden parachutes" for directors of marketized public companies; the numerous scandals concerning financial license and/or sex involving the directors of municipal limited companies and/or municipal politicians; etc.

In the modern welfare state, democratic theory concerns opportunities for formal participation in three major aspects of modern life, but not a fourth (Saltman & v. Otter, 1992). Participation can be expressed in relation to political institutions via elections, to social institutions, particularly social insurance via trade unions, and to economic institutions via co-determination and trade unions. What is excluded, however, is formal participation in civil institutions, particularly residence-related human services such as health care, education, child care and elderly care (*ibid.*, p. 99). Following the introduction of political democratization through the institution of universal suffrage in the 1920s in Sweden, there was an extension of social rights to all citizens in the middle of the century. Finally, efforts were made to establish formal co-determination and economic democracy with the Wage Earner Funds in the mid-1970s. The latter resulted in complete failure, and the issue of economic democracy was effectively dead and buried for many years to come. In spite of that, the time has now come to consider a fourth form or wave of democracy, namely civil democracy.

Large organizations will pursue their own internal objectives and self-interests rather than meeting diffuse consumer needs, unless, of course, public accountability or market-driven accountability are better developed. (See Chapter 6 on social accounting.) Civil democracy becomes a necessary corrective to empower individuals, enabling them to redress the adverse decision-making balance within human services (*ibid.*, p. 100). But Saltman & v. Otter reject attempts to incorporate citizens directly into the local decision-making process through improved local representation, or to increase citizen involvement in the design and delivery of community-based services. Rather, they suggest the exit alternative, combined with *lateral re-entry*. They propose to introduce market forces by making public providers compete with each other, but without any private competition (*ibid.*, 103).

Their exclusive focus on state and market solutions to the detriment of a third sector alternative for direct citizen participation as co-producers is in part explained by the fact that their main concern is health care. They argue that hospitals are so capital intensive that voluntary organizations in Northern Europe probably will not be able to accumulate the necessary capital to successfully compete[2]. So, they simply refuse to consider either voluntary organizations or cooperatives as viable alternatives to states or markets for providing all types of residential social services. By focusing exclusively on the capital intensive end of personal social services, i.e., hospitals, they "throw out the baby with the bath water". It is at the opposite end of the scale, i.e., in the personnel intensive care, that local social services can hope to find their market niche.

While their discussion is enlightening, we feel that it falls short of the mark. Their alternative brand of empowerment goes exclusively via the market and the power attributed to exit, not via the third sector and the power of collective voice. We would like to suggest another type of civil democracy, our own brand of it, one that puts emphasis on voice, the third sector and cooperative self-management of social service provision through small local social enterprises.

Civil democracy could provide the grounds for a fourth wave of democracy, a democratization of civil institutions and personal social services. We propose that the third sector and cooperative self-management

[2] While we share their apprehensions about the capital intensity of hospitals, the four hospitals in the Saitama Medical Cooperative outside Tokyo, with over 1,000 beds discussed in Section 4.D.3 or the 414 bed cooperative hospital in Barcelona, discussed in more detail in section 5.D.2, plus several other cooperative hospitals in Canada, Japan and Latin America, provide clear exceptions to their negative expectations concerning cooperative health care.

of personal social services would provide a durable base for creating institutions to facilitate the accumulation of social capital. Thus, the term *civil democracy* will be employed here to refer to *citizen empowerment through cooperative self-management of personal social services, where the citizens become members in social enterprises, where they participate directly in the production of the local services they demand, as users and producers of such services, and where they therefore become co-producers of these services*.

One of the main underpinnings of "civil democracy" is a realization that democracy is interactive in its nature; i.e., in the relationship between the rulers and the ruled. A democracy that only permits its citizens to vote every 2nd, 3rd, 4th or 5th year, and expects little or nothing else of them will lead to an atrophy of the democratic spirit of its citizens. Moreover, a democracy that attempts to meet most or all of the needs of its citizens without also expecting them to actively participate in the provision of public services, at least occasionally, turns its citizens into passive consumers of public services rather than active co-producers of the services they demand.

Democracy rests on a moral base, which grows when exercised, but dwindles when left fallow for too long. Unless Putnam's (1993) concept of social capital clearly includes civil democracy and participation in local decision-making, etc., it also faces the risk of becoming a passive resource. If the provision of personal social services and other local services remains exclusively the domain of professional civil servants, and if it does not directly involve and concern the citizens in their daily-life, then social capital will atrophy. In Sweden citizens often become the passive objects of a well-intended and well-organized universal welfare state, but one decided upon and run by professional bureaucrats. Paying taxes is not enough to keep solidarity, social capital and civil democracy alive. In order for social capital to be turned into a resource available to many citizens in the economic, political and social spheres it must be exercised more often than at annual general meetings or in general elections.

Stakeholder democracy promoted by the Labour Government in Britain is interpreted here as a way of giving all groups in society, i.e., all citizens clear rights and responsibilities, and thus a clear stake in society, the way it is run and the way it functions (Hutton, 1995). The democracy deficit and the professionalization of the provision of social services in Sweden have resulted in an unintended and undesirable situation where most citizens are pacified and become objects of social programs, rather than active subjects in meeting their own service needs. Citizens have several roles vis-à-vis the state and/or municipal authorities today, most of which are passive, including their roles as tax payers, service users and/or clients. Their activity and influence is limited to participating in general elections and becoming a member of a political party.

Civil democracy and the idea of enabling citizens to become co-producers of the personal social services they demand are part of a strategy for increasing the stake of the average citizen in the existence and effectiveness of the welfare state and public sector. Such a strategy attempts to turn passive citizens who pay their taxes and receive social services from the public sector and who vote regularly into active stakeholders in the society where they live. It proposes both to enable and empower them by providing them with opportunities to play an active role as co-producers of some of the most important personal social services they demand. It provides them with an individual stake in collective solutions and the collective provision of basic social services. It provides them with obligations, responsibilities, but also rights and influence in the democratic decision-making structures set up to govern these services. (See Chapter 3 for further discussion.)

Furthermore, in order for citizens to temper their demands and expectations they must actively participate in real world situations where they sometimes are forced to make hard choices. They may have to choose between one hour longer child care service per day, higher parent fees or an unacceptable deficit that threatens to close their parent cooperative day care center. They may have to decide whether to allocate more funds for trainers and sport activities for girls or for football and ice-hockey rinks for boys. It is from these everyday, but sometimes tough choices that the moral resources are derived which are so necessary to nourish a thriving social capital and civil democracy. Without regular exercise and without active participation neither the citizens, social capital nor civil democracy will become an active resource for democracy and a welfare society.

1.E Plan of the Book

The subject of welfare state reform is vast and comprises many aspects or dimensions. We can only hope to cover a few of them in this book. We are primarily concerned with exploring three sets of topics here. They are related to renewal of working life, to the changing relationship between citizens and the state and to the transformation of the welfare state into a welfare society. Enriching working life includes an improved work environment, increased co-determination and empowering workers. The changing relationship between citizens and the state includes empowering citizens as co-producers of the public services they demand and the development of civil democracy. The transformation of the welfare state into a welfare society includes the rejuvenation, renewal and reorganization of the welfare state through the development of social enterprises and civil democracy.

Related topics could include a re-organization of the public sector, promoting new models of work in public sector, decentralization of the provision of personal social services, the role of voluntary organizations in the welfare mix and in renewing the welfare state, contracting out, gender perspectives on empowering women as providers and consumers of social services, and the social economy's changing nature and roll plus its contribution to local economic democracy and community development. Yet other topics could comprise the contribution of social enterprises and the third sector to economic efficiency and the costs of providing social services, to alleviating unemployment and job creation, or to helping the socially excluded by projects for solidarity and insertion.

Most of these topics are directly or indirectly related to each other. By focusing only on the first group of topics, we do not mean to imply a lack of importance of the other groups. Many of them will in fact be touched upon in the chapters that follow. But they will not be the main focus of attention in this book. This choice of focus is primarily motivated by the need to concentrate our efforts and economize our resources. Hopefully students of these and other topics will nevertheless find some new knowledge and inspiration in the pages below.

The main reason for proposing to study social enterprises and civil democracy in their own right are, of course, the enrichment of work life, the improvement of the psychosocial work environment, the development of good jobs, the empowerment of citizens as co-producers and the transformation of the welfare state into a welfare society. Persons who do not value such social goals will of course not be attracted by social enterprises and civil democracy. Others might argue that the same social goals could be promoted by public services or private firms, but we strongly disagree with them. The following chapters might then contribute to helping to place these important social values on the social science research agenda in Sweden and elsewhere, and perhaps also may make a contribution to the public debate about the future of the welfare state and its the transformation into a new participatory welfare society.

Keeping in mind the differences between various type of social enterprise and the values associated with each type of cooperative and voluntary organization, we will now begin our conceptual journey before considering many of the details of practical world of social enterprises providing social services in Sweden. We will begin in Chapter 2 by reflecting on civil society, the third sector and shifts in the welfare mix. We will explore the politics of civil democracy in Chapter 3 by discussing citizen's numerous roles in modern societies and the possibilities for their gaining control and influence of the public sector. In Chapter 4 we discuss economic aspects of civil democracy, including market failure, government failure and third sector provision of social services, exit and voice in relation to various types of goods and services, the transaction costs of exit from enduring services, co-production and cooperatives as a forum.

In Chapter 5 we explore the development of multi-stakeholder organizations from both a theoretical and practical perspective and include examples of the same in Canada, Italy, Spain and Sweden. In Chapter 6 we discuss accounting for the performance of social enterprises in terms of performance evaluation and goal displacement. We also consider different types of social reports and audits and present some practical experience in developing social accounts from cooperatives in Canada and Italy. In Chapter 7 we conclude our theoretical discussion by examining the psychosocial work environment of social enterprises providing social service. The control/demand/support model of Karesek & Theorell is developed and refined, and recent signs of deterioration in the pyschosocial work environment of women in the public sector providing day care services are documented. Finally good jobs are contrasted with bad ones.

The empirical part of the book starts in Chapter 8 with a brief overview of social enterprises and their work environment in Sweden. First the growth of social enterprises providing day care services is traced, then the WECSS Project and its three studies are presented. They include an Organization Study, a Staff Study and a Parent Study. The Organization Study sets the parameters for social enterprises providing day care services, while the Staff Study compares the psychosocial work environment of these three types of social enterprises. Chapter 9 addresses the enrichment of women's work environment by comparing the experience of those women who worked for both a social enterprise and municipal day care services. Chapter 10 refines the concept of citizens as co-producers with the materials from the Parent Study. It compares parental involvement and their motives for choosing a particular type of social enterprise. It also compares the services provided by social enterprises and municipal day care services, for those parents who have experience with both forms.

The evidence presented here from the Project on Work Environment and Cooperative Social Services and its study of the staff and clients of publicly financed social services shows that they could contribute to the transformation of the Swedish welfare state into a welfare society. The strategy presented here calls for promoting greater worker participation in the production of social services, and for promoting greater citizen participation in production of the social services they demand. This strategy gives these groups a vital stake in the survival of publicly financed welfare services. The WECSS Project demonstrates that it is possible to develop an alternative to both the market and state. It provides a vision for moving beyond the market and state and for transforming the Swedish welfare state into a welfare society in the New Millennium.

Without a vision for rejuvenating and developing the welfare state, without the development of a new participatory welfare society, without greater worker participation in the production of social services and without the development of civil democracy, the universal welfare state of today faces a serious risk of collapsing under its own weight and becoming a relic of the past. In addition to the current crises of the welfare state and a growing resistance to increasing taxes, growing possibilities for capital to avoid high tax countries and the rapid internationalization of the Swedish economy will erode support for the universal welfare state. Internationalization of business not only facilitates social dumping, but the isomorphic tendencies promoted by global competition and multi-national companies often result in their outright rejection of the universal values of the welfare state. The massive "roll-back" campaigns of organized business can only be met by an invigorating vision for the rejuvenation of the welfare state and its development into a welfare society in the New Millennium. Hopefully this book will make a small contribution to developing that vision.

Part 1
Theoretical Considerations

2. Civil Society, the Third Sector and the Welfare Mix

The purpose of this chapter is to discuss some the main concepts necessary to our study of social enterprises, civil democracy and the transformation of the welfare state. The concepts introduced here are civil society, nonprofit organizations and the third sector. First, the concept of civil society is deliberated. Then voluntary and nonprofit organizations are considered as a social institution from an ideal typical perspective. Later, the concept of sectors and the third sector is introduced. Following this, the relations between the third sector and other sectors are discussed and finally shifts in the welfare mix are considered. Similarly, the concept of "citizens as co-producers" will be introduced in Chapter 4, while two additional concepts of relevance for our study, namely "multi-stakeholder organizations" and "social accounting", will be discussed at greater length in Chapters 5 and 6.

2.A The Concept of Civil Society

The concept of civil society can claim a long and rich theoretical heritage, although it has been employed in widely different contexts and with widely different meanings. It disappeared almost completely from the public discourse for long periods, only to reappear with a new definition and with new implications for the relationship between the state and the third sector. Much of the contemporary attraction with the concept may lie in the fact that it appeals to many levels and layers of meaning. However, the disparity of definitions results not only in shifting usage of the concept, but also in uncertainty. Kumar (1993) seriously questions the potential contribution of such a rich historical term in today's public discourse. The concepts of civil society is problematical due to its elasticity, since it means so many different things. This causes serious difficulties in distinguishing it from most conventional statements of liberal democratic theory, and from concepts of constitutionalism, citizenship and democracy (*ibid.*, 392). Although civil society is not a neutral social-scientific category for everyday analysis, an awareness of this can perhaps help to avoid too far reaching or categorical conclusions about the nature of the relationship between the state and the third sector.

Henriksen (1994) points to the pit-falls of overlooking or combining three different aspects of the concept of civil society. It can be seen as a special sector of society, as an economic legal category along side the state and market, and as a sociological structuring principle. However, initially it was a philosophical concept with a specific political character and its critical potential may still be its most useful contribution. The ideological nature of the concept, especially as it is currently used provide a fourth aspect that should not be ignored in academic discussions.

Civil society is perceived differently by liberals like Locke, democrats like Rosseau, conservatives like Hegel or socialists like Marx and Engles. These differences can have both scientific and political consequences. Freedom and individuality are centrally held values in Western political thought, and that they are often related to private property and a distinction between the public and private spheres (Berg, 1987). The theoretically loaded concept of "civil society" has been (re-)introduced in the Swedish debate and contrasted with the state. This development was inspired by events in Central and Eastern Europe at the time of the fall of Communism (*ibid.*). The perception of a dichotomy between the public/private spheres and an inevitable conflict between them varies with different theoretical traditions in European political thought.

For some theorists, like Rosseau and Hobbes, civil society was synonymous with the state; while others, like Locke and Paine, elaborate a distinct sphere of society with its own forms and principles, based on inalienable human rights that could be defended against an evil state, if the need arises; yet others, like Hegel and Marx, considered civil society equivalent to the market, while Gramsci provides several definitions, including not just economic, but also social and civil institutions (Kumar, 1993).

Comte, de Tocqueville, Durkheim, Tönnies, and others also attempt to create an alternative to "the atomization of competitive market society", on the one hand, and "a state dominated existence", on the other. Their efforts generally point to voluntary groups and organizations through which individual citizens develop the sense of social solidarity and civil participation. Thus, de Tocqueville adds a third region to the state-society dichotomy. The state is a system of formal political representation, with its parliamentary assemblies, courts, bureaucracy, police and army. Civil society is essentially the arena of private interest and economic activity, which also corresponds more or less directly to the capitalist economy that Marx identifies with civil society.

But, while Marx makes this the whole of non-state society, de Tocqueville critically adds another dimension, the dimension of "political society" (Kumar, 1993, 381), that draws on what he calls the most important "law" controlling human societies, "the art of association". In civilized societies there are political associations, such as local governments, juries, parties and public opinion; and there are civil associations, such as churches, moral crusades, schools, literary and scientific societies, newspapers and publishers, professional and commercial organizations, organizations for leisure and recreation. The life of *all* these associations constitutes political society. Political associations can be thought of as "...great free schools to which all citizens come to be taught the general theory of associations." Civil associations pave the way for political ones. It is through political society that the potential excesses of the centralized state, especially in democratic societies, are controlled. Thus, political society educates us for politics, tempers our passions and curbs the unmitigated pursuit of private self-interests (*ibid.*, 382). Ambjörnsson (1988) expresses a similar view of the role of popular movements in the development of democracy in Sweden at the turn of the last century.

For Hegel civil society stands in contrast to the state and comprises the sphere for individuals and particular special interests. At the center of this sphere was the capitalist market, the growth of which gradually eroded traditional religious, ethical and political ties. But, the state is not the only power that can keep together and integrate the particular wills of civil society into a rational social order, since civil society contains both integrating and disintegrating forces. In a market people enter into egoistic competition with equally egoistic persons. Integration is achieved through voluntary organizations or social corporations which generate solidarity, collective identity and public commitment. Thus, social integration can be achieved through state intervention into civil disputes and by setting the rules of the game, or by civil society's own institutions, which educate and socialize their members into the society as a whole (*ibid.*, 375).

Marx's reduction of civil society to economic matters, on the other hand, led Marxism away for the social structure of civil society (*ibid.*, 380). The diversity of Gramsci's attempts (1971) to formulate a position concerning the State leads to various definitions that delimit it from civil society: e.g., the State "as political society plus civil society", where political society is the arena of coercion and domination and civil society is that of consent and direction or "leadership"(*ibid.,* 208). He also conceives the State as "a balance between political society and civil society"; "civil society and the State as one and the same"; while "between the economic structure and the State with its legislation and its coercion stands civil society" (*ibid.,* 208). Finally, he says "by the 'State' [we] should understand not only the apparatus of government, but also the 'private' apparatus of 'hegemony' or civil society" (*ibid.*, 261).

Kumar concludes that:

> Hegel's concept of civil society, as the realm of association interpenetrated by the state, remains one of the most satisfactory. It has the merit of acknowledging the complementary nature of state and civil society, of their need of one another in the maintenance of both individuality and sociability, private interest and communal purpose, freedom and regulation. (Kumar, 1993, p. 389)

Kumar (1993) and Henriksen (1994) underline the need of reducing the sociological emphasis of the concept of civil society. Henriksen considers Nisbet's concept of "community" more relevant for describing the sociological phenomena many now call civil society. Community, according to Nisbet, is:

> something that goes far beyond mere local community. The word, as we find it in much 19th and 20th century thought encompasses all forms of relationships which are characterized by a high degree of personal intimacy, emotional depth, moral commitment, social cohesion, and continuity in time. Community is founded on man conceived in his wholeness rather than in one or another of the roles, taken separately, that he may hold in a social order... Community is a fusion of feeling and thought, of tradition and commitment, of membership and volition. It may be found in, or given symbolic expression by, locality, religion, nation, race, occupation, or crusade. Its archetype, both historically and symbolically, is the family. (Nisbet, 1966, 47-48, as quoted in Henriksen, 1994, 366)

The traditional distinction between the state and civil society and the difference between public and private sectors was not highly controversial in Sweden until recently. Voluntary organizations have had a decisive impact on our understanding of which problems and responsibilities were public and of how to resolve them, in the Nordic welfare states since the 1930s. Moreover, they have, positively affected the welfare state's organization development and value base (Henriksen, 1994). In so-called "state-friendly societies" of the Scandinavian type (Grindheim & Selle, 1990; Kuhnle & Selle, 1992) civil society and voluntary organizations played an important integrative function in the new social/political project of the 1930s (*ibid.*). Thus, previously, there was no confrontation between civil society and the state in Scandinavia over the development of the welfare state. This is no longer the case today, as demonstrated in the recent record of the Swedish Confederation of Employers and their efforts to bring about a neo-liberal paradigm shift and to replace the universal welfare state with a residual safety net based on subsidiarity and means-tests.

However, Henriksen, following Habermas, claims that civil society deals with opinion formation by associations with democratic and political goals, which are not part of the public administration, but nevertheless manage to have a political impact via the mass media, either in the form of direct participation in public communications or, through projects advocating alternatives to conventional wisdom, since such activities provide examples through which they implicitly contribute to public discussion (1994). Habermas, argues that the public discourse of civil society concerns:

> a constitutionally instituted formation of the political will and the spontaneous flow of communication unsubverted by power, within a public sphere that is not geared toward decision-making, but toward discovery and problem resolution and that in this sense is unorganized. (Habermas, 1992, p. 451, as quoted in Henriksen, 1994, 373)

The public discourse in Sweden the past two decades, however, suggest the necessity of modifying this particular aspect of Habermas' view of civil society. In recent decades the Swedish Confederation of Employers (SAF) has spent considerable amounts of money on promoting a neo-liberal paradigm shift. SAF's opinion formation promotes ideas and arguments calling, among other things, for the drastic curtailing of the welfare state and introducing more market mechanisms in the public sector. It has spend twice as much on opinion formation as all the political parties taken together in election years, and it has done so for 25 years (Pestoff, 1995b). Thus, SAF's role is not confined to "the discovery of and resolution of problems by civil society itself", but rather toward influencing the content of public policy-making.

We agree with Henriksen that the universal welfare state has been the dominant integrative power in society in the Scandinavian countries during the past 30 years. But, we argue that civil society is no longer a forgotten problem. SAF is now actively promoting a neo-liberal or at times even a libertarian concept of civil society in the Swedish debate; one which frames welfare state problems in terms of public vs. private, state vs. the third sector and individual freedom vs. collective bondage. Their efforts began to bear fruit in the late 1980s, and by the 1990s the negotiated economy (Neilsen & Pedersen, 1988; Nielsen & Pedersen, 1989) was replaced by market mechanisms in a growing number of central areas in Sweden, like the labor market, agriculture, housing policy, consumer policy, etc. (Pestoff, 1995b).

Thus, the concept of civil society has once again become highly controversial and ideological in the Swedish public discourse. There is therefore every reason to keep in mind warnings about this concept and to reserve it for philosophical questions with a specific political character and critical potential, rather than treating it as a special sector, an economic or legal category or a sociological structuring principle.

2.B Social Orders and Associations

Polanyi (1944 & 1957) refers to four basic social orders in modern societies: a) the market, b) the state, c) autocracy and d) symmetry. The main function of each social order differs. For the market, it is to promote exchange; for the state, to promote redistribution; for autocracy, to promote domestic administration, and for symmetry, to promote reciprocity. The four related principles of economic behavior designed to insure the production and distribution of goods and services are: a) exchange, b) redistribution, c) domestic housekeeping and c) reciprocity (*ibid.*). Barter, payment-in-kind and exchange comprise a principle of economic behavior that depend on the market for its efficiency. The principle of redistribution assigns production to a central authority, which also has the responsibility of distributing it. Domestic housekeeping consists of producing for your own consumption, according the needs of your group, while reciprocity builds on durable mutual-relations established among several persons (*ibid.*). These social orders, and the economic behavior associated with them, have developed in mutual adjustment to each other.

Laville (1992) distinguishes between three types of economic institutions i.e., commercial, non-commercial and non-monetary, that broadly correspond to Polanyi's model of social orders. Each of them has its own special role in assuring order in the production and distribution of goods and services. The commercial economy is reserved for the market; the non-commercial economy promotes the redistribution arrangements of the welfare state; while, the non-monetary economy is based on reciprocity, and is promoted by voluntary associations, and domestic housekeeping. All three types of economic institutions exist, or co-exist alongside each other in mixed economies.

Similarly, Streeck and Schmitter (1985) spell out the basic governing institutions of the market, the state and community, while exploring the role of associations as an emerging potential fourth governing institution.

According to them, each governing institution has its own guiding principles, predominant actors and resources, and principal motives and pay-off, etc. (*ibid.*). Different rules of inclusion (or exclusion) apply to the different social order: ownership and/or purchase provides the basis for inclusion in the market; citizenship and/or minimum residence comprise it for the state; while kinship and/or friendship provide it for community. The criteria for inclusion in associations is membership and/or sponsorship.

Similarly, we find a division among social scientists studying different social orders. The activities and functions of market institutions are the focus of economics, the activities and functions of state institutions comprise the material of political science and the activities and functions of community institutions provide the focus of sociology. The mixed nature of associations is perhaps underlined by the fact that they are not the main focus of any single academic discipline, but rather receive marginal interest in several of them, which also contributes to their interdisciplinary nature. Associations can, of course, be understood from an economic, political and sociological perspective. For economists, voluntary organizations can be understood in terms of the logic of collective action and selective incentives (Olson, 1965 & 1971) or market failure (Hansmann, 1980 & 1988; Weisbrod, 1988). For political scientists, voluntary associations both comprise part of community and mediate the interests of their members-cum-citizens vis-à-vis the state (Truman, 1951; Lipset, 1960 & 1963; Schmitter, 1974). For sociologists, associations exist in-between society and isolated individuals, permitting the construction of community vis-à-vis the state (Riesman, 1948; Kornhauser, 1960; Coser, 1956; Simmel, 1912).

Evers and Wintersberger's (1990) welfare triangle helps to depict these social orders and the relationship among them, and, therefore, provides a good starting point for this phase of our inquiry. Evers (1993) also argues that voluntary associations are found in the intermediate area between the state, market and informal sectors. However, their model requires further specification, as it is necessary to define the limits of various social orders and to clarify the position of associations in relation to the three major social orders at the micro, meso and macro levels. It is necessary to keep several important social distinctions in mind when examining the welfare triangle and the inter-relatedness of these social orders. The essential social dimensions are: public/private, for-profit/nonprofit and formal/informal (Pestoff, 1996a). These three social dimensions help to delimit and to distinguish the three main social orders from each other and from associations, as ideal types. They also contribute to depicting associations as a mixed order.

2.B.1 Sectors, the Third sector and its Definition

The concepts of social orders or governing institutional should not be confused with that of sectors, in particular not when considering the provision of personal social services. The former comprise abstract ideal types, while the latter refer to empirical phenomenon (Henriksen, 1997), and may or may not be providing personal social services. We now want to shift our focus to the empirical world where voluntary associations and nonprofit organizations exist, in order to explore their relation with the real world's of the state, market and community. In doing so we will also shift our terminology from the abstract, and speak of "the third sector", conceived of herein as a somewhat broader category than the ideal type associations. As illustrated by Figure 2.1, the third sector extends, in practice beyond the strict domain of associations and shades the domains of the state, the market and community.

Evers (1995) discusses the specific rationality of each major social sector, the state, the market, the community and the intermediate or third sector. Grindheim & Selle (1990) maintain that:

> it is useful to divide social welfare-producing institutions into four main sectors: the informal sector of the family or community; the for-profit sector, where social goods are offered by profit-seeking and profit-distributing institutions; the formalized sector of voluntary organizations; and the public sector. (p. 63)

Similarly, Klausen (1989) distinguishes between four types of providers of welfare services: the state, providing public or statutory services; the market, providing for-profit services; the third sector, providing formalized nonprofit services and the informal sector, providing services through family, kinship and local social networks (*ibid.*, 245). Henriksen (*op cit.*) argues that voluntary organizations as actors or providers of welfare belong to a distinct class or group - a sector - with certain features that are distinct from those of other actors and that can not be traced back to the state, the market or the community (*ibid.*, 1).

Aside from classifying the third sector, how do we define it? The third sector can be defined in relational terms from its position vs. the other sectors. It is delimited here by the shaded circle that partially overlaps with other sectors, where it both interfaces and interacts with them. These social sectors are sometimes referred to as the first, second, third and fourth sectors, where the state comprises the first sector, the market the second, associations the third and community the fourth. The third sector, which consists of the shaded circle in the figure below, is placed at the cross-roads in-between the other social sectors, denoting its mixed nature. But at the same time this very mix or heterogeneity makes the concept of the third sector more problematical.

English terms used for actors found in the third sector include:

> voluntary associations, non-profit organizations, private non-profit organizations, non-governmental or non-statutory organizations, philanthropic bodies, foundations charities, charitable trusts, local or community initiatives, third or independent sector agencies, the commons, and doubtless many more. In other languages there are terms which do not have exact or obvious English counterparts; examples would be the French *économie sociale*, the German *gemeinnützige Träger, Vereine und Nicht-Erwerbsbetriebe*, and the Italian *organizzazioni senza fine di lucro* and *terzo settore*. (Anheier & Knapp, 1990, 4)

We should hasten to add the Swedish *folkrörelser* or the Norwegian *folkebevegelse*, which are roughly translated as "popular movements". However, already with the French *économie sociale* and equally so with the Scandinavian terms certain problems of definition occur, as will be seen below.

There is an extraordinarily diverse set of organizations found in between the market, the state, and the community i.e. formal organizations that are not strictly governmental agencies nor profit maximizing enterprises. This explains why that the term "the third sector" is so widely used in Europe and the USA, rather than the "voluntary sector" or the "nonprofit sector" (Girdon, *et al.*, 1992). The concept of the third sector is usually taken as shorthand "...for a myriad of organizational forms, governance structures, activities, sources of income and other support, expectations, intentions, constraints, histories and futures" (Anheier & Knapp, 1990, 3). The use of such a conventional summary expression, such as the third sector, is only legitimate if we keep this diversity in mind.

Some of these organizations provide services to members and non-members, while others have an essentially advocacy representative role. The services they provide may take many forms, including day-care centers, universities, symphony orchestras and theaters, handicap care, adoption agencies, health care and hospitals, but also trade associations, labor unions, political parties, neighborhood organizations, self-help groups, and groups advocating for a wide variety of causes, from environmental protection to the preservation of civil rights. What distinguishes these organizations is not only that they are constitutionally independent from the government, and that they are not primarily commercial or profit-seeking in purpose, but also that they have their own procedures for self-government, and serve some public purpose.

For comparative purposes Anheier & Knapp distinguish between street definitions, legal definitions, statistical convention and academic definitions (*ibid.*). The latter can either be based on a residual definition, as is the case herein, or on first principles. Efforts of exclusion, i.e., what is left over once governmental, commercial and informal sectors have been put aside, are sometimes associated with theories of the market and government failure. Definitions by first principles attempt to specify the common characteristics and emphasize the core components and attributes of the organizations of interest (*ibid.*, 5).

Figure 2.1 The Third Sector and the Welfare Triangle

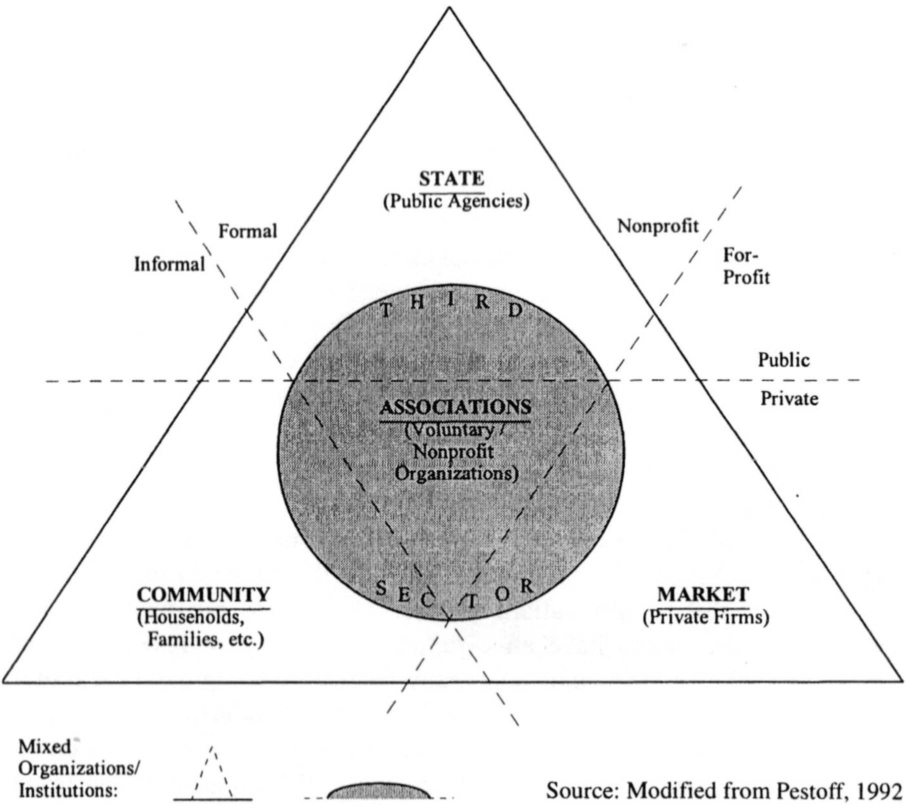

Source: Modified from Pestoff, 1992

©V. Pestoff, 1996a.

One of the main characteristics of voluntary organizations, as they are now defined around the world, is their adherence to the requirement of the non-distribution constraint, or the inability to distribute any surplus revenue to owners or other individuals who exercise control over an organization, such as members, directors or trustees (*ibid.*, 6; Hansmann, 1980). Profits or a surplus can be earned, but they must be reinvested into the organization or its activities.

However, different countries have different legal requirements and tax policies for such organizations. The definition based on first principles proposed above by Anheier & Knapp, takes its origin in American tax law. It provides legal non-profit status and subsequent tax exemptions to organizations which do not distribute their surplus. US tax law is very complex and Weisbrod (1988) notes the great diversity of categories of nonprofit organizations; ranging from those receiving contributions by individual donors which are eligible for deductions from personal income tax, to those with income which is not subject to corporate taxes, and organizations with taxes on non-related activities, etc. Tax relief to certain types of organizations can also be found in many European countries, but the rules are far from identical with those found in the US. Taxes on non-related income is also dealt with quite differently in different countries.

Thus, a first principle definition of the term "nonprofit" based on a single country's tax laws is not useful for comparative work, due to its American bias (Gidron *et al.* 1992, 3-4). Moreover, the non-distribution constraint also has unintended theoretical, legal-cultural and empirical implications not behooving comparative academic inquiry. It encourages the study of benevolent activities by well-to-do groups in America and Britain, where they play an important role in the production of social welfare services; but, by the same token, it discourages the study of cooperative, mutual or self-help actives by ordinary citizens in Europe and elsewhere.

Furthermore, American scholars consider restraints on the distribution of profit as a condition necessary for gaining the trust of consumers of certain welfare services and of the public-at-large. Profits and their distribution must, however, be related to the purpose of an organization. Cooperatives also gain trust among their members and the public-at-large, in spite of distributing a small part of their economic surplus. Thus, the non-distribution constraint should be related to who, or which group of stakeholders, benefits most from the activities of an organization. Is it the majority of the users themselves or is it a small and anonymous group of financiers? Cooperatives and mutual societies distribute a small portion of the surplus that their own collective efforts and economic activities produce. Selective economic incentives for members are an essential ingredient of collective action (Olson, 1965 & 1971). Dividends are distributed to members in accordance with their own economic activity within the organization, and thus, indirectly with their own contribution to the joint economic surplus or added value they create together. The non-distribution constraint fails to take this into account; thereby placing cooperatives in the same category as multi-national conglomerates.

The alternative principle of "one-member/one-vote" is deemed more important for studying cooperatives. Thus, the major regional consumer cooperative societies in Sweden, have recently separated their commercial activities from the membership organizations. But, by re-organizing the commercial activities as limited stock companies, members no longer have any say in the management of their local consumer cooperatives. Membership influence has been effectively eliminated in most Swedish consumer cooperatives, and the very term "member" means little more than "membership" in the American Express Company.

In Europe "the third sector" tends to be understood more inclusively and it means something broader than "nonprofits", e.g., it also includes cooperatives and mutual societies, as well as associations (6 & Pestoff, 1994). In much of continental Europe the inclusion of these three constituent parts of the third sector is self-evident, since cooperatives and mutual societies can claim between 55-60 million members each in Western Europe (EC, Economic & Social Committee, 1986). Moreover, they are usually considered an integral part of the not-for-profit sector in many European countries (Borzaga & Mittone, 1997). They are also considered part of *l'économie sociale* in France (Defourny & Munzon, 1992) and of Scandinavian *folkrörelser/folkbevegelse* (Pestoff, 1977; Pestoff, 1991 & 1996; Stryjan & Wijkström, 1996). The cultural appeal of cooperatives and mutuals is found in the fact that they practice direct grass-roots economic democracy. The culturally given identities of the third sector are more varied in Europe. However, given these cultural differences, the choice of the non-distribution constraint as the first principle appears less obvious in Europe. For many Europeans researchers, differences between personal/individual membership organizations, along with considerations of internal democracy, may be more relevant for their research focus than non-distribution constraints.

Despite decades of extensive discussions and debates about the most appropriate definition of the voluntary, nonprofit and third sectors, there are still several problems in the use of definitions to determine the scope of the field of research; particularly given cultural and political ideas about the scope of the sector (6 & Pestoff, 1994). Research can easily become the prisoner of various definitions (Lundström & Wijkström, 1994). More intensive efforts to reach truly general first principle definitions than those based on the institutional or cultural limits of any single nation or group of researchers would, of course, be very welcome. But, until such time first principles, implicitly or explicitly, serve more as cultural blinders than as guiding lights. Thus, the residual approach to defining the third sector will be maintained herein and both cooperatives and mutual societies, as well as voluntary organizations constrained by non-distribution requirements will be treated as parts of the third sector.

2.B.2 Relations between the Third Sector and Other Sectors

The third sector is an intermediate sector, which is intimately interrelated with the other three sectors, the state, the market and the informal sector. Conceiving of the third sector, as an intermediate sector, makes an important difference for research in at least four respects (Evers, 1995):

a) it calls attention to the importance of the social and political role of third sector organizations, which are otherwise usually only recognized by most American scholars in their economic role as alternative service providers;

b) it underlines the intermediating role of third sector organizations, in relation not only with states and markets, but also with the informal or community sphere;

c) it emphasizes the synergetic mixes of resources and rationales available to organizations in this sector, rather than a substitution or assimilation process between clear-cut sectors; and

d) it leads to a recognition of the great variety of ways in which intermediary organizations act as hybrids, intermeshing different resources and connecting with different areas, rather than trying to set boundaries around the sector and to map its size, etc. (*ibid.*, 160).

Historically the third sector develops different roles in different welfare systems. The role of organizations with social and service related purposes varies according to the historical and political traditions, as a brief comparison of the US, Germany and Nordic countries shows. The characteristics of the third sector are simultaneously shaped by and shape the respective influences of state institutions, the market actors and the informal sector of families, etc. (*ibid.*, 162-63). Thus, there is a constant tension at the border between the intermediate area or the third sector, on one hand, and the market, state and informal sectors, on the other. The first type of tension concerns the conflict between the instrumental rationality of the market and the solidaristic, social and democratic values of both the third sector and the state. The next type of tension is related to state institutions and their universalistic values, which are contrasted by the particularistic logic of the third sector. Finally, there is the tension between the third sector and the informal worlds of the family, personal relationships, neighborhoods, and social networks, etc., which make it harder to draw a clear line between the two in areas of help and self-help, etc. (*ibid.*, 167). This gives a polyvalent and hybrid nature to third sector organizations, which must act under the multiple influence from and dependence on the other three sectors, and in extreme cases it may result in organizational transformation. Thus, third sector organizations often pursue multiple goals simultaneously, i.e., providing service to members and others, lobbying for changes in the law or regulations, etc. (*ibid.*, 170-71). Balancing various activities can be very difficult, and also require greater transparency between the managers of third sector organizations and their strategic stakeholders, a topic to which we will return at greater length in Chapters 5 and 6.

Given the diversity of the organizations embraced by the third sector and their intermediary nature, there is good reason to question whether it constitutes a distinctive sector at all. However this is equally true of the other sectors found in Figure 2.1. The market is made up both of small "Mom & Pop's" country stores and huge multi-national corporations operating on all continents. The state is made up of public agencies at local, regional and state level, national or federal governments, interregnal governments like the European Union, and even international bodies like the United Nations, the IMF, World Bank, etc. Community is made up of traditional extended families, core families, single-parent families, single person households, etc. Thus, thc sector concept is problematic, but not necessarily more so for the third sector than other sectors of society.

Finally, different parts of the circle in Figure 2.1 comprising the third sector are closer to one of these other three social sectors. Actors within the circle can express varying degrees of privateness/publicness, nonprofitness/for-profitness and formality/informality, placing them closer to one or the other of the other three social sectors. Thus, according to Henriksen (1993a), it is possible to find voluntary organizations that are very highly oriented to the public sector, employing similar methods of work, having similar service delivery and similar institutional composition (*ibid.*, 13). It is equally possible to find voluntary organizations that have part or most of their activities oriented toward commercial pursuits ranging from holding raffles and lotteries to owning factories or stores and producing or selling goods, as cooperatives normally do. And it is possible to find voluntary organizations which express greater or lesser degrees of spontaneous solidarity, as self-help groups or organizations providing shelter for the homeless or comfort for persons afflicted by disease or disaster.

We can also note some overlap between the third sector and the other sectors. Organizations found in these overlapping areas have special characteristics. Taking them one-by-one we see an area of overlap between *the third sector and the market*. Here we find illustrations of mixed organizations, such as commercial non-governmental or nonprofit organizations, NGOs/NPOs. Consumer and agricultural cooperatives constitute a central component of this sub-category and illustrate the dangers inherent in such intermediary positioning. A multiciplicity of goals increases the risks of goal displacement or organizational atrophy associated with pursuing conflicting goals. Cooperatives in effect can become like ordinary private firms, as the Swedish consumer cooperatives illustrate. (See Pestoff, 1991 & 1996 for details.)

Also at the border between nonprofits and for-profits, we find business interest associations. They often exist in pairs and they function as twin organizations in Sweden, mainly for the purpose of tax exemptions. Both of them, however, normally serve the same member firms. One is a NGO/NPO that collects annual dues and can therefore maintain untaxed reserves, while its twin is established as a service company, permitting members to deduct the service fees. In addition to serving the same members, such twin organizations usually have the same executive boards, the same president and CEO, etc. (Pestoff, 1988 & 1989). Legally one of these twins is nevertheless a NGO/NPO while the other a private for-profit firm. However, treating one as a nonprofit and the other as a for-profit ignores their twin nature and seriously distorts our understanding of their combined activities and resources.

Turning to the organizations found in the overlap between *the state and the third sector*, we can note the increased blurring between public and private results in new or hybrid organizations. One example is found in quasi-public organizations, or what Streeck and Schmitter refer to as "private interest government" (1985), where the division between public and private almost disappears. Private nonprofit organizations are explicitly given official public responsibilities in terms of defining, deciding and implementing public policy. Such quasi-public organizations often comprise the nexus of networks of public and private bodies with strong mutual interest in regulating a certain field (Kenis, 1990). This is seen in the case of NGOs/NPOs which become involved in the regulation of certain public matters, such as farmers' organizations that become involved in regulating agricultural production, prices, import quotas and export subsidies (Pestoff, 1991 & 1996).

Still at the border between the state and third sector we find political parties. They demonstrate a unique capacity to transform themselves in to public authorities and assume major governmental functions for a limited period of time (Pestoff, 1977). They can form a government, in accordance with election results and coalition negotiations, and, later freely return to the ranks of the opposition, given different political outcomes. Few other voluntary associations are required to be so systematically flexible.

Finally, when examining to the overlap between *the community and the third sector*, we note numerous examples of mixed organizations. One such example is found in the area of HIV/AIDS (Walden Laing & Pestoff, 1997; Marin & Kenis, 1997). Here a formal nonprofit organization may attract the support of numerous individuals who are not formally members of an organization, but who nevertheless contribute their time and/or money to support the activities of an organization and to help achieve its goals. Another example is found in a variety of mutual-aid and self-help groups. Here the "members" either have not formed a formal association or the associations do nor restrict their activities to "dues-paying members" of a formal organization. Rather, they are opened to all relevant persons in the community served by such mutual-aid or self-help group. Social enterprises and consumer cooperative social services will be found closer to the overlap between the community and the third sector, than other types of cooperatives.

Wc want to round off this part of our discussion by considering the relationship between the third sector and the other three sectors. Starting with the relationship between the state and the third sector both Gidron *et al.* (1992) and Kuhnle & Selle (1992) categorically reject what they perceive as the dominant, but thoroughly inaccurate and uninformed paradigm of competition and/or conflict between the third sector and the state. Drawing on in depth in numerous countries, including France, Germany, Hungary, N. Ireland, Israel, Italy, the Netherlands, Norway, Switzerland, Slovenian and the USA, they refer to "dubious, long-lived myths" about the encroachment of an expanding welfare state into the domain of the voluntary sector (Kuhnle & Selle, 1992,1). This belief is based more on ideology and political opportunism than empirical documentation (*ibid.*, 6). The unprecedented expansion of the welfare state in the post-W.W.II period should, according to the competition paradigm, have led to the disappearance of the third sector in most European countries, something which is clearly counter-factual.

Gidron *et al.* propose four models of conceivable relations between the third sector and the state in the provision of personal social services, based on a distinction between financing and delivering social services. They range from: a) government domination, b) dual provision, c) collaborative relations to d) third sector dominance (*ibid.*, 17-19). They find no evidence supporting the existence of the latter model. Similarly, five distinct patterns of interaction were found between local authorities and voluntary organizations in social work in the Danish City of Aalborg (Henriksen, 1997). Three of them are based on varying degrees of collaboration with public authorities and two of which involve minimal or no cooperation with the public sector.

Furthermore, the relationship between the government and the third sector normally includes the flow of resources, directly via grant aid or purchase of service through contracting-out, and indirectly via tax exemptions and third party reimbursements; regulatory and accountability requirements; the encouragement of contributions from individuals and corporate donors through income tax laws; the planning of complementary or substitute services; and the impact of public policy on governance structures and organizational autonomy.

Links with the for-profit sector like corporate philanthropy or sponsoring are an important source of income for the third sector. But, growing competition in some countries between the third sector and the for-profit sector can result in increasing tensions between the two. Tax benefits for US nonprofit organizations are more frequently being questioned by their for-profit competitors, under the claim of unfair competition with small private business in the US and elsewhere (Rose-Ackerman, 1990).

The household or informal sector also has strong ties with the third sector. It supplies volunteers and paid employees and it participates in the management of voluntary organizations. Moreover, it donates large sums of money on a regular basis; it purchases services, pays membership fees and it is also obliged to pay much of the taxes which help to subsidize the third sector. Finally, in many other ways it demands or receives services and support from the third sector (Anheier & Knapp, 1990).

2.C Shifts in the Welfare Mix

The concept of the welfare mix provides a set of coordinates to assess the changing configuration of providers of welfare services. At the macro level, the idea of the welfare mix expresses variations in the importance attributed to the institutions of community, market, state and associations in the governance of society (Evers, 1993) and at the micro level in the role played by various sectors in delivering social welfare. The separation between public and private, for-profit and nonprofit or formal and informal is not the same everywhere nor fixed once and for all, but rather varies both in political, societal and temporal terms. What is seen as an appropriate role for the state in one country or period may not hold for another country or period. Much of the contemporary political struggle concerns the issues of what the state should do, what the market should do and what should be left to the third sector. Universal welfare states attribute many more responsibilities to the public sector and fewer to the market than do residual welfare states. Some countries, such as the Nordic countries, are well known for their highly developed welfare states, while others, like the United States, are associated much more closely with commercial provision of basic social services. Yet, traditional patterns of governance change with time and political shifts. Thus, in the early 1990s Sweden experienced determined attempts to dismantle the welfare state, under the auspices of a conservative coalition, while the United States, under President Clinton, experienced the first serious, but aborted, attempt to provide most of its citizens with access to medical care.

The institutional choices can also vary at the meso-level or between policy areas. A certain mix of public, commercial, not-for-profit and informal may be found in one policy area, while another may be prevalent in another area. Thus, one type of welfare mix may be found in social policy (Pestoff, 1996a), another type may exist in industrial policy and a third type may dominate consumer policy (Pestoff, 1984; Pestoff, 1989). The role attributed to various social orders can also shift dramatically with changes in regimes, as seen in the transformation of the post-socialist countries in Central & Eastern Europe. Previously, the state dominated the welfare triangle and there was very little room for the actors and institutions associated with community, the market and independent associations (Pestoff, 1978). Széman (1995) refers to a shift from a state dominated to a state centered, or even a voluntary sector centered, welfare mix in Hungary. However, it is no easy task to establish the new institutions necessary for a successful transformation. North (1993) estimate that it may take longer than expected to bring about fundamental changes in Central and Eastern Europe, and much longer in the former Soviet Union.

Much of the recent debate about privatization of the welfare state often fail to take into account the characteristic differences of various social orders. Moreover, a shift from one type of social order to another for providing goods and/or services also implies a shift in the dominant values associated with each social order. Both the proponents of and opponents to privatization in Sweden have conceived this phenomenon in a black/white terms. This highly polemic debate fails to recognize the different paths to privatization, nor their divergent values and consequences. It is therefore necessary to clarify such differences and the far-reaching consequences associated with each one, both for the theory and practice of the welfare state.

Privatization of the provision of personal social services can follow one of three distinct paths or trajectories, each with different values and implications for society. These distinct social values require different social institutions for their fulfillment. First, a privatization that results in*a greater role for the market* implies a commercialization and commodification of social services. This alternative depends on the ability of consumers or clients to pay for the service, thus excluding many groups in society from such services. Second, a privatization that is based on *greater community responsibility* implies a subsidiarization, feminization and deprofessionalization of the provision of social services. Women are either forced off of the labor market or kept off it, and compelled to provide personal social services to relatives without pay. This is the main path for privatizing social services in Central and Eastern Europe (Pestoff, 1996b). Third, a privatization that depends on *a greater role for nonprofit organizations and voluntary associations* can imply a democratization and cooperativization of the provision of social services. Under certain circumstances, this type of privatization can promote civil democracy and empower citizens as co-producers of the services they demand. Furthermore, all three types of privatization also imply lower taxes and a reduction in the power and redistribution functions of the state, to a greater or lesser degree. Moreover, privatization also implies greater individual contributions by consumers of goods and services and, therefore, a shift in financial and power resources between different individuals and groups in society.

It would be a mistake to interpret this simply as a case of a zero-sum game, in which the growth of one sector automatically means the diminishment of the other. First, it is not so easy in the real world to shift the production of services from one sector to another. A greater reliance on the community, market or third sector is more that a question of merely redirecting resources from public to private provision of social services. New institutions must be established, and the community, market or third sector often lack the capacity and resources necessary to assume new responsibilities on short notice (Grindheim & Selle, 1990; Pestoff, 1996a;

Henriksen, 1993b; Henriksen, 1997; Stryjan, 1995; Stryjan, 1995; and Stryjan, 1997). Secondly, greater reliance on the community, market or voluntary organizations for the provision of social services does not automatically imply a diminished role for the state. The state is still primarily seen as the financier of social services, even if they are contracted out or provided by competing bodies. Finally, both the third sector and the government are embedded in an institutional setting and a national style of politics and policy-making (Seibel, 1990). Thus, the government/third sector relationship is far less flexible in terms of mutual substitution than economists often suggest.

A key issue in the discussion of finding a more appropriate "mix" between the sectors and organizations providing social services is the search for more synergetic welfare mixes, both at the micro and macro levels (Evers, 1995, 173). At the micro level hybrid solutions that mix the benefits of more than one sector can result in more "intelligent" solutions, where public and private contributions are intermeshed in a fashion promoting both professionalism with voluntary cooperation and general norms and standards with specific ways for caring according to a given situation (*ibid.*). The cooperative social services studied herein provide a good example of such synergies. At the micro level the need for synergetic solutions will vary with the circumstances, attitudes and priorities of citizens. Some citizens may be more interested in actively participating in the provision of the services they demand than others. Some will also be more able to do so. Thus, both for elderly care and child care a number of circumstances can facilitate more active user participation in providing care.

Different mixes are conceivable, allowing for greater flexibility, or even tailor-made solutions in individual cases. Salamon (1987) suggests a "nonprofit federalism" for the US, that enables voluntary organizations to provide service delivery advantages in a highly pluralistic and fragmented society, with the revenue generating and democratic priority setting advantages of the state. This is possible since the strengths of the voluntary sector correspond with the weaknesses of the state and vice-versa. State-based services with their uniform character have serious troubles responding to specific needs and are seldom capable of providing a quick response. Community based voluntary initiatives can, however, respond more quickly to new needs. The growth of cooperative day care services in the 1980s and of other cooperative social services in the 1990s in Sweden provide a good example of this type of synergy effect both at the micro and macro levels. On the other hand, state provision stands for reliability, where voluntary efforts are often unevenly spread, or tend to exclude certain groups. Thus, the state, through its rule setting capacity can make availability of services to everybody a prerequisite for funding (*ibid.*, 174-75).

Evers argues that combining market mechanisms and state provision can bear with it certain benefits; e.g., greater flexibility through the use of service vouchers. Evers asks if the welfare mix or welfare pluralism contributes something that is fundamentally different from étatism or economic liberalism? His answer focuses not only on the costs of providing services not on a greater openness to different solutions, but also the degree to which the third sector is given an explicit role in service provision on the basis of its own virtues (*ibid.*, 176). We will take a closer look at the nature of these differences in terms their potential political and economic contribution in the chapters below and also briefly in terms of their actual performance toward the end of this book. But, Evers argues that merely conceiving of voluntary organizations or cooperatives as cheap service providers due to volunteers or a work obligations, etc., completely misses the point. Organizations found in the third sector are more than just service providers. They have a role in preserving and cultivating public virtues like participation, solidarity, etc.; they also promote economic, political and social change through pressure group activities; and their experiments often serve as innovators in service delivery, etc. (*ibid.*, 177).

Ever's emphasizes the long-range implications of the changing relationship between the state and third sector. Expenditures on third sector provision of social services can be seen as "... a long-term investment in the basic stock of social capital, not merely as a form of social spending". (*ibid.*, 179). The social capital represented by communities, social net works, voluntary organizations and cooperatives can and will erode without the continuing support of the state. However, there is a clear danger in shifting government grants to voluntary organizations, from those with a wide variety of activities to contracting out for specific projects, like service delivery. Such a shift could result in the third sector becoming"... colonized and used as a dumping grounds for simple load-shedding operations" (*ibid.*, 179; see also Kuhnle & Selle, 1992 for a similar warning).

2.D Conclusions

Much of the current debate about the role of the third sector in providing personal social services, about the nature of civil society, and about the relationship between the third sector and civil society reflect a clear neo-liberal bias that is based on a distorted and misconstrued paradigm of competition and/or conflict between the third sector and the state or between civil society and the state. Not only is this perspective inaccurate and uninformed; it also leads academic pursuits down ideologically loaded, but dead-end paths. The main goal appears to be to delegitimatize, curtail, and eventually replace the universal welfare state in the Scandinavian countries with a means-tested minimal safety-net. The purpose of such efforts appears more political and ideological than academic. With regards to the concept of civil society, it would appear, is best reserved to philosophical discussion, rather than to employ it as a sociological research. Thus, the relationship between the third sector and civil society at the concrete level remains obscured by the lack of precision or relevance of the latter.

The concept of the third sector was explored at length, and related to the other social orders, i.e., the market, the state and community. Both American and European research traditions contribute to our study of the third sector. First principle definitions of the "nonprofit sector" were rejected for being too relativistic, i.e., they are based on American tax laws and they, therefore, lack relevance outside the USA. The third sector was then related to shifts in the welfare mix. Different paths or models of privatization were considered in terms of the social values they promote. The third sector can promote the democratization and cooperativization of the production of personal social services, while the other two sectors promote other values. The market promotes the commodification and commercialization of personal social services, while a privatization that relies mainly on community promotes a deprofessionalization, and feminization of the production of personal social services.

3. The Politics of Civil Democracy

Civil democracy was defined earlier in section 1.D as citizen empowerment through cooperative self-management of personal social services, where citizens participate directly in the production of the local services they demand, and therefore become co-producers of these services. This chapter explores in greater detail various political dimensions of civil democracy. In order to do so we will first examine the divided citizen and his/her different channels of influence. Following that, we will look at the various roles as citizens, consumers and clients and their relation to classical ideas of citizen control of the public sector and public services, and how such control is modified by contracting out. Next, we will consider differences between the terms citizen and customer and issues of power and influence in consumer and client relations with the public sector. Finally, we will discuss the separation of the financing of from the production or provision of social services and developments in Denmark in terms of greater citizen participation in the provision of social services.

3.A The Divided Citizen: Various Channels of Influence and Accountability

Citizens' lives are divided into several different roles, each of them is regulated by separate social governance structures and there are separate organizations or actors associated with each governance structure. The inter-relatedness of these roles is an important feature of modern welfare states. However, they are usually studied separately and most academic disciplines only focus on one of them. Such a narrow focus only presents part of the complexity of European society at the end of the 20th Century. While it may be justifiable for teaching and research purposes, it nevertheless only comprises a small part of the multifaceted reality. The mixed economic matrix helps to depict the interrelatedness of several different roles and social institutions in Northern Europe.

Five of the most important roles citizens have in Scandinavian countries were chosen for closer examination by the Norwegian Power Study in the 1970s. These were their roles as consumers, members of interest organizations, clients of the public bureaucracy, voters and activists. This matrix can be extended to include two additional roles, i.e., the roles of

Figure 3.1 Citizens' Roles and their Channels of Influence in Mixed Economic Networks

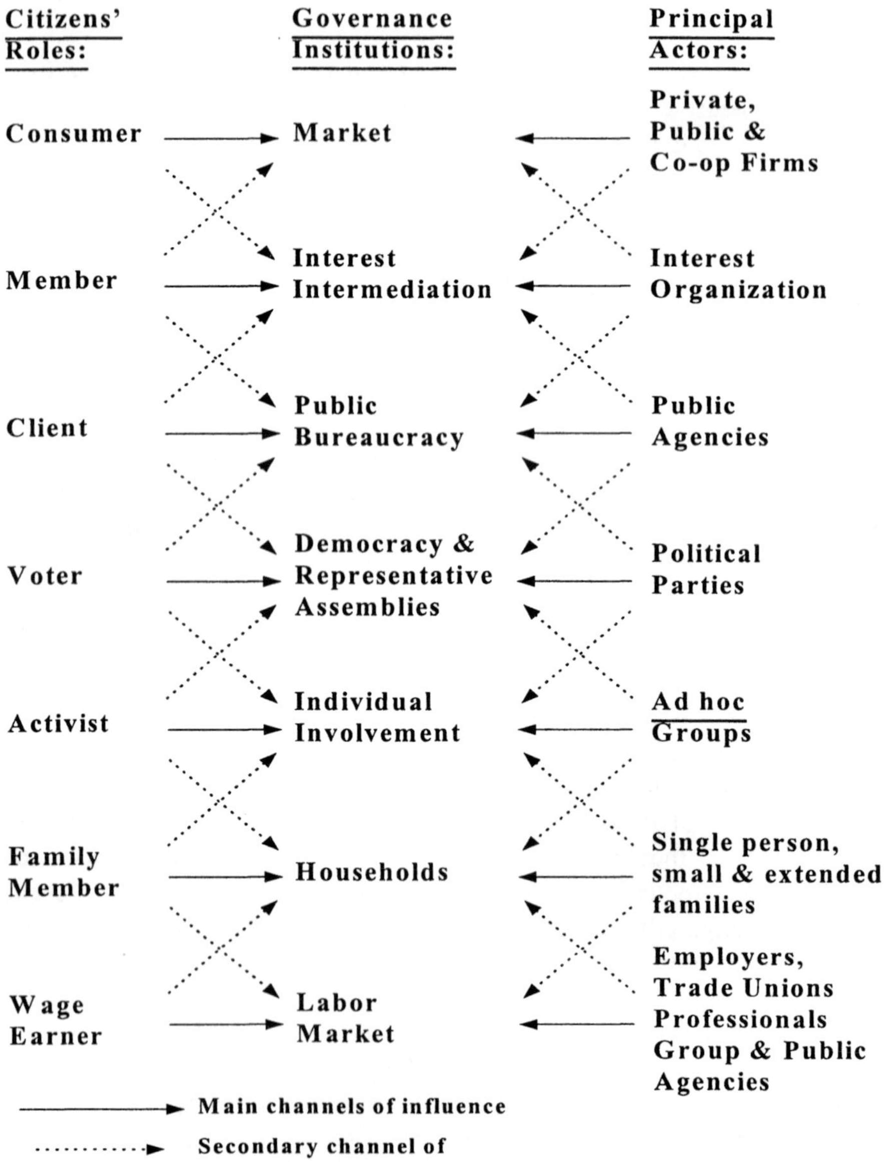

Source: Pestoff, 1996a, adapted from Berrefjord, NOU

family member and wage earner. A modified mixed economic network is presented above in Figure 3.1.

Separate channels of influence are associated with each of these roles and the governing structures of society. Taking the role of consumers as an illustration, the main channel of influence for it is the market, indicated here by the solid line in the figure. But if consumers should, for one reason or another, be dissatisfied with how the market functions, they can turn to various secondary channels of influence connected with their other roles, indicated here by the numerous broken lines in the figure above. They may be members of an organization that demands certain changes in the quality and prices of goods and services or the way the market functions. They can turn to the consumer authorities and urge them to enforce certain minimum standards of product safety or anti-monopoly legislation. They can vote for political parties that call for greater price control or more stringent consumer legislation. If everything else fails, they may even engage themselves in *ad hoc* consumer or environmental groups that promote their interests as consumers more directly. Finally, family members can coordinate and plan their purchases, hoping not only to save money, but also to gain more influence in the market. Wage earners can also band together and demand higher wages to compensate for inflation and increased consumer prices.

The diversity of roles opens numerous channels of influence to citizens in mixed economies. Normally, resourceful citizens do not limit their efforts to redress an unfavorable situation to a single channels of influence, but will try to pursue them in several different channels. Similarly, if we are not satisfied with public services, we can seek redress via our roles other than as clients. We can turn to political parties, various interest organizations, become directly involved, and/or by turning to private providers of the services we need. We will now look more closely at the political channels of influence on public services and explore possibilities for greater citizen control and influence of them.

According to classical theories of public administration, the political process traditionally provides several channel of influence for citizens in democratic societies, as illustrated in Figure 3.2 below. Traditionally expression of dissatisfaction with public services is channeled through the electoral process, shown here as a), where citizens indirectly influence or control the public sector through their choice of political parties. The effectiveness of this channel of citizen influence varies, of course, from country to country, and with the frequency, intensity and nature of electoral competition. An elected government is held responsible for the functioning of the public sector, and it in turn holds the civil service accountable to certain standards of services, as shown by b). Citizens may also express their dissatisfaction with public services directly through individual, spontaneous, *ad hoc* voice, c), i.e., by complaining directly to the service providers or to their supervisors.

Figure 3.2 Alternative Models for Citizen Control of the Public Bureaucracy

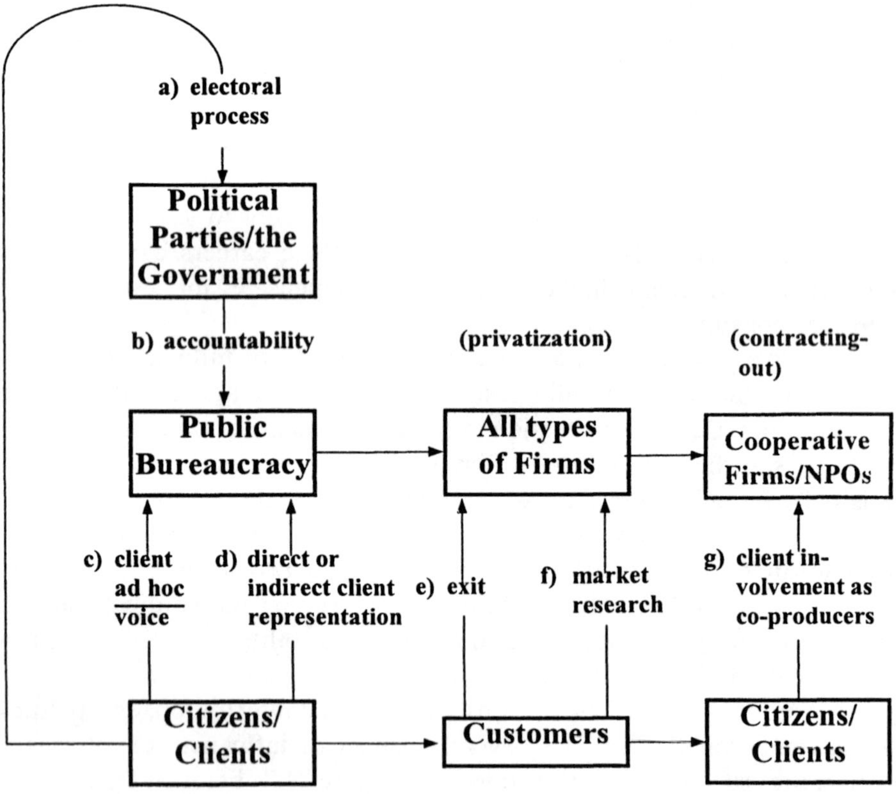

Source: V. Pestoff 1996a

The shortcomings of indirect citizen influence has sometimes led to the institutionalization of client representation in advisory councils attached to various public services, d). Several public utilities in Britain, such as the coal board, the gas board, etc., included this type of consumer representation for some decades after the war. No systematic evidence is available about the functioning of this type of direct client representation; however, more often than not the problem of "entrenched cranks" surfaced. A spokesman for a particular group of clients would gain representation on an advisory council and remain in that position for a long period, gradually loosing touch with the ordinary consumers of a particular service. Rather, they pursued their own private battles against a particular perceived shortcoming of the public service in question.

Swedish consumer policy attempted to facilitate the articulation of the weak consumer voice during the entire post war period, but it traditionally excluded public services (Pestoff, 1984; Pestoff, 1989a). Initially, the post-war governments promoted such aims through efforts to overcome various hurdles for consumer organization. Later, it attempted to bolster consumer voice by a creating countervailing consumer power and integrating consumer representatives into the public bodies charged with overseeing Swedish consumer policy. The neo-liberal government in the early 1990s, however, prepared proposals to redirect consumer policy by "privatizing" it and turning much of the responsibility for it over to voluntary associations (dir. 1992:63). They were poorly prepared to mantle such responsibility, and these plans were put on ice by the Social Democratic government which was returned in 1994 (Prop 1994/95:100). Moreover, the old Swedish model for organizing consumers lost much of its earlier importance due to Sweden's membership in the European Union.

The Citizens' Charters, were initiated in Britain by J. Major as a means of augmenting consumer influence over public services. We need to distinguish among three types of accountability, i.e. 'upward' accountability to superiors and elected officials, 'outward' accountability to professionals and other colleagues and 'downward' accountability to those receiving the goods and services (Elcock, 1993, 19-20). Citizens Charters' mainly provide for greater downward accountability, by extending certain rights, such as the right to complain, to the public, albeit as consumers or customers rather than as citizens. But they do not provide greater 'upward' or 'outward' accountability.

Service management also tends to focus on the individual consumer, who can express her/his view through consumer surveys. Consumers have a say in choosing or putting together their own package of services, although their access may vary greatly. They may also have a say through complaint procedures. But the users of public services are not generally customers in the true sense of the word, unless they freely choose to pay for a public service rather than a private one. In recognition that public services have captive customers, many local authorities in Britain have begun to introduce "Service Standards", which make explicit what to expect and how to complain if the standard is not fulfilled, similar to the Citizens' Charters at the national level. Individual citizens and consumers vary, however, considerably in their ability to make their voice heard and make their choices count (Taylor, *et al.*, 1992).

Is it possible to be accountable to both to the citizens-at-large and the consumers of particular services, and what happens if there is a conflict between the two? The fragmentation of the welfare state is not likely to lead to a dilution of upward accountability (Day, 1992). Citizens have the ability to hold those who produce services to account for what they do and to impose sanctions if they fail to perform, i.e., voters can still turn out politicians. However, when it comes to the notion of downward accountability, this is another matter. It is not only the obligation to explain, but also the existence of sanctions that is the core of accountability. It makes little sense to speak of being accountable to captive consumers of various social services.

The customers of public services are not always the direct recipients of the service provided, a situation that is evident in the case of law enforcement (Chandler, 1993). The desire of the immediate recipient of the service must be balanced against those of numerous other members of the public. Citizenship implies both rights, such as equal treatment and provision of services, and duties, such as paying taxes to finance public services. Participation in the formation of policy is a further and critical right (*op. cit.*, 9). The Citizens' Charters divert attention from schemes that encourage greater participation through decentralization of government. They emphasize the role of the individual consumers of services, but not their collective role nor their rights as citizens to participate in public policy-making.

In the Swedish debate, it is often maintained that more radical solutions are needed to improve the quality and reduce the costs of public services. The accountability of public services and civil servants can be improved if the production of public services is transferred to private firms or non-governmental organizations, either through a process of privatization or of contracting-out. Here political control of the provision of public services is still more indirect. Public bureaucrats are still accountable to politicians and the government for the quality of services themselves. These services are no longer produced by the public sector, but rather by private firms, cooperatives, nonprofit organizations, etc. An already weak or indirect channel of citizen/client influence becomes, therefore, more tenuous than before. Thus, it could be argued that privatization and/or contracting-out of public services must be accompanied by a simultaneous reinforcement of direct citizen influence over the quality of services to compensate for the loss of indirect accountability. Renewed direct accountability to clients is of course what the spokesmen for market and for cooperative solutions promise to deliver. However, there may be grounds for skepticism towards both claims. Both privatization and cooperativization open numerous new problems for political accountability.

In the case of privatization, market mechanisms are supposed to provide the managers of the newly privatized service firms with information about the preferences of the clients or consumers in the market terminology. It is consumers' market behavior, or their exit, e), that is supposed to provide the managers with the information necessary to allocate scarce resources and to make investment decisions. However, most commercial firms making consumer durables and non-durables also spend considerable amounts of money to obtain alternative sources of information to the signals provided by the market. In particular, the marketing research industry, f), focuses on providing alternative sources of information to market signals.

We must also distinguish between purchasers, providers and customers, when considering accountability (Day, 1992). In the United Kingdom the purchasers, i.e., the government, remain accountable, and nothing has changed here, but the quasi-markets and contracting-out practices change many other things. The quasi-markets introduced in the National Health Service and the social services in Britain, based on the separation of the purchaser and the provider roles, raise different issues for accountability. The real change is found in the relationship between purchaser and provider.

Whereas in the past providers were part of the same hierarchy of accountability, they will no longer be so in the future. Accountability will therefore be exercised through contracts, and only effective at the time of their renewal. In theory purchasers have sanction powers, but in reality many purchasers only have limited scope for changing their providers, due to local monopoly conditions of service provision (*ibid.*) and the length of the contracts awarded. The new relationship between purchasers and providers of social services greatly increase the transaction costs of political control, not to mention the transaction costs of negotiating and monitoring contracts. Such costs are explored in greater detail in the next chapter.

The idea of accountability to customers is not logical. The market analogy does not hold for publicly financed services, since the links between upward and downward accountability are in effect broken by the introduction of market mechanisms. In private commerce managers must be sensitive and responsive to their customers because of competition, but if they are accountable to anyone it is to their shareholders and board members. This is exactly why they are sensitive to customer reactions, otherwise they would be punished by their shareholders (*ibid.*).

Contracting-out often involves cooperatives or other nonprofit organizations as providers of public services. Here too political control is usually indirect and weak. Contracts are normally granted for a given period of two, three or more years. However, contracting-out to nonprofit organizations opens-up yet another option for greater citizen/client influence. Clients can also become involved as co-producers, g), in the production of the services that they demand, since they are often members of the social enterprise providing them with service.

3.B Solidarity and Greater Citizen Participation

This book is devoted to exploring the theoretical and empirical implications of greater consumer influence when citizens become co-producers. In order to pursue this aim, we will now consider the solidarity relations of welfare states, a model for greater citizen participation in public services and citizens as co-producers of public services.

3.B.1 Horizontal and Vertical Solidarity

Institutionalized solidarity between different social groups is one distinctive feature of the welfare state. Durkheim distinguishes between mechanical and organic solidarity, where the former is based on traditional society and the latter is associated with industrial and urban society. A discussion of the various uses of the term solidarity suggests several alternative aspects or dimensions: institutional and spontaneous solidarity; symmetric and asymmetric solidarity; traditional class and cross-class solidarity; and local and global solidarity (Juul, 1996). Another approach refers to horizontal and vertical solidarity, taking the historical class position of a given group as the logical starting point (Christensen, 1996). Thus, working class solidarity is termed horizontal since it transpires within the same class, while upper class philanthropy is termed vertical, since it is represented by the rich giving to poorer individuals in society.

However, in this book we provide a different interpretation of horizontal and vertical solidarity, i.e., from the perspective of individual or group relations with other citizens or groups of citizens. Welfare states build on the idea of redistribution and therefore normally involve transfers of resources from one group to another, i.e. some sort of institutionalized solidarity between social groups. This solidarity can be manifest between younger and older persons in society, between the occupationally active and those not active, between the better-off and the not-so-well-off persons in society, between the healthy and the sick or handicapped, etc. Solidarity relations between the social groups are institutionalized differently in different types of welfare states. The two main patterns are either articulated through vertical, or horizontal solidarity relations. *Vertical solidarity* is based on active involvement of the state in transferring resources from one social group to another. Differentiated taxes, usually progressive, are levied on most citizens and funds are transferred directly or indirectly by the state to the objects of group solidarity. The government is normally involved in vertical solidarity, in its capacity as revenue collector and financier of social programs, while individual citizens are not necessarily engaged directly in such solidarity relations.

Horizontal solidarity implies greater personal involvement, active citizen participation in the production of welfare services and less direct government involvement in the provision of public services, but not necessarily in the financing of them. Horizontal solidarity is an expression of individual or collective preferences and can have different objectives and objects. Horizontal solidarity between individual consumers/clients of various social services could be called "participatory"; solidarity between employees in a given branch or category could be termed "mutual benefit"; while solidarity between better-off citizens and less well-off groups might be referred to as "benevolent".

All welfare states combine both vertical and horizontal solidarity relations, to a greater or lesser extent. But there is often a correlation between the type of welfare state and the type of solidarity relationship. Solidarity relations are primarily institutionalized in a vertical pattern in the universal welfare state, they are more or less equally divided between vertical and horizontal solidarity relationships in industrial achievement welfare states, while they are primarily expressed through horizontal patterns in residual welfare states. Universal welfare states do not exclude benevolent solidarity relations. Rather, they consider social welfare services as entitlements of citizenship that are provided to all citizens, primarily through the public sector; thus, reducing the necessity of relying on charity. Industrial achievement welfare states normally include pronounced elements both of mutual benefit and of self-help, through collective employee insurance schemes, etc., and the role of NPOs in the delivery of social services (Fölster, 1996). Residual welfare states normally rely extensively on the activities of benevolent and charitable groups, and only provide public welfare services to the "deserving poor", often on a means-tested basis. Two additional types of welfare states are included here, the "enterprise" and the "rudimentary" welfare states.

It should be kept in mind that these different types of welfare states and solidarity relations are ideal types. Reality is of course much more complicated and most welfare states will combine the features of two or more of these ideal types. These differences in the type of welfare state and the type of solidarity relations are depicted in the figure below[1] . It should be made clear that an enterprise welfare state in Central and Eastern Europe bore/bears no similarity with the universal welfare state found in the Nordic countries, despite a similar pattern of solidarity relations in the figure below. The universal welfare state is/was a result of a long struggle by the trade unions and labor movement for improving the benefits of their members and the population in general in Europe. No such possibilities were available in Central and Eastern Europe due to the monopoly of power previously granted to the Communist Party in the constitutions of the Communist countries. Thus, trade unions were normally prevented from protecting or promoting the interests of their members through industrial action, etc. (Pestoff, 1978). Moreover, the benefits of the enterprise welfare state were best known for their meagerness (Deacon, 1992).

Changes in welfare state regimes and shifts in the welfare mix can either imply a transition from one type of welfare state regime to another in terms of the coverage provided to citizens, and/or shifts in terms of greater or lesser vertical and/or horizontal solidarity relations or both. Which of these strategies is pursued remains primarily a political and ideological question. An enterprise welfare state in a postcommunist country can be replaced by a minimal safety net for the "deserving poor", according to the recommendations of the World Bank and IMF, moving it closer to the Latin Rim model of a rudimentary welfare state. However, neither family, charity nor nonprofit organizations can fill the gap left by the disappearance of universal social benefits. A universal welfare state could be dismantled and replaced by an industrial achievement welfare state, by a residual welfare state, or by a mix of both, as neo-liberal critics of the Swedish universal welfare state usually propose. Certain features of universality can remain in

---

[1] Note that the broken lines indicate the existence of a marginal phenomenon above or below the line, as family in the Central and Eastern European enterprise welfare state or minimal state support in the rudimentary Latin Rim welfare state.

some sub-sectors, while industrial achievement may replace it as the guiding principle in other sectors and targeted benefits in yet other sectors.

Figure 3.3 Type of Solidarity Relations and Welfare State Regimes

Solidarity Relations:	ENTER-PRISE	UNIVER-SAL	INDUSTRIAL ACHIEVE-MENT	RESID-UAL	RUDI-MENT-ARY
Horizontal	(Family)	Participative	Mutual Benefit	Bene-volent	Family & Charity
Vertical	All Citizens via their Work-Sites	Public-in-General	Employees & their families	Targeted	Minimal
Countries:	Central & Eastern Europe	Scandinavian	Continental	UK & No. America	Latin Rim & Greece

Source: V. Pestoff, 1996a.

Shifts from vertical to horizontal solidarity or vice versa can also promote a greater institutional mix within the same welfare regime. Universal welfare states can either encourage a larger role for social enterprises and other nonprofit organizations and/or promote greater citizen participation in the production of the services they need or demand, like social enterprises providing day-care services, elderly care, health care, etc. A residual welfare state can extend or contract its coverage to more or fewer needy groups and/or provide them with more or less services and benefits.

3.B.2 User Empowerment: the Market or State?

We want to consider in greater detail the implications of greater citizen participation in the production of the services they demand. Following recent changes in the public service in several Anglo-American countries (Peters, 1994) and presents four alternatives to the classical model of a neutral public service; i.e., the market model, the participatory state, flexible government and deregulated government. There are several reason for the emergence of these alternatives: first, the principle of an apolitical civil service no longer holds; secondly, assumptions of hierarchical and rule-based management within the public service no longer apply, now that various alternative sources of organizational power and authority exit; and thirdly, partially as a result of these developments civil servants no longer respond mechanically to the policy directives given them by their nominal masters, i.e., the politicians. Rather civil servants have become managers in their own right, which is related to changes in possibilities to control and achieve accountability of public services (*ibid.*). There is some similarity of analysis in these alternative models and all of them imply a "hollowing" out of the State and a reduction in its significance as an actor in society.

We will primarily concentrate on presenting the participatory model, which is most germane to our purpose of exploring the implications of citizens as co-producers. However, first we note some similarities with the model presented by Taylor, *et al.*, (1992, 16-17). They discuss the development of four possible models of welfare for the provision community care at the local level, based on different combinations of financing and providing social services. Social services can either be financed by public funds or individual citizens and services can either be provided by public bodies and/or NPOs or mixed or private providers. The four models are:

a) the *welfare state model*, where the state is the financier and dominant provider of care. Users exercise influence through the democratic system, which includes only limited mechanisms for participation;

b) a *quasi-market model*, which is in the process of being established in Britain. This designates the state as the purchaser of care, but the choices of the consumer are mediated through a care manager, backed up by a system of redress related to quality standards set by the purchaser;

c) a *pure market model*, which would make the consumer or client the purchaser of care, if necessary through the provision of vouchers (although this is technically a quasi-market). The consumer would have a contract with the provider, services would need to conform to public standards and there would be a system of redress in the event of faulty service; and

d) an *enabling model*, where an authority acts as the orchestrator of a diversity of flexible care in a locality; stimulating through funding and other powers a market of alternative providers which offer choice to the user and care-giver; ensuring advise, information and advocacy to help users through this range of provisions to ensure their rights to a quality service, and to help providers to meet these requirements (*ibid.*, 17). These alternative models imply very different roles for citizens, e.g., citizens as tax payers in the welfare state, citizens as clients in quasi-markets, citizens as consumers in private markets and citizens as participants in the enabling model. Differences in the roles of citizens, consumers and clients ware discussed in greater detail in section 3.C below.

The intellectual roots of the market model are closely interwoven with the public choice or rational choice schools, which provide the most popular alternative view of the state and government. It:

> assumes that one of the principle problems with the traditional structure of the public sector is a reliance on large, monopolistic departments that respond ineffectively to signals from the environment. The size and complexity of government organizations, combined with their delivery of unpriced goods and services, is seen especially by students of public choice to be the root of a good deal of the (perceived) inefficiency and ineffectiveness of government.(Peters, 1994, 5)

The solution to these problems is rather obvious, e.g., decentralization, contracting-out to private or quasi-private organizations to deliver goods and services, and replacing equal pay scales by more market-like differential rewards related to performance. In spite of general difficulties in accurately measuring individual contributions, a more important problem is related to policy-making, particularly to coordination and control, which becomes difficult, if not impossible, once public services become decentralized (*ibid.*, 8). There is also a problem of conceiving citizens as consumers, when their rights and legal status becomes diminished, and government becomes reduced to buying and selling, a problem to which we will examine in greater detail in section 3.C below.

Experience of the Conservative Party privatization program in the United Kingdom provides some useful conceptual clarifications regarding some of those roles as consumers, etc. Concerns for consumers has been driven by the challenges of users themselves - most notably perhaps by these voters who brought in a government in 1979 committed to rolling back the welfare state in the name of choice and efficiency (Taylor, *et al.*, 1992, 5), and who also repeatedly returned it until 1996. Following its first election, the Thatcher Government put into practice its own version of user empowerment, based on neo-liberal arguments that the market would be both more efficient and more sensitive to the needs and preferences of service users (Flynn, 1992). Against this background, state-owned businesses were privatized in transportation and public utilities.

Market principles have also been introduced into welfare and education with the separation of the purchaser from the provider, compulsory competitive tendering in some areas, the introduction of "opting out" in others, internal markets in health and the development of a "contract culture" in community care (Giddens, 1994 & 1996; Le Grand, 1990). Policies encouraging independent service provision have taken place against a background of parallel policies seeking to reduce responsibility for expenditures on welfare where possible, through benefit reform, through reform of local government finance and through promotion of individual responsibility and active citizenship (Taylor *et al.*, 6; and Gastere & Taylor, 1993, 23).

The "participatory state" model is less familiar and, there is, therefore, good reason to rely heavily on Peters' presentation (*ibid.*). It may appear to be the antithesis of the market approach in terms of political ideology, but some of its recommendations appear very similar. It is often discussed under different names, such as "communitarianism", the participatory state, the "empowerment state", "discursive democracy", etc., where various groups, normally excluded under more hierarchical models, are permitted greater organizational involvement. Hierarchy is also considered a severe impediment to effective management and governance. However, rather than concentrating on the managers of public services to provide the solution, this approach concentrates on the lower echelons of workers, as well as on the clients of organizations (*ibid.*, 11). He notes that:

> The fundamental assumption in this approach is that there is a great deal of energy and talent being underutilized at the lower echelons of hierarchies, and that the workers and clients closest to the actual production of goods and services in the public sector have the greatest amount of information about the programs. It is assumed that if those ideas and talents are harnessed government will work better. The general prescription, therefore, is greater participation and involvement on the part of those groups within government who are commonly excluded from decision-making. (*ibid.*, 11-12)

It bears some similarity with the "ladder of empowerment" proposed by the School of Advanced Urban Studies in Bristol, and provides an alternative to privatization and greater competition in providing social services (Taylor, *et al.*, 1992). It contains seven steps for facilitating citizen involvement in the provision of social services. This democratic approach, which gives citizens greater voice in the provision in services, can be contrasted with the market approach to consumer empowerment, based on more alternatives for exit.

The participatory state proposes much flatter structures since better quality goods or services would require fewer controllers from above. There needs to be a variety of structures to channel participation, especially for clients and lower-echelon employees. Thus, a variety of councils, advisory groups and the like have to be created. This model appears to enhance the role of the citizen and to attempt to induce democratic participation by means other than voting (Peters, 1994, 13).

We can, thus, distinguish between market and democratic approaches to consumer empowerment: the *market* approach seeks to empower consumers by giving them choice between alternatives and the option of "exit" from one service and/or providers, if he or she is dissatisfied; whereas the *democratic* approach would keep more services in the public sector but seeks to empower users by giving them a voice in the services and thereby the chance to change (i.e. transform) the existing service or service organization (Taylor, *et al.*, 1992, 8).

Thus, the participatory state is dependent upon citizens themselves being involved in making some choices about policy. It too would give citizens more consumer choice and direct control over programs, similar to the market model. The manner in which consumer choices would be exercised in the participatory state would be through some sort of political process. This participation might take the form of referenda on policy or it may be in local structures, like parent involvement in school committees, etc. (Peters, 1994, 15).

> In summary, the participatory model is not as well articulated as is the public choice model. Still, it is possible to extract some implications of this "vision" for the role of the civil service in governing society, as well as for the nature of governance itself. This version is ideologically very different from that of public choice, as well as in its assumptions about human behavior within organizations. Even with these differences, the prescriptions for design in the two approaches are not all that dissimilar. In particular, the principal prescription is for decentralization, and some transfer of power to the lower echelons of organization, as well as to the clients of the organizations.... (*ibid.*, 15-16).

Although the prescriptions of neo-liberals and those proposing a participatory state may bear some similarities, the meaning attached to them is definitely not the same. Rather than a means of creating competition among service providers in order to facilitate the market, decentralization in the participatory model is intended primarily to channel control to a different set of bureaucrats, or to the clients (*ibid.*, 16), through new direct democratic or participatory institutions. While Peters' presentation discusses distinct models or alternatives for organizing the entire public sector, one could of course consider a greater mix of all four models in relation to governmental tasks.

3.C Consumers, Clients or Citizens as Co-Producers?

We will now consider the implications of various terms like citizens, clients and consumers. Then we will discuss power and influence in consumers and clients relations with the public sector.

3.C.1 User Empowerment: Citizens, Consumers or Clients

Because of their different roles in modern society and many people have a legitimate interest in the functioning of public services at the local level. This ranges from the municipal tax payer to the local business, from the person who chooses to use one of its leisure or transportation facilities to the child in school, from the voter to the person applying for community social relief. There is a great deal of difference in the influence that these various individuals and groups can exercise in their relationship with the local authority. The words *customer, citizen, consumer, service user* tend to be used interchangeably, but they imply very different things in service relations (Gastere & Taylor, 1993, 7). It is, therefore, important to be careful about language:

> Consumer describes the relationship of a person to a product... Customer describes a relationship of a person receiving services to another person offering services [in the private sector]... Client also describes a relationship of a person receiving services to another person offering services [in the public sector]... Citizen describes the relationship of a person to the State (Burns, as quoted in Taylor, *et al.*, 1992, 2).

The distinction between citizens and customers is not merely a question of semantics nor rhetoric. A key problem is that, while perceiving citizens as customers may indirectly serve important purposes of increasing public sector efficiency and responsiveness towards individual choice and preferences, it distorts a delicate and sensitive system of mutual entitlements and obligations between the state and individual (Pierre, p. 58). Citizenship denotes a system of entitlements, both material and non-material, which are complementary, not contradictory, to those related to the concept of customer (*ibid.*, p. 59). The terminological shift of emphasis from citizens to customers can have far reaching implications that need to be spelled out more clearly. For sociologists and political scientists, a major problem associated with citizenship is how political democracy can be accommodated and sustained within a capitalist economy (Marshall, 1977; Marshall, 1981, Lindblom, 1959). For Marshall (1977, 1981) the welfare state provides an answer to this question, since it ensures redistribution of the wealth generated by the capitalist system both by spreading the fruits of growth to all socio-economic groups and by bringing in the potentially alienated social groups into the community (Turner, 1986 & 1994, as quoted by Pierre, 1995, 60-61).

The neo-liberal "rolling back of the state" has generated a "vacuum" with regard to the rights of citizens; as the material elements of citizenship were abolished or transformed into services provided under private auspices. Thus, citizenship has to be redefined and reaffirmed at the same time the welfare state is reformed. Most definitions of citizenship tend to stress the inclusion of individuals into a social community and the entitlements and responsibilities associated with membership. For example Turner states that: "citizenship may be defined as that set of practices (juridical, political, economic and cultural) which define a person as a component of society, and which as a consequence shape the flow of resources to persons and social groups" (Turner, 1994, 2, as quoted by Pierre, 1995, 62)

Thus, in an analysis of the difference between citizen and customer-driven models of public service delivery, a key dimension of citizenship should be the material entitlements that are associated with it. Such material connotations are much stronger in the European view of citizenship than in the American view. The notion of "social citizenship" (Esping-Andersen, 1990; Pierre, 1995) refers to citizenship as comprising both the constitutional and membership aspects typical to the American debate on this topic, as well as a specific European codified system of material rights, like freedom from poverty. Thus, "social citizenship" in Europe often includes entitlements in the form of benefits from the many welfare state programs. What makes "social citizenship" an important concept is the comprehensive and non-selective nature of the more extensive welfare state provision in Europe (Pierre, 1995, 64-65).

Shift from citizenship to customers implies a clear loss of social and material rights. This provides a plausible explanation of recent overt reaffirmation of "citizenship", necessary in the rolled back state. In Britain these measures were introduced as compensation for the substantial reductions of social citizenship, in the form of "citizens' charters" that were proposed for strengthening citizens' rights vis-à-vis the public service in terms of quality of service, but also for redefining the relationship between individuals and the state (*ibid.*, 65).

Citizenship carries with it political capabilities, which individuals otherwise do not enjoy, thus it can be referred to as the democratic approach to consumer empowerment or *political empowerment*, while the customer model carries with it certain rights, but few or no obligations and thus promotes the market approach or *economic empowerment*.

> However, the important point here is that political empowerment relates to the political dimension of citizenship, with all that entails of universalism. Economic empowerment, on the other hand, essentially refers to strengthening the position of a customer in a market,...[which]...is a much more selective and individualistic measure than political empowerment (*ibid.*, 16-67).

Allowing for choice between different services and different service providers leads to "public markets" like those suggested by Saltman & von Otter (1992), or the creation of a competitive space within which public and private providers compete for customers of various services. However:

> the 'marketization of the state' also means the depolitization of the state. While the traditional system of public services produced goods which were designed and redesigned through a communication channel from citizens via policy-makers to the bureaucracy, the customer-driven model aims at opening up a channel directly from the citizen/customer to the providers of public services (Pierre, 1995, 68).

The "public or planned market" refers to processes of resource allocation between the public and private sectors of society with special regard to services delivered under some form of public auspices, e.g. regulatory, administrative or financial control (Saltman & von Otter, 1992). Most British scholars, however, prefer term "quasi-markets", introduced below in section 4B. The "public market" sees citizens as customers choosing between different public or private providers of different services. "[T]he concept of 'public market' is employed here to indicate the commodification of public services, new forms of the production and distribution of public goods and services, and the notion of the beneficiaries of such services as 'customers' rather than citizens" (Pierre, 1995, 73). The emergence of a "public market" also means that the system of accountability is shifted from one involving elected officials, political parties and political institutions to accountability measured primarily in terms of customer satisfaction.

The "customerization" of citizens also introduces the notion of selective or restricted public services, services made available to some citizens, but not to others and not distributed equally to all of them. This is clearly in conflict with the traditional meaning of citizenship (*ibid.*, p. 73). Moreover, redefining citizens as customers will deprive citizens of their rights to use their voice. But, in most core welfare policy areas, clients can not exit without incurring financial or other losses, and "...given the oligopolistic and regulated nature of the 'public market' - exit in the 'public market' will probably inflict more damage on the customer than on the provider" (*ibid.*, p. 74). There are often large transaction costs associated with exit from enduring social services (see section 4.C.3 below). Thus, it is ironical that "public market" advocates should argue that it will promote two-way communication between the service provider and clients, since this it both inconsistent with the very logic of the market and contrary with the factual circumstances in most oligopolistic markets. Rather, there is a real risk that silence will replace the voice of citizens, once transformed into mere customers.

The "marketization of the state" builds on a simultaneous depoliticization and re-politicization of the public administration. Politics must both be down-graded or down-sized in general by restricting the domain of politics. Such changes are not made in a vacuum, they are brought about by political processes intended to redesign both the size of the state and the functions of citizenship. Moreover, replacing a political signals with a market-signals is also a political process (Pierre., 1995, 77-78).

3.C.2 Power and Influence in Consumer and Client Relations with the Public Sector

Consumer and client power and influence are usually treated as self-evident and unproblematic. It is often assumed that consumers obtain power and influence on the market in modern societies by their purchase of goods and services. Equally, it is often assumed that clients obtain power and influence on public sector in democratic societies through their voice and vote. Power and influence are there just for the taking; all that is required are rational consumers and active citizens. Power and influence are not considered as "zero-sum" nor relational phenomena. More power and influence to consumers and clients is not conceived as meaning less power and influence for private businessmen and/or public bureaucrats. Both the hidden hand of the market and political accountability of the public sector ensure that power and influence are readily available to consumers and clients at will. Such representations stifle serious efforts at analyzing consumer and client power and at increasing their influence on markets or in public services.

Power and influence are often considered as synonymous terms. A classical political science definition of power refer to the power of person "a" to influence the behavior of person "b" to do something the latter would not otherwise do. Preference is shown herein for distinguishing between power as a macro attribute and influence as a meso or micro attribute of a relationship. At the individual level, a consumer or client may have influence on the decisions of the private organization or public agency providing him or her with goods or services, but we will not speak of individual consumer or client power. Rather, power is reserved for collective or structural attributes. Consumers and clients obtain influence to the extent they are able to participate in decisions concerning the goods and services produced and thereby to influence their quality. This is sometimes referred to as consumer empowerment.

Power is related to structural attributes of the market, like the number of actors on the demand and supply side, their resource specificity and convertibility, the asymmetry of knowledge between suppliers and buyers of goods and services and the existence of "externalities" (Sjöstrand, 1993, 40-44). While individual consumers or clients can influence the quality of the goods or services of a particular producer or provider, without having power in the market or on public services; the influence they have may be sharply constrained by the power of structural attributes of the market or of public policy-making. Thus, having influence and having power are not synonymous from a consumer and client perspective.

Likert's discussion of the system of organizations and the involvement of employees in decision-making is germane for our efforts to analyze client influence on public services. Likert classifies firms into four basic types on the basis of their system of labor relations, and he develops four corresponding models of employee involvement in decision-making. *Exploitative authoritative* organizations do not permit any employee influence on firm decision-making; *benevolent authoritative* organizations never permit employee involvement in decision-making, but they do nevertheless occasionally consult them on some work-related issues; *consultative* organizations normally consult employees on important matters, but they are not, however, directly involved in decision-making; and finally, *participative group* organizations fully involve employees in all decisions related to their work (Likert, 1959 & 1961). The latter would probably be best represented in the real world by employee ownership or worker cooperatives. These relationships are depicted in the figure below.

In a similar fashion, it should be possible to study systems of organizations providing public services in terms of the varying degrees of client influence, from those with the least to those with the greatest client influence on the public services provided. *Authoritative bureaucratic* public agencies allow for no direct client influence or involvement in decision-making at all, and, thus, they demonstrate the typical client/bureaucrat pattern of a clear top-down relationship found in many public services. The growth of *benevolent bureaucracy* in public services occasionally involves clients in consultation, although they are not given any influence on decisions made by the agency. This may include facilitating client complaints and suggestions for improvement, the use of client questionnaires to evaluate service quality. *Consultative bureaucracies* go a step further in consulting their clients by establishing consultative mechanisms for involving "consumer" representatives on consultative boards, or in some well defined projects. *Citizens as co-producers* provides the clearest model for client power and influence. Social service provision throughout the Western world is beginning to involve greater clients participation, as seen in the growing reliance on various self-help groups, social service enterprises and the contracting out of social services to cooperatives and various nonprofit organizations (NPOs). These relationships are also depicted in the figure below.

Figure 3.4 Involvement in Private and Public Bureaucracies' Decision-making

a) Likert's System of Organizations and Employee Involvement in Decision-making:

Exploitative authoritative	**Benevolent authoritative**	**Consultative**	**Participative group**
No employee involvement at all	Never in decisions, but occasionally consulted	Usually consulted, but not ordinarily involved in decisions	Fully involvement in all decisions related to their work

b) Bureaucratic Organizations and Citizens Involvement in the Provision of Public Services:

Administrative bureaucratic	**Benevolent bureaucratic**	**Consultative bureaucratic**	**Citizens as co-producers**
No client influence at all	consumers occasionally consulted	mutual goal definition and consumer enabling	contracting out of social services to NPOs
Typical top-down client/ bureaucratic relationships	customer questionnaires and reference groups	Holma tenant project, with tenant participation in maintenance	parent day care, handicap care, elderly care co-ops, Managing AIDS and NPO services

Source: V. Pestoff, 1996a.

One example of a consultative bureaucratic relationship might be found in the efforts of the City of Stockholm to involve unemployed immigrants in practical language and skill training projects designed to facilitate their (re-) entry in the labor market. Another is to create a local job-resource bank and job-center for unemployed persons in immigrant dense areas of Stockholm. A third is seen in the efforts of the municipal housing authorities to involve tenants in the maintenance of the buildings and grounds in the Holma residential area of Malmö.

The concept of citizens as co-producers will be discussed and defined in section 4.D. A good example of citizens as co-producers is found in the efforts of many European countries to meet the challenge of HIV/AIDS (Marin & Kenis, 1997). In Sweden and elsewhere, nonprofit organizations can perform a unique reach-out function and both getting the message out and helping "high-risk" groups, which were already subject to social stigma, prior to the additional stigma manifested by HIV/AIDS. Self-help groups and NPOs were, thus, in a unique position to influence both public and private decisions concerning collective and individual efforts to meet this new challenge (Walden-Laing & Pestoff, 1997). Another related phenomenon is found in the growing provision of social services through client based cooperatives, social enterprises and voluntary organizations. These organizations are charged with providing the very services their members demand. In Sweden social enterprises provide day care, handicap care, elderly care, etc. The public sector continues to finance these services, but it no longer provides them directly. Rather, members are given responsibility for administering and providing certain social services themselves. Thus, they have greater influence on and involvement in decision-making related to the provision of these social services than in any of the other models. Here we find citizens-cum-clients-cum-members as co-producers of the very social services they both demand and pay for, through taxes and the time they devote to the running of cooperative social services.

3.D The Separation of Financing from the Provision of Social Services

In universal welfare states of the Scandinavian or Nordic type, social services are normally financed, produced and regulated by the public sector; while the Bismarckian or continental model often separates financing from the provision of social services and provision from the regulation of the quality of services provided. In Sweden it is often taken for granted that the three functions of financing, production and regulation are by definition reserved for the state or public sector, in spite of the fact that it is not normally the same public organization or authority that fills two or more of these functions simultaneously. Thus, financing is often made possible by taxes collected by the central government and these funds are transferred to municipal governments. Services are then provided by municipal authorities and these services are controlled or overseen both by national and local authorities charged with regulating such services.

Sweden provides some good examples of a clear division of labor and partnership between the public and nonprofit sectors concerning the financing and provision of social services; i.e., of public financing and nonprofit provision of social services, both for services in kind and services in cash. Public authorities also control the quality of services provided and the use of public funds, both when they are provided by public authorities as well as by nonprofit organizations. Adult education is traditionally provided in Sweden by private nonprofit adult education associations or *bildningsförbunden*, rather than by municipal education authorities or local school districts. A large proportion of their courses are financed by public funds, rather than by course fees. Unemployment insurance is traditionally provided by "guaranteed unemployment funds" or *erkända arbetslöshets kassor*, organized and run by the Swedish trade unions, as separate legal entities, and financed mainly by public funds. Now that Sweden no longer has the lowest unemployment rate in Europe, but one of the highest, the sums administered by and transferred via such unemployment funds are very significant indeed.

Another example of a public/private partnership concerning very substantial economic resources is found in the price regulation associations for foodstuff, or *prisregleringsföreningarna*, which take the legal form of economic associations in Sweden. Eight of them exist for domestically produced foodstuffs, like milk and dairy product, grains, meat, eggs and poultry, sugar, etc., and they regulate the import and export fees on food (Pestoff, 1991 & 1996). Numerous other examples of such a partnership between the public and nonprofit sectors could be provided. The main point to keep in mind is that already today there is a clear division between, yet partnership involving, the public and nonprofit sectors in terms of financing, providing and regulating some major services in Sweden. This type of partnership has existed in these and other areas at least since the end of W.W.II, if not longer. The typical bureaucratic view where the three functions of financing, providing and regulating the production of services are integrated into one organizations, is just one of several possible models for organizing the welfare state. Another one is based on a clearer division of labor and partnership between the public and nonprofit sectors, or a fragmented model. Fragmented service delivery need not be seen as a goal or value in itself. But, if it were possible to promote other values, such as greater citizen involvement and community engagement, then a more fragmented model for financing, providing and regulating social services could make a substantial contribution to the renewal and rejuvenation of the welfare state.

Hirsh (1994) discusses "associative democracy", which is based on a continuous collaboration between the pubic and nonprofit sectors in terms of providing social welfare. He maintains that big government has grown at the expense of individual rights and freedoms and that the attempted uniformity of state policy and forms of social provision had meant the imposition of common rules and standard services on the increasingly diverse and pluralistic objectives of the members of modern societies (*ibid.*, 5-6). "Associative democracy" provides a new form of economic and social governance, a system that combines citizen choice with public welfare, and that is well suited to meet the triple challenges of high unemployment, the diminishing political and financial importance of the nation state and the growing marginalization of many citizens, so wide-spread in Europe at the end of the 20th Century. Social planners identify welfare with state provision, and demand more public services as a patent solution to all social problems, both old and new; while spurning the nonprofit sector as old-fashion charity and religiously motivated benevolence. Étatists emphasize public sector solutions and have long since lost sight of the possibilities found in the social economy or the mutual and cooperative sector. The left or social democrats in many parts of Europe appear to have abandoned mutual and cooperative solutions in favor of social planned and étatist models (*ibid.*, 11).

The "associationalism" proposed by Hirsh both recognizes the challenges facing Europe today and attempts to combat further development of social planing and étatist solutions to pressing social problems. "Associationalism makes accountable representative democracy possible again by limiting the scope of the state administration, without diminishing social provision" (*ibid.*, 12). It is based on voluntary self-governing associations gradually and progressively becoming the primary means of democratic governance of economic and social affairs (*ibid.*, 24), while retaining the financial support of the public sector. This means the devolving of the provision of public welfare and other services to the voluntary sector and enabling associations to obtain public funds to provide such services for their members (*ibid.*, 167). Behind the issues of public vs. private and welfare vs. taxes looms a more important issue of citizen involvement. Regardless of the quality of service delivery, citizens have little access to public institutions other than in the capacity as clients and objects of the public administration.

Changes in local service delivery in Denmark (Bogason, 1994), relate to Hirsh's proposals. School boards are now required by law to include representatives for both teachers and pupils, while a 1992 law provides for a parental majority on the boards of public day care services (*ibid.*, 11). Similar developments are under way in terms of elderly care and other areas of personal social services in Denmark. There is a clear tendency towards strengthening the user by turning over responsibility to a user board. Thus, the traditional consolidated system of municipal government as a financier, producer and regulator is being split up with regard to some of the most expensive services: day care, schools and elderly care, often with the users gaining considerable power and influence (*ibid.*, 12).

However, some established interest organizations and power spheres in Denmark, such as the political parties, trade unions, etc., see little immediate gain from such changes, or perhaps even a loss of power (*ibid.*). In our high level of welfare services, based on public intervention and finance, "...it may become necessary to involve citizens more in a process of deciding and implementing service decisions, because if one fails to do so, nothing but materialistic claims for more may be the overarching result" (*ibid.*, 18). Without greater citizen participation there will be little understanding for costs of making decision, nor the trade-offs involved in choosing between two highly desirable alternatives. Hence demands for service become unrelated to limits in public funding and the abilities of the staff to provide services (*ibid.*, 18).

A similar interpretation is found in Abrahamson's (1991) discussion of trends in welfare provision at the turn of the century. He sees three clear alternative developments: 1) the *dual welfare state* in the US and Great Britain, where an affluent majority gets many benefits thanks to social insurance, but where the marginalized only have access to the remnants of a residual welfare state; 2) the *corporate welfare* state based on tripartitism and active participation in the labor market; and a 3) *community welfare* or welfare socialism, based on strengthening local community and social networks.

Advocates of the community welfare are critical both of public intervention schemes and reliance on the market, but they champion the principle of self-management. In Europe such proposals are supported by a "red-green" alliance - that is, between new and old labor movements, which do not emphasize equality in the traditional social democratic sense; i.e., of everybody being alike. On the contrary, he notes that welfare is provided through various local organizations and that it depends heavily upon the active participation of the members of the community. However, as he points out the plausibility of this scenario depends on shortened work hours, on a much more even distribution of paid work, and on the existence of altruistic ethics in the population (*ibid.*, 261).

Development of greater citizen influence has proved much slower and more arduous in Sweden than Denmark. An overview of recent Swedish developments documents that the current reforms of the Swedish welfare state did not start with the coming to power of the non-socialist Bildt Government in 1991 (Möller, 1996). Historically welfare state reforms can be traced to the early 1980s, when the Social Democrats first demonstrated a growing interest in renewing the public sector. The most important aspect of this renewal was democracy: the citizens influence in the public sector was too weak. This could pose a serious legitimacy problem over time, since support for the welfare state might diminish, if citizen participation and control did not increase (*ibid.*, 17). A main goal was to decentralize responsibility and decision-making. Ideas about user influence (*brukarinflytande*) were introduced, under Bo Holmberg, then Minister of Civil Affairs. Those citizens who used public services should also be permitted to participate and influence them. This represented a clean break with the ideas of the "strong society", social rights, universalism and equality, which had dominated Social Democratic welfare policy during the post-W.W.II period. However, opposition to such changes was strong, especially within the trade union movement (*ibid.*, 18; see also Melborne, 1986).

Eventually, some adjustments were made in the mid-1980s in the direction of limiting the public monopoly on providing social services. This primarily took the form of cooperatives and ideal or voluntary associations, which were allowed to provide day care services without a profit motive. *Demokratiberedningen* (the Democracy Commission) of 1983 provided several suggestions for increasing user influence; some were implemented, but most were not, including suggestions for institutionalizing councils of employees and consumers. Thus, in 1988, when the *Riksdag* made its decisions on this issue not much was left of ideas about "user influence". The Law on Municipalities was, however, amended to include a recommendation that local councils and boards "should promote collaboration with those using municipal services" (KL kap. 1. §5) and conditions for the establishment of "conditional delegation" (*ibid.*, 19). KL, kap 3, §13 refers to the consultation with and the potential representation of users on municipal boards and commissions (*ibid.*, 19-20).

Although these requirements were repeated in the new 1991 Law on Municipalities (KL, kap. 6 §38), they are not very constraining. According to the *lokaldemokratiberedning* (the Local Democracy Commission) provisions for conditional delegation have rarely been employed and user influence has not been exercised often. The interest among local politicians is simply too weak. The non-socialist Bildt government proposed similar means for increasing user influence, where the municipal council could turn over the administration of a municipal service or institution to a *self-administering body*. Such bodies should be composed of users and employees at the institution in question and users should comprise the majority. The motive for this long-going proposal is interesting: "[p]articipation also increases understanding for the difficulties which can be associated with running certain activities when personnel and economic resources are limited (Prop. 1993/94:188, p. 72; as quoted by Möller, *ibid.*, 20).

3.E Conclusions

Civil democracy was defined in Chapter 1 in terms of citizen empowerment through cooperative self-management of personal social services, where they become co-producers of such services. We have explored the political dimensions of civil democracy in this chapter. We saw that it is related to the various roles citizens have in modern societies, the diversity of channels of influence and alternative models for citizen control of the public service. It is also based on greater horizontal solidarity between groups and individuals in a participatory state. Civil democracy is anchored in the concept of citizen and the rights of citizenship, rather than in the concept of consumer. In terms of citizen empowerment in their relationship with the public sector, we prefer to speak of citizens as co-producers. The latter terms is defined by the changing relation between producers and consumers of personal social services and by the value added by this changing relationship. Civil democracy provides a policy objective both for increasing public sector efficiency and strengthening citizenship. We discussed the separation of financing from the provision of personal social services. We also found that certain aspects of civil democracy could be identified in developments in neighboring Scandinavian and European countries. But, we noted that similar ideas have made little real progress in most areas in Sweden, except for day care services.

4. Economic Aspects of Civil Democracy

We previously considered political aspects of civil democracy in Chapter 3. We now want to discusses economic aspects of civil democracy in this chapter. We will start by considering market failure, government failure and third sector social services. This is followed by a discussion of quasi-markets. Then we turn our attention to exit and voice in relation to goods and services, followed by considering the transaction costs of the exit alternative. Finally, we go beyond exit and voice, to examine citizens as co-producers, cooperatives as a forum and reach some conclusions.

4.A Market Failure, Governmental Failure and Third Sector Social Services

From a transactions costs perspective, variations in ownership are related to the costs of market contracting. The costs of ownership, i.e., monitoring the behavior of managers, collective decision-making and risk-bearing, should be weighed against the costs of market contracting (Hansmann, 1988; Hansmann, 1996). The latter are related to market power, being locked-in and asymmetric information, commonly referred to as "market failure". Markets do not manage to achieve allocative efficiency nor *Pareto* optimal allocation when (at least one) of the five following characteristics is present: the failure of competition particularly linked with increasing returns to economies of scale; the existence of public goods; and the presence of externalities, of incomplete markets or of imperfect information (Stiglitz, 1988). This results in the sub-optimal production of public goods, the creation of externalities and the existence of asymmetric information.

Enjolras (1993 & 1995) identifies the asymmetry of information between the providers and consumer of personal services as a general source of market failure. When producers have more information than consumers, the former can take advantage of their superior knowledge to obtain excess profit in a market situation or relationship. Such an asymmetry is typical of personal domestic services that are strongly relational, such as care for the elderly or day care for children. An elderly person or their family finds it difficult to evaluate *a priori* the quality of the services provided by a certain organization or by certain visits to the home. Similarly, parents find it difficult to evaluate the quality of day care service prior to enrolling their child.

Modes for providing domestic personal social services that are currently developing in France, Italy, Spain, Sweden and other European countries are largely a result of informational constraints inherent in the type of services produced and exchanged. A refusal to relinquish domestic bonds and to establish impersonal dependencies is a major problem associated with such services (Enjolras, 1993; Enjolras, 1995). Another problem is related to the role asymmetric information in determining the quality of service. The quality of the service does not entirely depend on a certain number of material activities according to predetermined norms. The quality of human relations established between the producer and consumer of services plays a crucial role, but the quality of these relations can not be determined before hand.

It is possible to distinguish between two types of asymmetrical information situations; moral hazard or the lack of control of the value of the service rendered and adverse selection, which depends on knowledge necessary to perform services, that one party has and the other lacks (*ibid.*). Adverse selection comes in to play when the clients do not *a priori* know anything about the quality of the service, and are not able to measure quality at the time of purchase. Price signals may not provide a clear indication of quality. If services are priced too low, good providers will be excluded from the market. Also, when services are priced too high, the inferior providers will receive excess remuneration from clients.

An additional weakness of the market model is the unrealistic nature of its assumptions concerning consumers, especially when it comes to personal social services. Underlying the consumerist or market model is the assumption that the consumer has a "real" choice. The market analogy posits that an active consumer, who has a choice between products or providers is in a position to withdraw his/her custom (i.e. exit) of a product or provider, if it no longer satisfies him/her. These assumptions which must be questioned. In the demand for care many people are dependent, frail or mentally handicapped, which prevents them from behaving as "true" customers. They are not able to compare competing suppliers and exit from one if it no longer satisfies them. In the majority of cases, the recipient of care only has a theoretical choice between several alternatives; and he/she is not in a position to exercise effective choice or to exit. The frail people can only be assured influence on the supply of service if their advocates or they themselves have a voice in the organization of the services. The participation of the recipients of personal social services or domestic care, or of their representatives, is a safeguard that services will adapt to their needs. The development of quasi-market regulation is based on a consumerist model of market participation, which undermines the development of a model for social power, or empowerment, that allows for the active participation of recipients in the running of services (*ibid.*).

If consumers demand similar services, public provision is simple, but if their demands are different, the public provision will satisfy some, but not others. There will always be certain persons who want more and others who want less service, something that is difficult for the public sector to cope with (*ibid.*). The provision of rapidly expanding service or different kinds of service due to heterogeneous demand often results in public failure, i.e., citizens' needs go unmet.

Economists propose that associations and nonprofit organizations tend to develop in areas or activities that are either subject to market or public failure. Associations, by their not-for-profit nature and the fact that they are often based upon voluntary activities, are particularly well suited to develop responses and provide services where other forms of production fail (*ibid.*). This is so because associations can promote trust between the consumers and producers of services. It is commonly assumed that associations will not engage in opportunistic behavior, given the absence of the motive to maximize profits. However, it should be kept in mind that the voluntary or third sector is not immune to failure (Salamon, 1987), nor to breaching trust relations (Gulliam & Perrow, 1992).

However, market failure can be corrected by public efforts, either by financing services, through subventions, or by regulating the provision of certain services. The state can create norms concerning the provision of private services, or it may provide them itself. While the state may correct market failure, the provision of services by nonprofit organizations has the potential advantage of protecting consumers against most abuses of the asymmetry of information and they become a means for reducing uncertainty about quality stemming from the asymmetry of information. A consumer who is aware of the asymmetric information situation may, therefore, prefer to deal with a family member, an old friend or someone who is recommended by a nonprofit organization, on the assumption that such providers of service will not normally take advantage of the ignorance of the consumer. Producers who choose to provide services through nonprofit organizations give a possible signal of quality and a potential guarantee that the asymmetry of information will not be exploited nor lead to super-profits. In addition, a nonprofit organization can satisfy minority needs not catered to by the public sector (Enjolras, 1993; Enjolras, 1995).

4.B Quasi-Markets

Numerous reforms in the provision of social services in Britain in the late 1980s introduced "quasi-markets" (Le Grand, 1990) into the delivery of welfare services. The state stops being both the financier *and* the provider of services, and becomes primarily a financier of services which are now provided by a variety of private, voluntary and public suppliers, operating in competition with each other (*ibid.*, 2; Bartlett, 1996, 3). They are considered markets, because:

> they replace monolithic state providers with competitive independent ones. They are 'quasi' because they differ from conventional markets in a number of key ways. The differences are both on the supply and on the demand sides. On the supply side, as with conventional markets, there is competition between productive enterprises or service suppliers. Thus, ...there are independent institutions ... competing for customers. (Le Grand, 1990; 2)

The introduction of quasi-markets is supposed to encourage a more economic use of resources, thus improving service efficiency. Competing suppliers means that welfare users, or their agents, have an alternative. This not only extends choice to users, but, it is claimed, gives them real power (Le Grand, 1990, 8-9; Saltman & von Otter, 1992). The method of funding also changes, i.e., resources are no longer allocated directly to providers through the public bureaucracy. Instead, in some cases the state continues as the principal purchaser, but resources are allocated through a bidding process. In other cases, an earmarked budget or 'voucher' is given directly to potential users, or to an agent acting on their behalf, who can then allocate the budget as they choose between the competing providers (Le Grand, *op cit.*, 2) This is a major break with the past and it represents a challenge to social policy. Thus, in the 1990s numerous social areas have become subject to quasi-markets in Britain, like voluntary sector residential homes, schools and housing associations. In Sweden we find examples of social enterprises and NPOs providing social services.

The defining characteristic of quasi-markets is therefore not privatization *per se*, but rather marketization, i.e., the attempt to mimic market mechanisms within a system of public ownership, or, where ownership is transferred to private or nonprofit providers, through a system of regulation (Bartlett, 1996, 6). Proponents claim that quasi-markets provide greater efficiency, responsiveness and choice. However, the adherents of quasi-markets present an idealized version of markets, that fails to correspond to real developments. Privatization may, in fact, have the opposite effect for a wide variety of reasons. For example, in terms of price and efficiency:

1) the costs of setting up the infrastructure for markets to operate efficiently, like billing, contracts, etc.;
2) marketing and advertising also cost money;
3) switch from monopolistic providers to competitive ones may raise labor costs, since monopoly labor supply will no longer be matched by a monolpoly purchaser of labor; and
4) difficulty in assessing the quality of outcomes in many areas of welfare services often leads to focusing on *inputs*, but in effect it is outcomes that count for the clients (*ibid*., 9-11).

Indeed, private providers may discover many possible mechanisms for cream skimming, thereby worsening the outcomes of the services which is provided in terms of equity. Studies of quasi-markets and the use of vouchers in Britain, show that there was little if any noticeable improvement in responsiveness and choice, as most users couldn't discriminate among providers in their use of vouchers. The cost of the scheme were extremely high due to administrative costs of organizing and distributing vouchers. At the same time, increasing government regulations which impose targets for service delivery, reducing budgets and reducing consultation times will all lead to reductions in the quality of service provided to users (Bartlett, 1996, 17). Increased regulation will also lead to increasing the costs of negotiating such contracts or regulations and increasing the costs of overseeing them.

The separation of purchaser and provider has created a "contract culture" which increases the administration necessary through promotion, negotiations, and monitoring of contracts. It has been argued that market mechanisms are inappropriate for the delivery of social services, since information about quality of services is difficult for the users to collect and evaluate. Moreover, the choice of provider is normally made only once and a wrong decision can have lasting consequences. Certainly, switching providers can be costly and disruptive. Often the costs of "shopping around" become prohibitive, and these high transaction costs may end up promoting monopoly or oligopoly outcomes. The 'market' will consist of a monopsonist (the buyer authority) and a monopolist (the favored provider) (FES 1995, 17).

In terms of greater consumer choice it is questionable whether they can provide it or not. Distance and travel time are often the main limits on choice, since there is often only one local (monopoly) provider. Additional providers at a greater distance means greater expenses for consumers in terms of travel, time, and other inconveniences, etc. (*ibid.*, 12). In terms of equity, quasi-markets would function just like traditional markets, i.e., they would result in creaming off the most able or least demanding clients and leave the rest to sink (*ibid.*, 13).

Welfare reforms should not be evaluated on narrow economic considerations of efficiency, but also in the extent to which users needs are met in a broader social sense i.e., responsiveness, choice and equity considerations (Le Grand & Bartlett, 1993). Equity is of particular importance in any evaluation of welfare systems, since welfare services are often provided precisely in order to overcome adverse distributional effects of market determined economic transactions (Bartlett, *op cit.*, 14-15).

In some cases, marketization is only a first step on a path which logically will lead to the eventual full privatization of service providers, due to the successive inflow of private capital, and the transition from public funding to private insurance arrangements. There are many examples and signs that such "creeping privatization" is occurring, and that the quasi-market experiment is a transitional phenomenon which will lead to a more privatized and individualized approach to the provision of welfare services. The welfare state may not be dead, according to Bartlett, but it is expiring rapidly (*ibid.*, 6).

The potential contribution of the third sector differs greatly from that of the for-profit sector:

> the goals of efficiency, responsiveness and choice may be better met by nonprofit providers, who have internalized some of the interest of user groups into their own decision making criteria, and so may be less prone to take opportunistic advantage of their monopoly market situation. (Bartlett., p. 16)

Third sector and NPOs providers should, therefore, not be seen primarily in terms of improving efficiency and increasing consumerism, but rather in terms of augmenting social power and facilitating civil democracy.

4.C Exit and Voice in Relation to Goods and Services

We now turn our attention to exit and voice in relation to the nature of goods and services. Differences between various types of goods and services make exit and voice more or less relevant as a means for consumer redress if they are dissatisfied. In particular the transaction costs of exit from enduring services has not previously been given ample consideration.

4.C.1 EXIT, VOICE, LOYALTY AND GOODS

Almost 30 years ago, A. Hirschman (1970) initiated a discussion of exit and voice as alternative responses to decline in the performance of firms, organizations and states, with his seminal book,*Exit, Voice and Loyalty*. Exit is a typical market response, where disappointed customers quietly change their patronage to other suppliers of the goods or services they purchase. Voice is a typical political response, where customers verbally express their disappointment about poor quality, either individually or collectively (*ibid.*). Both exit and voice can be brought to bare not only to protest declining quality, but also can be based on expectations of better quality goods or services (Stryjan, 1989; Pestoff, 1992; Möller, 1996). Voice can express both complaints and suggestions for improvements.

Exit and voice correspond essentially to different social roles in modern societies, i.e., our role as consumers and as citizens and/or voters. Hirschman notes that voice is more costly to individuals than exit, but also that voice is much more rich in information than exit. Exit may, however, at times be more unambiguous. Voice is, moreover, conditioned on the influence or bargaining power that consumers can bring to bear within the firm or organization (1970). One shortcoming in his argument is the failure to discuss the role of organizations in amplifying the voice of individuals (Pestoff, 1984; Pestoff, 1989a). One reason for the greater costliness of voice is related the costs of collective action (Olson, 1965 & 1971). This will be discussed in greater detail below.

Loyalty serves to mitigate between exit and voice, holding exit at bay. A loyal customer will continue to buy a product that demonstrates declining quality, in the hope that it may soon improve. Möller (1996) distinguishes between instrumental and value loyalty. A combination of the two results in the strongest form of attachment to goods or services, while either type of loyalty provide greater attachment than if none exists.

In *Shifting Involvement* (1982a), Hirschman addresses consumer disappointment as the source of shifts from private interests to public action and back again, underlining the unstable nature of consumer involvement. Different expressions of consumer disappointments are associated with specific types of goods. It is necessary to distinguish between truly non-durable goods, different kinds consumer durables and services. Disappointment is seldom permanent with everyday non-durable items, where daily learning processes can calibrate expectations downward. But, they also tend to be pleasure intensive. The contrary situation is associated with goods that are durable, unique and/or with a high value. Their potential for generating disappointment is related to the pleasure/comfort (p/c) ratio, and the regularity with which they are used.

Disappointment prone goods are much more likely to result in the use of voice than non-disappointment prone goods. Truly non-durable goods will facilitate the exit response in case of consumer disappointment, thereby relieving the necessity for voice. Irregularly used durable goods will only remind the user of his/her dissatisfaction occasionally, and are therefore not likely to engender the need for voice. Durables put to continual use or those used at regular intervals are more disappointment prone and more likely to result in voice than exit. Such goods are not frequently purchased, and therefore provide very few opportunities for using exit. Voice is more likely where exit is restricted, so disappointed consumers of regularly used durables have little other recourse than voice.

The various consumer reactions, depending on the type of good and the multiple roles played by adults in Western democracies, i.e., both as consumers and citizens, etc., rule out either exit or voice as *the* exclusive channel of redress. Exit and voice, are complementary consumer reactions, rather than mutually exclusive alternatives or rival consumer reactions. The development and refinement of his concepts would significantly contribute to a more comprehensive mapping of the alternatives open to citizens/consumers, in particular for services.

4.C.2 Type of Services: Non-Enduring and Enduring

First we want to briefly consider the distinguishing characteristics of services. Grönroos (1990) attempts to define services and provide some common characteristics. He maintains that for most services, several basic characteristics can be identified:

1) services are more or less *intangible*;
2) services are *activities* or a *series of activities* rather than things;
3) services are at least to some extent *produced and consumedsimultaneously*; and
4) the customer *participates in the production process*, at least to some extent (*ibid.*, 29).

Hirschman fails to clearly relate his concepts of exit and voice to his discussion of consumer disappointment with different types of goods and services. This is, however, relevant to our discussion of consumers as co-producers in the provision of social welfare services. Although he introduces services briefly in his discussion of consumer disappointment, he does not compare and contrast consumer reactions to them in the same fashion as durable and non-durable goods. Services also have a high potential for generating disappointment, although not because they fail to deliver pleasure, but rather because their performance tends to be uneven and unpredictable, or they have a highly variable degree of quality and efficiency (Hirschman, 1970). His distinction concerning the regularity of use of goods should be adapted to our analysis of services, and we will distinguish between two categories of services: non-enduring and enduring services.

a) Irregular or *non-enduring services* are minor services which are used on a daily basis or other services which are used irregularly and do not depend exclusively on an enduring interaction, nor result in a long-term relationship between the consumers and providers of the services.

b) Regular or *enduring services* are regularly used major services that depend extensively on enduring interaction, and often result in a long-term social relationship between the consumers and producers of the services. Enduring services often include attributes of greater intimacy and more extensive social contact than non-enduring services. The figure below illustrates these differences.

Figure 4.1 Exit, Voice and the Type of Goods or Services

	G O O D S	S E R V I C E S	
REGULAR DURABLES	exit & voice (p/c ratio)	**V O I C E**	ENDURING
IRREGULAR DURABLES and NON-DURABLES	**E X I T**	exit & voice (service management)	NON-ENDURING

Source: modified from Pestoff, 1994a.

One problem is how to further distinguish between non-enduring and enduring services. Often repeated and relatively inexpensive services belong to the former category, like hair cutting or hair dressing, getting laundry or the car washed, baby sitting, meals out, transportation, using the telephone and fax outside home or the office, etc. Enduring and important physical or social needs belong to the latter category, like regular child care, education, chronic health care, handicap care, elderly care, etc. Services found in the first category can readily be bought and sold in a spot-market like situation. They are subject to supply and demand.

Services in the latter category have different attributes requiring more enduring personal and social relations between buyers and sellers than normally found in a spot-market. Here it is necessary to establish stable long-term relations between buyers and sellers, to guarantee some minimum demand for the provision of such services on a continual basis. Day-to-day market fluctuations would make the minimal provision very difficult (Pestoff, 1994a).

4.C.3 The Transaction Costs of Exit

Following Barry (1971), Möller (1996) notes that there are costs associated with practicing the exit alternative. By focusing on simple consumption goods, Hirschman does not pay enough attention to the hurdles or thresholds applicable to more complicated products. Due to practical considerations children, sick persons and the elderly do not change day care centers, schools, hospitals nor rest-homes at a snap of the fingers. If dissatisfied with current services, you still need to get information about alternatives, systematize and analyze it. Then you must convince yourself that the alternative(s) make the effort to change worth the continued investment of energy and time. All these efforts can be seen as transaction costs of obtaining services (see North, 1990; and Williamson, 1985; Williamson, 1992).

The transaction costs of continuously shopping around for the best buy in personal social services, would soon prove prohibitively high from a consumer perspective. Taken to the extreme, if each individual purchaser of child care, elementary or higher education, chronic health care, elderly care, etc., had to shop around once a week or once a month in order to get information about next week's or month's service bargains and where to get the best quality for their money, there would be little time to do anything else on the week-end or at the end of the month. Endless hours would be spent shopping around between various offers, only to discover later that the claims of one service provider did not hold or that another provider had a better offer. Formalized or institutionalized relations between consumers and producers of enduring social services are preferable from a consumer perspective because they help them to reduce the transaction costs of obtaining these services.

In addition to transaction costs associated with the purchase and re-purchase of social services, the individual exit and re-entry costs of changing from one service institution to another would also be considerable. Small children, pupils, students and sick or elderly persons would have to be moved from one service provider to another, from one week or month to another. Such costs would in most cases be shared by the consumer and purchaser, if they were not the same person. Both parents and their small children would have to be re-socialized in a new day care center, parents and pupils would have to be re-socialized into a new elementary or high school, the sick into new medical facilities or the elderly into new senior residences, etc. Such social costs would necessarily restrict the free flow of customers/clients from one service provider to (compare with Möller, 1996, 217-18).

Exit costs of regular and enduring social services are considerable higher than those of simple goods (Möller, 1996, 218). Moreover, much social service in Sweden is assigned on the principle of proximity or closeness, i.e., your child or elderly parents go to the nearest facility providing the services desired. For children that means near to where their parents live, for the elderly than means near to where they resided prior to becoming incapacitated or near to their relatives who might be expected to visit them occasionally. Nearness is, however, not merely a question of transportation nor travel costs and expenses, but will increase the chance of greater social contacts both for children and elderly persons.

In addition to these practical costs of transferring custom from one provider to another, we can add the "emotional costs" for the child or elderly person and their guardian or relatives. The "customer" of such services must tear up old social ties and develop new ones, while the guardians or relatives who must confront the staff of the old provider to motivate or explain the need to change service providers and the staff of the new provider to get to know them, etc. Thus, there are considerable costs associated with the exit alternative, and although they should not be exaggerated, neither should they be ignored.

One way to reduce the transaction costs for the purchase of enduring social services is to remove some of the uncertainties of a spot-market by establishing formal contracts between the sellers and purchasers of personal social services for a certain period of time, i.e., either half a year or one year at a time. Moreover, there would also be clear transaction costs for the firm with the repeated exit and entry of consumers of enduring social services. Small children, pupils, students and sick or elderly persons would have to be socialized into the receiving institution. If they leave the institution shortly after such costs would be lost. The new clients that fill the vacancies would have to be socialized anew. Keeping order books up to date would pose another problem to managers, not to mention keeping an optimal stock of the requisite productive resources for quickly increasing or decreasing production of services.

The market analogy is also tenuous from a societal perspective, as seen in attempts to introduce market solutions in British education with the use of school vouchers, that guarantee an adequate education for the mass of the population. Parents are free to supplement vouchers with money of their own, either in the private sector or through supplementary lessons and courses at the local authority schools. This introduces something like market competition between schools, even within the public sector (Crouch, 1985, 410-11).

Thus, the transaction costs of a free flow of market signals for major personal social services may prove equally problematic from a consumer, a producer and a societal perspective. Unless a formal contract exists between the buyers and sellers, it would prove impossible to provide a minimum of day care, education, health service or elderly care. The necessary resources for long-term planning of day care, education or chronic health care would not be available if children, pupils or students and patients could freely resort to the exit alternative at any time to communicate their preferences to the managers of day care, school or health care units.

4.D Beyond Voice: Co-Production

We now want to discuss voice as mechanisms for consumer influence and explore the importance of the negotiated economy, ways of promoting voice, citizens as co-producers and cooperatives as a forum.

4.D.1 The Negotiated Economy

There are rival interpretations about the impact of the market on society. Some argue that it is a civilizing force, while others say it is a destructive force (Hirschman, 1982b). A pure market based on perfect competition would be comprised of anonymous buyers and sellers supplied with perfect information and without any room for bargaining, negotiations, mutual adjustment nor for repeated or recurrent contacts. Long-term personal social contacts and frequent encounters that lead to the formation of ties between the buyers and sellers are considered a substantial departure from the ideal competitive model (*ibid.*). The fact that such ties are so frequent and important has often led economists either to regard them as aberrations that should be castigated or belittled as imperfections or to ignore them. However, the great frequency and importance of negotiations in market transactions should result in a situation where more attention was paid to such phenomenon. One welcome exception to this professional ignorance is the "Negotiated Economy School" in Scandinavia.

The concept of the "negotiated economy" (Hernes, 1978) was first introduced by the Norwegian Power Study in the mid-1970s. It was somehow different from both of the other main types of economies, i.e., the market and the planned economy, and it had many of the features later termed "democratic corporatism" (Katzenstein, 1985). The negotiated economy was first described in terms of polar opposites to the school book market economy (Hernes, 1978; Berrefjord, 1981; Berrefjord, 1982). The three most distinguishing features of the negotiated economy in Norway were that a few big firms, through their interlocking directorates both cross-owned each other and had complete information as to how their "competitors" would behave both in the short and long run. They also invariably had frequent political contacts. The negotiated economy is constantly undergoing development, and thus, is not a state nor fixed structure, but a process, one where large firms clearly play a central role.

Later this field of research was expanded to other areas and the neighboring Nordic countries (Nielsen & Pedersen, 1988; Nielsen & Pedersen, 1989; Pedersen, 1992). The negotiated economy is defined as "...a structuring of society where an essential part of the allocations of resources is conducted through institutionalized negotiations between decision-making centers in state, organizations and or corporations" (*ibid.*, 7). In terms of structures they speak of five complementary institutions which provide the basis for its institutional arrangements. These are: a) institutions for policy making, b) discourse, c) campaigning, d) negotiation, and e) arbitration or sanction. All five types, or at least their functional equivalent, are necessary for the negotiated economy. Existing institutions may, however, cover more than one function (*ibid.*).

In subsequent comparative efforts this concept has been applied to various phenomena in the Nordic countries, including labor negotiations in Denmark (Pedersen, 1989), income policy in four Nordic countries (Elvander, 1989), consumer policy in Sweden (Pestoff, 1989a), agricultural policy in Norway and Sweden (Steen, 1989), pension funds in Denmark (Petersen, 1989), etc. Later it was extended to compare developments in different sectors in Sweden, like industrial relations, consumer policy, housing policy, etc. (Pestoff, 1995b), and finally to analyze the demise of the Swedish Model and the negotiated economy in Sweden (Pestoff, 1994a; Pestoff, 1995b). Thus, the Scandinavian negotiated economy provides an alternative both to the neo-liberal and the planned economy models for organizing society (Nielsen & Pedersen, 1989; Pestoff, 1989a), and perhaps for organizing enduring social services. Thus, social enterprises in particular can become institutions for policy making, discourse and negotiations between the various stakeholders, in particular the local authorities, clients and staff.

The view of contracting out of social services as one of the most attractive quasi-market alternatives to traditional bureaucratic service delivery, has been criticized. (See Section 4.B above). This view is normally based on the assumption that it provides better services at lower costs. But the decision to contract out to outside firms or agencies does *not* necessarily result in lower costs nor better services, since the ideal conditions for competitive contracting do not always hold. Only where a strong market for services exists, when resources are abundant and where service production is certain can the competitive contracting model hope to fulfill its promise. If not, then two alternative models exist, a negotiation and a cooperation models (Dehoog, 1990). Both these other models keep the perspective of the government as the "principal" or buyer and usually a non-governmental organization as an "agent" or seller. The negotiation model involves relational contracting, where consensus and incremental decision-making are the norm. Contractors are limited to a few previous suppliers, who submit a general proposal, which is then negotiated in greater detail. Such a model can accommodate uncertainty and complexity. If there is only one supplier with high capital investments or if the supplier has much more knowledge about the goods or service to be provided, then they will most likely have a long-term relationship with the relevant governmental agency. Here the government and firm are more like equal partners. Such a model is highly flexible and adaptive to change and uncertainty.

Given a small number of potential suppliers, limited organizational resources and high uncertainty and/or complexity, alternatives to competitive contracting appear necessary. However, rather than quasi-market alternatives, why not consider a combination of quasi-market and quasi-political alternatives, like those illustrated by social enterprises; in particular, those which are based on greater citizen participation in the provision of the services they demand. Such social enterprises could either negotiate and/or cooperate with the municipality over the details of a contract to provide certain services and involve citizens in the production process.

4.D.2 Citizen Involvement as a Way of Promoting Voice

Exit and voice should not always be seen as mutually exclusive alternatives, but rather as complementary responses to consumer disappointment, depending on the type of good or service. Voice is not a rival to exit, but rather a welcomed complement, i.e., consumer sovereignty (exit) often needs to be complemented by consumer participation (voice). Hirschman's discussion of the elusive optimal mix of exit and voice points out the difficulty of combining these two consumer responses. Too much of one input diminishes the impact of the other (1970). Exit and voice are not mutually exclusive, but they can in fact depend on or be predisposed towards each other, according to Möller (1996). The existence of one influences the other. Thus, exit may be necessary for augmenting consumer influence, but it is not sufficient for doing so. Collective voice is also needed to achieve real consumer influence (Pestoff, 1984; Pestoff, 1989a).

Consumers often have clear preferences about their food tastes and readily use exit to express these preferences. By contrast, expressing preferences about services, like day care, education, elderly care, etc., which are of an uncertain quality, both for the consumers and producers, requires more voice, and an active and constructive dialogue between consumers and producers. Ignorance about quality is not necessarily limited to consumers nor to goods. The demand for new services may arise more rapidly than the ability to meet them or the knowledge of how to satisfy them, in particular when they become popular. Under such circumstances, it is not so much a question of consumer redress, but of educating producers and providing them with as much information as possible about their performance in relation to consumer preferences. Voice provides much more information about performance and preferences and is also much richer in detail than exit, which remains silent about details (*ibid.*). Similarly, with products or services where there is asymmetric information or disproportionate knowledge between sellers and buyers, such as medical care, voice has an important role to play.

Customer voice is a more important component to services at the enduring end of the continuum, while exit gains greater importance at the non-enduring end of the service continuum. Consider briefly how price elasticity and quality elasticity differ. When prices increase, it is often those customers with the smallest means, i.e., the marginal customers, that exit first, since they are most price sensitive. However, when quality decreases, it is often those customers with the greatest means who leave first, because they are also the most quality conscious. Thus, if we want to avoid a situation where the most quality conscious and articulate consumers are the first to exit, then some means must be found to facilitate their voice and restrict exit (Hirschman, 1970).

Thus, we see that developing techniques for promoting the active and constructive voice of consumers can be an important, if not an essential aspect of enduring services. But, just as there are two types of voice, positive and negative, so too are there two ways in which voice can be expressed, individually or collectively. Positive *individual* voice, or making suggestions for improvements, is the type with which service management is normally concerned, but positive *collective* voice, or co-production, could also be more important in certain services, in particular in enduring services. Social enterprises and cooperatives can promote power sharing and a closer partnership between consumers and producers of social services. They could contribute greatly to improving the quality of social services, since they promote a collective institutionalized encounter and the continuous collective interaction between consumers and producers. The institutionalized encounter and continuous interaction between clients and producers of social services is also related to the process of quality improvements stemming from such interaction. Perceiving consumers as co-producers carries with it three major potential benefits, i.e., better quality products and services, shorter time required to develop new products or services and lower costs (Wikström, 1993, 8-11).

One essential way to promote greater citizen involvement as co-producers of social welfare services is to provide them with greater collective influence and bargaining power in the production process itself. Involving citizens as co-producers could result in a far-reaching form of consumer participation in the production of social services, one that goes beyond exit and voice, and facilitates active and creative consumer responses. Such responses will not always manifest themselves spontaneously among individual consumers, especially during periods of major reorganization nor curtailments of the public social welfare services.

The necessary structures or institutions must be created for facilitating citizen involvement. Additional structures are needed if citizens are going to become involved as co-producers of welfare services, and political support will be necessary.

4.D.3 Citizens as Co-Producers, a Conceptual Discussion

Co-production is a phenomenon that refers to greater consumer involvement and participation in the production of goods and services. The changing patterns of interaction between firms and their consumers open new possibilities of doing business, as well as new possibilities for consumer influence. Such changes bring about a much closer relationship between consumers and producers than traditionally found in industrial society, one in which the consumer increasingly assumes the role of co-producer (Wikström, 1996). The customer is no longer a passive receiver of goods and services, but rather an active and knowledgeable participant in a common process, on the marketplace. The company's role is no longer limited to providing goods or services, rather, it is a question of designing systems of activities within which customers can create their own value. The firm thereby compliments the knowledge and resources already possessed by its customers, as was normally the case in the pre-industrial period. From this interaction and cooperation in time and space, a value emerges that is the result of their cooperation.

Co-production is defined as "...company-consumer interaction (social exchange) and adaptation for the purpose of attaining added value" (Wikström, 1996: 362). Such social exchange is motivated in part by the perceived degree of uncertainty in the exchange relationship and the potential benefit accruing to the participants from eliminating this uncertainty (*ibid.*, 363). The interactive way of working generates different types of values than those created by the logic of mass-production (*ibid.*, 372). For our purposes we need to specify the value or values associated with co-production of personal social services. In Chapter 10 we examine the specific value-added for parents of children in various types of social enterprises providing day care services.

Co-production is a multi-faceted phenomenon comprising several different aspects. It includes differing means of consumer participation in production, differing stages for their participation and varying degrees of consumer influence on that process. For our purposes, we are as interested in the relationship between a municipal housing authority and its tenants in Malmö and between a health and medical cooperative and its members in

Tokyo, as a cooperative day care center for children and its members in Jämtland or Stockholm. Our research focuses on the influence of the final consumers of services; in particular that stemming from their membership in small social enterprises providing personal social services in Sweden.

Co-production means greater consumer voice and involvement and certain similarities can be found with the terms consumer enabling and consumer empowerment, but this similarity leads to some confusion in the business literature. Consumer enabling refers to greater access to a good or service, while consumer empowerment refers to greater consumer influence. The latter is not merely a question of influence through purchase power, but rather greater direct influence on the production and management of the firm providing the goods and/or services. Thus, greater consumer involvement may also entail consumer enabling, i.e., making possible the delivery of a service in a new way that involves the consumer more directly. Consumer enabling may be combined with greater use of computers and new information technology, such as automated telling machines or ATMs. Here the customer plays a more active role in executing the service, i.e., the withdrawal of funds from a bank; but this new role also requires new and often more sophisticated knowledge on the part of consumers, i.e., an access code, knowing when to press the correct button, etc. By interacting with this new computer technology consumers now normally have access to their own money all day long, all year round and in many different countries. In this case, the introduction of new technology required greater consumer involvement if certain potential economic gains were going to be realized. These gains were related to the reduction of the work-force needed to provide a particular type of service, the withdrawal of funds.

Co-production may, however, imply another type of involvement and be motivated by other reasons. Consumers may be interested in another kind of influence than that possible on the market and its purchase/don't purchase forms of influence. In fact, greater influence itself may be one of the values that greater consumer involvement promotes. For example, some parents may be motivated to choose cooperative day care services as a means for gaining more parent and/or personal influence in running of their daughter's or son's day care center, while others won't. The latter will most likely prefer some other form of day care services that is not as demanding, like worker co-ops, municipal day care facilities or private for-profit services. Consumer empowerment is, therefore, different than consumer enabling; the latter is more a question of power and influence than consumer enabling.

Enabling consumers is not only a question of greater consumer involvement through new information technology. Developing better communication structures within existing organizations, in particular communication between the front-line staff and consumers of particular goods and services may be equally as important. For example involving the tenants, as consumers of building maintenance services, in the daily maintenance of the grounds and apartment buildings in their municipally owned housing is primarily a question of enabling them to participate in the improvement of the services they expect and demand as municipal housing tenants (Cars, 1994; Alfredsson & Cars, 1996). However, empowerment, or providing tenants with greater influence in the decisions made by the local municipal housing authority, by giving them representation on the board of the local housing authority is quite another matter. In the Holma tenants' experiment in Malmö we find a good example of enabling, but clearly not of empowerment. Thus, enabling may be considered as a necessary, but not sufficient, condition of empowerment.

Co-production through patient involvement in Japanese health and medical cooperatives provides another example of the distinction between enabling and empowering, since they successfully represent both aspects. A staff of more than 1,000 persons in the Saitama Medical Cooperative in Kanagawa Prefecture, outside Tokyo, provides medical services to nearly 250,000 households/members, organized into nearly 5,000 *han* health discussion groups. Members can either visit one of the four Saitama Medical Cooperative Hospitals, the largest with nearly 400 beds, one of its twelve primary health clinics or its dental clinic. Involving patients in their own health care means among other things making them actively responsible for their own heath. These patients/members are no longer seen by doctors and nurses as passive objects; rather, they become active subjects and take their own blood pressure in a split second, by placing their arm in a digital machine in the reception of such health facilities. Then they inform the nurse and/or doctor about today's blood pressure reading. They probably remember both the last reading and know what their blood pressure usually is, as well as what it should normally be. Patients also test and keep record of the salt content in their urine and the sugar content in their blood. Moreover, the health cooperatives members are divided into small groups (*hans*), where health matters are lively discussed on a regular basis. The pedagogical implications of facilitating their own collection of such fundamental health information can not be underestimated in terms of enabling patients to play an active role in leading a more healthy life. By bringing them together regularly to discuss such matters they are also collectively enabled. This helps them to break, even if only marginally, the almost total asymmetry of knowledge in medical care between the professions, on one hand, and patients on the other.

In Japan, the medical cooperatives are patient or consumer cooperatives, not producer or worker cooperatives. Consumer empowerment is primarily achieved through the democratic structures provided by the patient health and medical cooperatives, where the patients are members of the medical co-ops. To the extent such cooperatives are run democratically, they can also empower their members. Members are represented in the cooperative's democratic structures and can influence decisions of the health and medical cooperatives. Member control of the elected officials is greater in the Japanese cooperative movement, than in many other cooperative movements (See Pestoff, 1991 & 1996 on problems of cooperative democracy in Sweden). Both the Chairman and CEO of two of the five or six largest cooperative societies in Japan were recently removed at the annual general meeting, i.e., in Kanagawa (just outside Tokyo) and Sapporo. Consumer empowerment implies formal representation of members and their participation in internal democratic decision-making structures. Thus, the Japanese health and medical cooperatives can combine both consumer enabling and empowerment in the same organization.

However, it is worth keeping in mind that employees do not always have the same perspective on and interest in co-production as do consumers, or employers. In particular, many organizational changes or greater consumer participation can be perceived as a threat to job security, during periods of high unemployment. Thus, the introduction of ATMs is clearly seen as a threat to employment in the banking sector, and many jobs have in fact been eliminated as a result of ATMs. Here consumers and employers share an interest, that is not shared by the banking employees. If, however, instead of introducing new technology, co-production implies greater consumer participation as a result of a major organizational changes designed to promote better communications between the front-line staff and clients, then it may bear with it the promise of a better work environment and a richer work-life, due to more intensive client contacts. We will explore theoretical aspects of the relation between improved work environment and greater client contacts in Chapter 7. The staff of the

Malmö Municipal Housing Authority in Holma clearly perceived such work environment improvements, as too does the staff of most of the cooperative day care centers studied herein. This does not however mitigate the fear felt by employees when faced with greater consumer participation in and perhaps even influence on the production of personal social services. Thus, co-production can often be, and in fact in Sweden is, a controversial topic from the point of view of employees and trade unions. High unemployment can make the perceived trade-off between jobs and improvements in work environment brought about by co-production either seem utopian and too costly for the workers or both. Employees may resist it for these or other reasons.

4.D.4 Cooperatives as a Forum

Much of the so-called privatization of the public sector in Sweden has in effect led to a "cooperativization" of social services. Cooperatives have rapidly become one of the most important alternatives to the public provision of social services in the current transformation of the welfare state and privatization in Sweden. Taking day care services as the prime example, the number of "non-municipal" day care centers more than tripled between 1988 and 1994, increasing from 538 to 1,768 centers, while the number of children attending them nearly increased five-fold during the same period, from 8,500 to 39,000. Nearly two-thirds of these "private" day care centers are in fact either parental or worker cooperative day care services.

Cooperative organizations offer a unique opportunity for creating a dialogue between the clients and personnel of social services, and under certain circumstances can involve the consumers as co-producers of social services. The financing of these "privatized" social services, however, remains primarily a public responsibility. A variety of vouchers have been developed or are under development in different parts of Sweden to pay for social services, e.g. day care vouchers, school vouchers, patient vouchers, home-help vouchers, etc. These vouchers are financed by public funds and provide access to basic social services; i.e., they constitute a quasi-market. Service vouchers are supposed to give individual consumers greater freedom of choice and to stimulate efficiency through competition, according to their proponents.

While service vouchers may facilitate "exit" reactions by clients, and introduce more market signals, they ignore "voice" reactions and indirectly discourage a dialogue between the consumers and providers of personal social services. Cooperatives and other nonprofit organizations can, therefore, make a unique contribution to bringing clients and personnel together and promoting an institutional dialogue between them. Such a dialogue could in turn help to eliminate some of the asymmetry of information and, thus, provide unusual opportunities for improving the quality of social services.

Such a scenario is not wholly problem free. Hirschman (1982a) warns of the excesses of involvement and of its high transaction costs. Involvement is intoxicating, but it can also with time lead to a reaction or withdrawal to private pursuits. It could be argued that greater consumer involvement in the production of social services could, in the long run, be detrimental to the quality of such services. The unstable nature of consumer involvement would be reflected in the unstable quality of the services produced. Certain natural cycles might, however, mitigate the unstable nature of involvement (Stryjan, 1989). Some parents might be involved in the provision of day care services, but not of the elementary education of their children, only to become involved again in educational matters when their children become teen-agers. Other parents may opt for the opposite patterns, choosing a public or private day care center, but then becoming involved in elementary education through a cooperative school, etc. However, Swedish experience to date suggests that there is a cumulative nature to collective action. The positive experience of participating in a parent day care cooperative is carried over to the schools when their children grow older and results in greater parental involvement there.

Parent cooperatives and other types of non-profit organizations providing day care in Sweden, not only facilitate a dialogue between the producers and consumers of social services and enhance the meeting between them, they also encourage the direct participation of consumers in the production of such services. It is common for parental cooperatives and other non-profit alternative forms of day care to include a work obligation for members in their statutes. Parents are not normally charged with actively developing the pedagogics of child care, but they are obliged to participate in maintenance, repairs and administration of day care centers. This work obligation provides greater insights into the running of individual day care centers and promotes a dialogue between the personnel and parents (see Chapter 10 for details). Parents also have a majority of the seats on the board of these day care centers, which gives them greater influence. They are able to formulate and discuss their opinions about the quality of the service with the personnel.

The recent development of greater cooperative and nonprofit production of social services in Sweden can facilitate the development of citizenship and citizens as co-producers of social services in several ways. The institutional involvement of members/citizens as co-producers of social services can extend their right to participate in the governmental process by facilitating their direct participation in the production of some relevant personal social services. It can clarify their duties as citizens and consumers of social service in terms of the obligation to contribute time and service. It can promote a decentralization of the public sector and maintain upward accountability of the producers of social services to politicians, it can also increase the downward accountability of these same producers to their consumers or users. Finally, it can strengthen the control of citizens over politicians and politicians control over the bureaucracy and the public service.

4.E Conclusions

Market failure and information asymmetries make personal social services well suited for provision by social enterprises and other organizations in third sector, since such organizations instill more trust in the relations between the consumers and providers of such services. Quasi-markets are also constrained by possibilities for opportunistic behavior on the part of the producers of personal social services. The enduring nature of some personal social services renders them better suited for voice than exit. Moreover, the transaction costs of providing such services via markets are prohibitive for the consumers, producers and society. All these considerations argue for third sector alternatives both to markets and politics. Here the negotiated economy at the local or micro level, citizens as co-producers, social enterprises and cooperative social services provide an alternative to markets and quasi-markets. They also contribute to the development of civil democracy and local cooperative self-management of social services.

However, when it comes to the new types of social services provided by the welfare state, it is not only a question of information asymmetry, opportunistic behavior and market failure, but also pure and simple lack of knowledge, both on the part of the producers and the consumers of these new social services. Both parties are ignorant of what is good quality service. They need to engage in a dialogue with each other in order to reach a mutual understanding of and agreement about what comprises good quality service. Quality is not something that can be codified, translated into numbers, nor programmed into the memory of robots. Rather it is something that must be learned and re-learned through the repeated interaction of the providers and clients of such services (Wahlgren, 1996). Repeated encounters and meetings between the providers and clients of services helps to reduce both the information asymmetries between them and their mutual uncertainty about the quality of the service.

Co-production facilitates the reduction of this uncertainty, as seen in Chapter 10. By involving clients as co-producers, their expectations about the services and the values they hope to realize by the services can be expressed and translated into practical activities. Their participation in the practical aspects of production of the enduring services they demand facilitates greater interaction with the professional providers of such services and makes a greater dialogue possible between them. This in turn helps both parties to eliminate their uncertainty as well as to facilitate their reaching an agreement about a common standard of good quality services. As a by-product co-production provides the clients with an opportunity to observe some important aspects of the provision of social services and to control against opportunistic behavior on the part of the providers.

Thus, by involving the clients in the provision of services, co-production reduces information asymmetries between the providers and clients of social services, it facilitates a dialogue between them, it helps them to reach a mutual understanding about the provision capacities of the providers and the clients expectations, thus, helping to eliminate uncertainty about the quality of the service, it provides clients with both insights and influence, and thereby helps to safeguard against opportunistic behavior.

5. Control and Multi-Stakeholder Organizations

Who or which groups control a firm is becoming important again in the American debate. The classical perspective argues that in the US it is very rare to find a firm in which control is shared among individuals who are at all dissimilar (Hansmann, 1996). Homogeneity of interests is an especially important consideration in determining the costs of ownership. Heterogeneity of ownership increases the political costs of owning a firm. From this perspective, voting and voting rights are not seen as a mechanism for aggregating and communicating the preferences of a firm's owners to its managers, but rather to provide some crude protection against gross opportunism on the part of those in power (*ibid.*). Accordingly, while there may be a need to improve communication between a firm and its patrons, giving them control over the firm is not necessarily a good means to that end, as it may create costly conflicts. On the contrary, one way of reducing conflicts among various stakeholders with heterogeneous interests is to appoint directors who are charged with the operation of a firm on the behalf of a given class of patrons or stakeholders, but who are not directly controlled or elected by those patrons. This is, in essence what a nonprofit firm is, an "ownerless" firm (*ibid.*). From a different perspective, increasing the representation of various stakeholders appears, nevertheless, to be one way to make US enterprises more competitive than those in Germany and Japan. The institutionalized accountability of US firms would be increased by the involvement of customers and suppliers in the governance of private corporations and this could greatly enhance their international competitiveness (Porter, 1992).

However, no single model can serve all sectors of the economy, all types of firms and all countries. Nor are we primarily interested in discussing the best model of ownership nor competitiveness for large multinational companies, but rather in exploring the potential benefits of extending control to various groups who contribute significantly to providing services in small social enterprises in Sweden and elsewhere in Europe. Multi-stakeholder organizations are seen as one model for increasing citizen involvement.

But who are the stakeholders in a social enterprise and what is their relationship with the firm? We will examine these questions first by presenting stakeholder theory, second by considering the logic of multi-stakeholder organizations and third by introducing a conceptual model of the differences between single and multi-stakeholder firms. Then we will examine multi-stakeholder organizations in Canada, Italy, Spain and Sweden and discuss the issue of membership in multi-stakeholder organizations, before reaching our conclusions.

5.A Introduction to Multi-Stakeholder Theory

The concept of stakeholder usually refers to various parties interested in or directly or indirectly effected by a firm's activities. Stakeholders are persons or groups that have a legitimate claim on the firm (Ackoff, 1981; Clarkson, 1995; Deetz, 1994; Donaldson & Preston, 1995; Hill & Jones, 1992). This legitimacy is established through the existence of an exchange relationship, which permits them to claim rights or interests in the firm and its activities, past, present or future (Donaldson & Preston, 1995). Stakeholders include stockholders, creditors, managers, employees, customers, suppliers, local communities, the government and the general public (Breton & Côté, 1995; Deetz, 1994; Gröjer & Stark, 1978; Hill & Jones, 1992). Each of these groups supply the firm with critical resources and in exchange each expects its interests to be satisfied (Hill & Jones, 1992). It is possible to distinguish between primary and secondary stakeholders (Clarkson, 1995), where the former include all those groups without whose continued participation the firm could not survive. The latter comprises groups who can influence or affect the firm, but with whom the firm does not necessarily engage in transactions, and who are not essential for its survival (*ibid.*).

Stakeholder theory can be seen as a more generalized theory of agency, i.e., as a theory of *stakeholder-agency* (Hill & Jones, 1992). Stakeholder theory goes beyond agency theory, in that it argues that *all* persons or groups with legitimate interests in participating in a firm do so to obtain benefits. Each group of stakeholders has its own expectations or stake in the activity of a firm. The economic and social purpose of the firm is to create and distribute increased wealth and value to all its primary stakeholders, without favoring one group at the expense of another (Clarkson, 1995). Therefore, the objective of a firm is not to serve any single stakeholder group, but rather "*...to serve all of them by increasing their ability to pursue their objectives more efficiently and effectively*" (Ackoff, 1981, 33, emphasis in the original). Thus, the firm should not pursue a purpose of its own, but be an instrument of *all* stakeholders. So there is no *prima facie* priority of one set of interests and benefits over another (Donaldson & Preston, 1995). This means that each stakeholder group has a right to be treated as an end in itself, and not just as a means to some other group's end. Therefore, they must all participate in determining the future of direction of the firm in which they have a primary stake (*ibid.*).

The managers are, however, in a unique position, since they are the only stakeholder group who are in contact with all other stakeholders and the only group that has direct control over the decision-making structures of the firm (Hill & Jones, 1992). In agency theory, managers only serve the interests of the principal or the providers of capital, while in stakeholder theory they should serve all of them (*ibid.*). The interests of principals and agents diverge, mainly since they expect different returns from the firm. This can lead to conflicts over how to use the resources of a firm. Stockholders are wealth maximizers, while managers want to increase their salary, job security, status, etc., and, thus, the latter tend to maximize growth. Stakeholder theory claims that the rewards other groups of stakeholders expect from the firm are also affected by the decisions of managers and the use to which management put resources. Employees want higher wages, customers lower prices, suppliers higher prices and reliable buyers, local communities and the general public lower pollution and enhanced quality of life. All of these things involve the use of resources that otherwise might be invested by managers in maximizing growth (*ibid.*), and/or stockholders in maximizing wealth.

As insiders, managers are in a position to filter or distort the information they release. This complicates agency problems and makes it more difficult for other stakeholders to gather information about a firm's activities. This is highly likely when stakeholders are diffuse, or when no group of individuals has command over a significant proportion of the group's total resources, common in consumer co-ops. Here, no one individual nor group may be able to finance extensive information gathering and analysis necessary to reduce in a meaningful way the information asymmetry between managers and other stakeholders. This in turn gives managers greater discretionary control over the firm's resources (*ibid.*). Stakeholder theory implies that all primary stakeholder groups have a right to complete information about the firm's activities.

Thus, it becomes imperative to develop institutions that can facilitate the alignment of the divergent interests of various stakeholder groups which are primary for a firm's survival. Monitoring structures and financial accounting provide information about the activities of managers, while legal enforcement mechanisms deter the management from maximizing its own utilities at the expense of other stakeholders. Audits, laws, and the exit and voice of various stakeholder groups are the classical institutions for curtailing management opportunism. But such institutions have a number limits, in particular with respect to the power differentials of various stakeholders. Power differentials are greatest when some stakeholders are "locked-in" to an exchange relationship, either due to asset-specific investments, when the costs of exit are very high or because of the information asymmetry that normally exists between managers and other stakeholders (Hill & Jones, 1992). Two additional mechanisms for safeguarding and promoting the interests of all primary stakeholder groups are the establishment of multi-stakeholder organizations and the development of social accounting. We will deal with the first of them here and the second the next chapter.

5.B The Logic of Multi-Stakeholder Organizations

The traditional model of the firm has been severely criticized for merely being based on economic representation (Ackoff, 1981; Deetz, 1994; Breton & Côté, 1995) and solely building on managerial control, since only the stockholders can sanction or remove the managers. Aside from investors, all other stakeholders lack a substantive voice in the firm. The only option available for most other stakeholders, like labor, consumers, suppliers, is either exit or loyalty, but exit can also be very costly to individual stakeholders. Their interests are usually perceived as external to the corporation and with this separation all other stakeholders are merely seen as a cost to the corporation, not as an asset. Thus, there are labor and training costs, equipment costs, tax costs, supply costs, natural resource costs, the costs of compliance with environmental laws, etc. Even consumers are conceived of as costs in terms of the need to advertise and market goods and services. Given this perspective of other stakeholders, it is easy to understand why cost containment becomes the predominant pursuit of managers. The figure below depicts different stakeholders, their stake or expectation in the firm and the typical management view of these stakes as costs.

In order to overcome these problems, the various corporate stakeholders must have an opportunity for greater direct involvement at the site where decisions are made. Greater democracy in corporate decision making is warranted by both political and economic conditions. Politically, if an increasing number of decisions made in corporations effect our personal, social, and national well-being, the public has the right to be represented in them (Deetz, 1994, 3).

Figure 5.1 Different Stakeholders, their Expectations and Costs

Stakeholder	Stake or Expectations	Costs*
Investors	profits, maximization of returns	return on investments
Financiers	repayment on schedule	capital equipment
Workers	fair income & good working conditions	labor & training
Suppliers	use of resources, fair prices & dependable buyers	resources & supplies
Consumers	goods & services at value for money	advertising & marketing
Communities	enhancing the quality of life for citizens	taxes, laws & regulations
Society	following laws and social values	laws & regulations
World Community	environmental effects & sustainable management	natural resources

Source: modified from Deetz, 1994, Figures 4.1 & 4.2, pp. 24 & 27; Breton & Côté, 1995; and Hill & Jones, 1992, p.133. * as perceived by managers.

A multi-stakeholder model (*ibid.*) is based on the conception of firms as having many different types of "owners"; i.e., persons or groups with an interest in or directly or indirectly effected by the activities of a firm. This drastically changes the relations among stakeholders and managers. Many additional groups must be considered as internal to the system of the firm. It becomes accountable to many "investors" or stakeholders, and they all must be consulted in a number of decisions, and not only the stockholders. Various stakeholders will have different interests and will want them represented in the firm's decision-making. Thus, a fully developed multi-stakeholder model changes the function of management radically. The main role of managers in the multi-stakeholder model becomes to find ways to align divergent interests and to facilitate conflict resolution, not to control nor eliminate costs and conflicts among various stakeholders. Management can no longer act as an interested party in the decision-making process (*ibid.*). This would put the many stakeholders in a firm on an equal footing. Domination and control will be replaced by co-determination and coordination, by participation and involvement (*ibid.*).

In Europe we find an important and growing number of social enterprises that are extending their membership to a plurality of stakeholders, including volunteers, workers, consumers and the local authorities who finance them (Borzaga & Mittone, 1997). Multi-stakeholder social enterprises in Europe have several distinguishing characteristics (Borzaga & Mittone, 1997). Their members consist of diverse stakeholder groups, they produce welfare services without the motive of providing profit to a single category of members, they practice internal democracy that permits all stakeholders to participate in important decisions, they lack a non-distribution constraint and can therefore distribute a limited amount of the potential surplus from their operations to their members and they take different legal forms, e.g., associations, co-ops, public companies, etc., which vary according to the law in different European countries.

Two major advantage of multi-stakeholder social enterprises are that their multiple composition helps both to dispel the information asymmetry between producers and consumers as well as to curtail the incentive of various groups to distort information about the nature and quality of the services provided. In addition the formal inclusion of diverse interests of different groups of stakeholders will act as checks-and-balances on each other. Each stakeholder group has its own motives for participating in the organization. The interests of consumers and volunteers for participating in a multi-stakeholder social enterprise will differ from those of workers and the presence of the former provides a certain amount of control of the costs of a firm's operations. Moreover, participation by consumers reduces certain production costs by directly engaging them as co-producers of the services.

5.C Multi-Stakeholder Organizations, a Conceptual Model

Most organizations, whether private firms, social enterprises, cooperatives or voluntary associations, are made up of or combine the interests and the contribution of several different groups, with different, sometimes conflicting interests. The goods and/or services they produce are the result of the joint efforts of many groups, i.e., owners, financiers, workers, suppliers, consumers, the local community, etc., but nevertheless a single group usually dominates them and reaps the fruits or benefits of these joint efforts. Thus, when all factors of the production have been compensated or paid for, any surplus or profit is retained by and solely at the disposed of its owners or stockholders. They can, therefore, be called single or uni-stakeholder organizations. Ownership of stocks conveys property rights and influence in the internal decision-making of such organization.

Cooperatives in many countries provide examples of alternative single stakeholder firms. One single group, e.g., the producers, consumers or workers, through its exclusive membership rights becomes the owner of the cooperative. Through their exclusive membership rights they are able to exclude other groups from claiming property rights in the cooperative. Thus, there are worker or employee cooperatives, where the employers are members and contribute some or most of the firm's capital, and therefore become its owners. Consumer cooperatives provide another example, where

Figure 5.2 Single-Stakeholder Models for Different Groups in an Organization or Firm

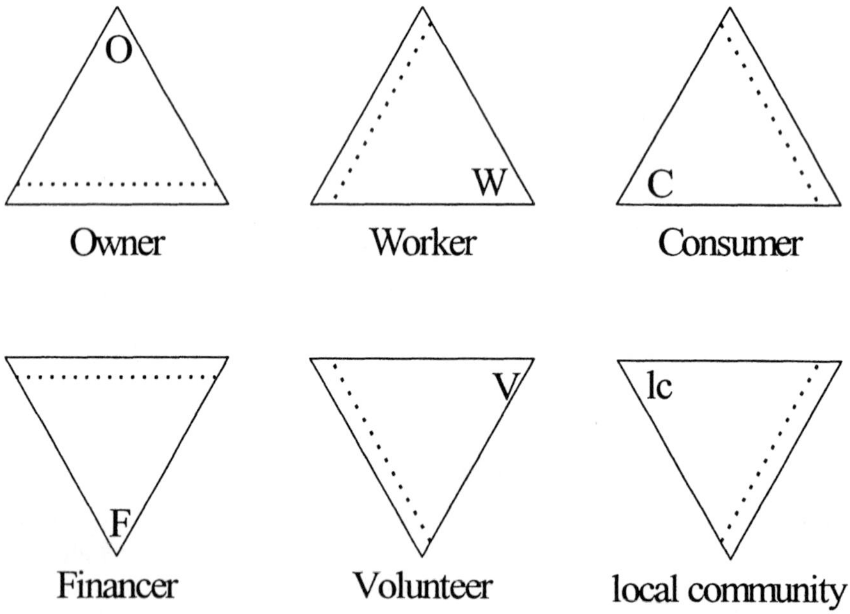

Source: Pestoff, 1995c.

the consumers are members, have an equal share in the cooperative, and therefore the owners of the cooperative. Agricultural producers or farmers pool their resources when selling or buying products, have shares usually in relation to their trade, and are therefore the owners of agricultural cooperatives All these models have in common that a single group has a monopoly of ownership rights and responsibilities. It and it alone can claim to make all the important decisions in the organizations, without any need to take into account the other stakeholders.

However, other stakeholders or groups make alternative ownership claims on the organization. It is possible to conceive of a firm or organization dominated by the workers, volunteers, consumers and other interested parties in the local community. Variations in the pattern of domination by a single stakeholder groups are depicted in the figure above. The dotted line indicates the extent of influence of any single dominant stakeholder and how much is left for all the other stakeholders.

In the world of single-stakeholding, whether it be a private firm, social enterprise, cooperative, voluntary organization, any formal recognition of the interests of other groups is seen as a loss to the owners. This is like a zero-sum model or game, where one's gain means another's loss. Single stakeholder models therefore result quite naturally in an inequitable distribution of power and allocation of benefits to the various contributors to the organization's or firm's production of goods or services. Thus, regardless of which group controls this type of organization, it will normally dominate the firm or cooperative and exclude the interests of other of groups that, nevertheless, contribute to the production of goods or services.

However, if we recognize the contribution, interests and formal rights of several different stakeholders to participate, we must include the multiple stakeholders who comprise most organizations, private firms, social enterprises, cooperatives or voluntary associations. Here one's gain does not automatically mean the loss of some or most other contributors to the joint product of the firm. Thus, multi-stakeholder organizations can be seen as institutions for changing the organizational dynamics of a zero-sum into a plus-sum game, where the interests of all, or most of the players are taken into account, where they can influence the outcome, and thus they can claim a share in the benefits and rewards of their joint production of goods or services. The multi-stakeholder organization, by contrast, can be conceived in the fashion below.

Multi-stakeholder organizations can provide both strong democratic and economic motives for reorganizing private firms, social enterprises, cooperatives and voluntary associations. They promote economic democracy since they recognize the rights of all groups. They give legitimacy and influence to all major contributors to the production of an organization's goods or services. Thus, they are both more equitable and democratic in their internal decision-making structure than single stakeholder organizations. This in turn should contribute to a greater legitimacy in the eyes of many of the organization's stakeholders, and, thus also result in greater loyalty from the many groups contributing to the production of goods and services, as they now all have a recognized stake in it. By representing all major groups in the internal decision-making structures, multi-stakeholder organizations internalize their interests in the organization, and can thus, potentially lower the costs of the transactions between and among these diverse groups.

Figure 5.3 The Multi-Stakeholder Cooperative

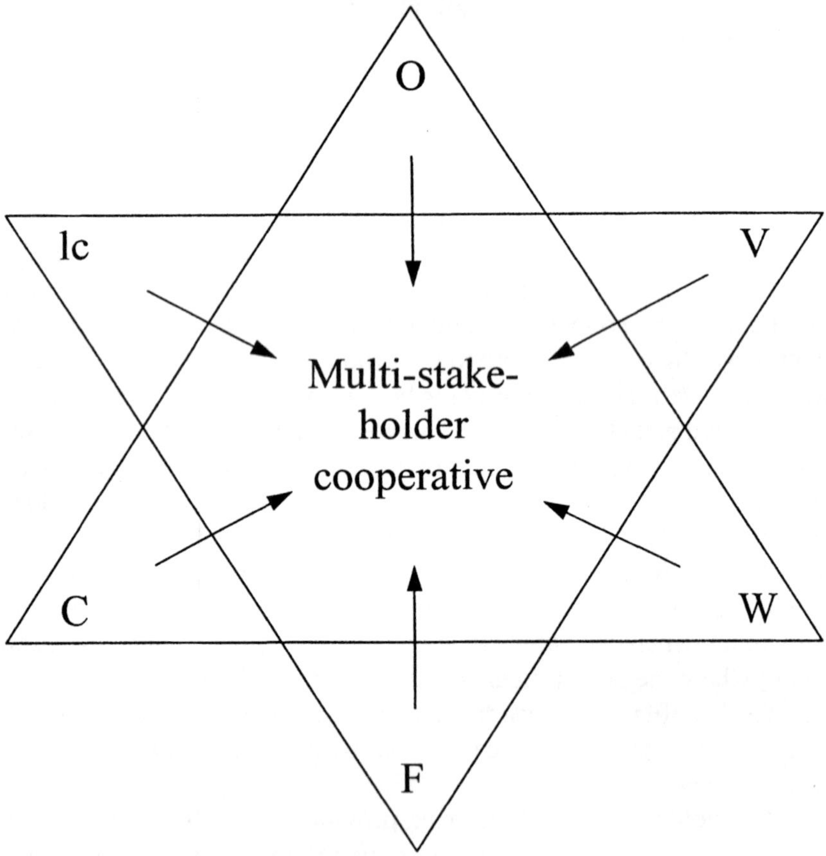

Copyright: Pestoff, 1995c.

The transaction costs for decision-making in the multi-stakeholder organization may, however, increase, as the interests of many divergent groups will now have to be taken into account (Hansmann, 1996; Borzaga & Mittone, 1997). But the costs increases immediately associated with internal decision-making will be set-off by the gains due to increased legitimacy and loyalty of all these groups to the organization or firm. As all of them are represented and can now influence decisions, opportunism can be reduced, if not eliminated. Everybody has a clear stake, with the accompanying rights and responsibilities of multi-stakeholding. Moreover, the necessity of negotiating separate contracts and then of enforcing them with each of these major groups will also be eliminated, as they are now all part of the organization, and partners in its success or failure. This too should help to lower the transaction costs, making for a more efficient and effective organization.

Such cost reductions can be significant, in particular when an organization produces services, rather than manufactures goods, since labor costs are crucial. When labor costs account for 75-80 per cent of the total costs, then worker engagement is important, if not decisive for producing a surplus. Without both qualified and engaged workers there will be a much smaller profit, if any, to distribute to the stockholders. Thus, in areas like personal social services, it seems obvious that a multi-stakeholder model promises greater rewards to all parties than is possible with single stakeholder organizations or private firms. Today workers in personal social services in Sweden choose their job primarily for reasons of self-satisfaction, and not merely in material terms. They prefer to have meaningful jobs, ones that are both challenging and rewarding in non-material terms, jobs that permit personal development and influence on the job and how and when it is done, jobs that fulfill meaningful social functions and/or that contribute to the satisfaction of others, etc. (See Chapter 9 for details). Permitting their participation in the internal decision-making, providing for greater co-determination will increase their satisfaction and loyalty. Thus, it is not so much a question of controlling for the opportunistic behavior of workers, as of achieving the greatest engagement by employees and of getting the greatest quality of services. This will also benefit the clients in terms of better quality services and the local community where such services are provided, in terms of more satisfied citizens.

Clients can make a significant contribution to turning bad jobs into good jobs. Engaged clients with both rights and responsibilities can become involved in the production of the very services they demand, and thus become co-producers. Their involvement can make a significant contribution to the well-being of an organization and can mean the difference between a surplus or loss in operations. Again, it is not a question of preventing opportunistic behavior by clients, but rather of providing the means for clients to become engaged in the activities of the organization providing services for them and/or their family. The rights and responsibilities of clients can best be promoted by recognizing their legitimate stake in the service organization and turning them into co-producers. The involvement of clients in the production of such services is important for maintaining the interaction necessary for good jobs and also contributes to satisfied citizens in the local community. It can also help to curtail the cost of producing such services.

5.D Multi-Stakeholder Cooperatives, Some Examples

Multi-stakeholder organizations are found in the cooperative movements of several countries, including Canada, Japan, Spain and Sweden. We will examine some examples of multi-stakeholder cooperatives from these countries below. More than one hundred years ago cooperatives were a large advance in economic democratization, but that the form they customarily take has the paradoxical effect of excluding some interested parties, usually the workers. This mismatch often leads to performance difficulties that contribute to the declining role of cooperatives in many sectors and countries of the world (Jordan, 1989).

The traditional consumer and producer cooperative relies on the conventional logic of the primacy of use, according to which, users alone are entitled to the benefits of their cooperation. By contrast, worker cooperative advocates often motivate their arguments by reference to the labor theory of value; the surplus is created exclusively by the efforts of the workers, and they alone are entitled to it. There is, however, one serious problem with the lack of congruence between the conventional structure of cooperatives and the various parties with a basic interests in them. Most cooperatives were established to meet the pressing needs of a particular stakeholder group that originally formed its membership base. They were normally small at the outset, but over time they grew and other interests usually came into play. The cooperative hired a staff that developed its own interest in the future of the cooperative as an employer. If it relied on external financing, the investors also developed an interest in the cooperative thriving, so it could pay back its loans. As it continues to grow its suppliers developed an interest in the cooperative's well-being and continued orders. If it was an agricultural or producer cooperative with long-standing, stable relations with its purchasers, they also developed an interest in the future of the cooperative as a deliverer of produce, etc. Thus, overtime cooperatives grow and attract new stakeholder groups that contribute to their continued well-being and growth.

The origin of this mismatch can be traced back to the dominant tradition of the International Cooperative Alliance, ICA, since its formation in 1895. The French and some other cooperators argued at that the practice of "co-partnership" should be adopted as a requirement for ICA membership. Their main concern was that the traditional consumer or producer cooperative did not adequately recognize the contribution and rights of a cooperative's employees. The Anglo-Saxon view of single-stakeholder cooperatives, however, gained the upper hand in the ICA at that time, and it still dominates today.

When a cooperative experiences difficulties, the significance of other parties becomes clear and their stake in the future of the cooperative becomes obvious Thus, the Berkeley Co-op, originally a consumer cooperative reorganized itself into a hybrid consumer-worker cooperative after persistent operating losses in the mid-1980s. The lack of congruence between the interests of various parties or stakeholders is particularly apparent in consumer cooperatives where members' financial stake are often very small - typically ranging from as little as $5.00 to $200.00.

5.D.1 Canada and the Cooperators

In weighing the opposing claims of various stakeholders, we need to ask if and why any of them should be excluded? After all, consumers often contribute extensively to product development, and in other ways which benefit the supplier. How, on the other hand, can user-owners of a consumer cooperative perceive the contribution of staff as external to the well-being of their organization? And in a market economy, how can the users and staff fail to see that some investors make a legitimate contribution to the success of a cooperative?

The question became one of whether a cooperative could be redefined so that it was a product of the various interests that contribute to its being effective? Could the legitimacy of multiple and even opposed interests be acknowledged? Could an organization be designed that specified the nature of the different interests and allocated them an appropriate role? The position taken by the Co-operators' Group (a Canadian insurance cooperative) was that the various parties with major interests in an organization should have a right to have their stakeholder status formally recognized and legitimized (Jordan, 1989). In a conventional corporate setting, these groups would represent customers, labor and capital. But that means that their interests are often opposed to each other. It is necessary to ask if their divergent interests could be aligned (Hill & Jones, 1992), or brought together in one organization? The difference in interests was real, but the question was whether the three groups could see that their interests in-common outweighed their particular divergent interests. This perception of common interests provided the starting point of the multi-stakeholder model, as it was designed to empower each of the three stakeholder interests (Jordan, 1989, 161).

The Co-operators' Group established the Canadian Data Service Limited, CDSL, on an experimental basis as a multi-stakeholder computer service cooperative. CDSL had 750 employees at most in the mid-1980s. However, once a multi-stakeholder model was defined and stakeholders were identified, one still faced a considerable design challenge. Several additional questions needed to be addressed. What form should stakeholder participation take? How were the three different interests to be positively related in an organization? How would potential conflicts be addressed? What should the balance between the three interests be? Three principle for the multi-stakeholder organizational design were developed (*ibid.*). They concerned commitment and balance between groups, their voice and representation, and financial aspects of multi-stakeholder cooperatives. Interestingly enough, representation in this multi-stakeholder cooperative comprised four members each on the board for the clients and financiers, and only two for the staff. The number of votes at the annual general meeting was fixed, regardless of the number of individuals in each group, but it varied between groups (*ibid.*).

The experiment was, however, terminated in the mid-1990s. Today the staff are no longer shareholders nor individual members of CDSL, and the stakeholder structures described below have been dismantled (Jordan, fax of 28/7, 1995). But, CDSL continues as a cooperative corporation, whose shareholders and members are other cooperatives. The failure of this experiment should be given greater attention in order to understand what went wrong, and how to avoid such problems next time around.

In Canada, the Ontario legislature passed amendments to the provincial cooperative act in the early 1990s, which included legal provisions for multi-stakeholder cooperatives, i.e. both staff and clients can join the same cooperative organization and have equal voting rights at annual general meetings (*ibid.*).

5.D.2 Italy: Multi-Stakeholder Cooperatives and Social Services

The Italian Law No. 381/1991 recognizes "social cooperatives" as a new cooperative form that developed spontaneously during the 1970s and

1980s and in part gained recognition through litigation (Borzaga, 1998). They are divided into two main groups:

a) those that provide social, health and educational services; and

b) those that carry out other types of activities (agricultural, industrial or services) with the purpose of employing disadvantaged persons. The latter are defined as physical, mental or sensorial handicapped, ex-patients of psychiatric institutions, persons undergoing psychiatric treatment, drug addicts, alcoholics, teen-agers with difficult family situations and convicts who choose to serve their time in this fashion rather than in detention. Disadvantaged workers must comprise 30 per cent of more of the employees of such multi-stakeholder cooperatives (*ibid.*).

According to this law social cooperatives have the following features:

a) their aim should be "the pursuit of general community interests in promoting human concerns and the social integration of citizens";

b) while traditional cooperatives legally are single-stakeholder organizations, the social cooperative can recruit members from both consumers and workers, and volunteers (but not exceeding more than half of the members); and public or private legal entities whose statutes permit the financing and development of social cooperatives; and

c) while social cooperatives can acquire multi-stakeholder features, they are not obliged to do so. In Italy there are both single-stakeholder (worker) social cooperatives and multi-stakeholder social cooperatives (*ibid.*).

Research shows that three-fourths of the 560 social cooperatives surveyed in 1986/87 had volunteers as members (*ibid.*). However, under the new law the situation gradually changed in the 1990s, as local and regional authorities began to contract out social services to these newly legalized social cooperatives. This development both favored the creation of social cooperatives with only worker members, and the professionalization of service provision, at the expense of volunteers. Thus, already by 1992 half of the social cooperatives had no volunteer members (CGM, 1994), and by 1994 two-thirds of them lacked volunteers as members (CGM, 1997).

Thus, in Italy today there are mainly two types of social cooperatives. The majority of them only have worker members, i.e. they are single-stakeholder cooperatives, and a minority of about one-third that members other than the workers, i.e., mostly volunteers (Borzaga, 1998). Another interesting feature of the Italian social cooperatives, according to the law No. 381/9991, is that they must prepare an annual social account of their activities.

5.D.2 Spain: Integral Health Cooperatives in Barcelona

In Spain there are several multi-stakeholder cooperatives in different parts of the country. The best known of them is *Eroski*, the retail co-op in *Mondragon*, which is organized with a dual membership base of workers and consumers so that the interest of each are recognized. It is described in numerous scholarly works and those details will not be repeated here. In Barcelona a multi-stakeholder cooperative health care organization was started in 1974. By 1990 it had 161,000 members and opened its first hospital (Castano, 1990), with 367 single-bed rooms. Its services cover surgery, intensive care, general medicine, pediatrics, obstetrics, gynecology, psychiatric, etc. According to Catalonian law any cooperatives may include both the employees and clients among the ranks of its members, and give them voting rights, if the statutes permit it (*ibid.*).

The organization of Integral Health Cooperation in Barcelona was started by Dr. Espriu and the Espriu Foundation. It was based on a (con-) federation of four separate cooperatives, one for doctors, another for consumers or health insurance clients, a third for other hospital workers and a fourth, which is a peak organization where they join forces and co-manage their integral health cooperative efforts (Espriu, 1995). The option of creating a multi-stakeholder confederation of separate single-stakeholder cooperatives stemmed from a fear among doctors that the non-doctor members, who would outnumber them, could perhaps gain the same rights, duties and status as the doctors (*ibid.*, p. 231). The doctors' ambition was, nevertheless, to provide "collective medicine". In medicine, as in many other professions, there are a minimum of two parties: the patient and the doctor. The patient is the one who pays and suffers because of illness, and it is the doctor who puts his knowledge and reputation into play, for which he gets paid (*ibid.*, 231). In spite of the differences between them, the Espriu Foundation emphasizes the harmony between these two groups. "To our understanding, this harmony will be impossible if one attempts to include both these collectives in a single cooperative, as well as the other workers who are not doctors. In this way the internal conflicts would be numerous and serious and, furthermore, the advantages proper to second and subsequent level cooperatives would be cast aside." (*ibid.*, 232).

5.D.3 Social Service Cooperatives in Sweden

The majority of the cooperative day care facilities studied here were run as consumer cooperatives, while worker cooperatives were a newer phenomenon. Only a few of the cooperative day care centers formally permit the representation of both consumers and producers on the board governing their activities (See Chapter 8 for more details). However, we find some examples of hybrid institutions for consumer representation in worker cooperatives or for employees representation in consumer cooperatives among the cooperatives studied by the WECSS Project (Stryjan, 1995). Additional examples of mixed cooperatives are found in certain parts of Sweden exist in other types of social services, such as health and medical care, handicap care and care for the elderly (Wahlgren, 1996).

This development has, however, been questioned in terms of the intensity and duration of the interests of these two groups, as they differ in one fundamental respect. Both the producers and the clients of social services may feel intensely involved in determining the quality of social services, and may feel an equal need to be involved in the decision-making process. Thus, neither group should be denied influence in the running of cooperative social services merely on the basis of the intensity of their involvement. However, the producers and clients of social services differ in terms of the *duration* of their involvement. The involvement of a producer can be indefinite, or as long as they work in the sector or a given organization, i.e., for several for years, if not decades. But, the involvement of clients is normally more short-term and limited, e.g., a parent's involvement is normally limited to a few years, or until his/her child starts school. So, both a producer and a client may share the same intensity of involvement in decision-making, but not the same duration of involvement in it, nor the same commitment for the organization's survival over time.

Thus, the parental cooperative form may be more prone to degenerate into an organization with little if any cooperative values and membership involvement. Parents who start a cooperative day nursery facility may or may not be replaced by other parents of an equally intensive involvement, when their child reaches school age. There is a greater risk of losing the cooperative commitment and involvement in a parental cooperative day care program, than in worker cooperative day care services. Parents in some cooperative day care programs in Sweden are aware of this risk and they are anxious to insure the continuation of the cooperative form for running such programs. Thus, they have initiated the institutional involvement of the employees in the decision-making process of their parental cooperative, to insure the survival of its cooperative values and democratic governing principles. Over time this is likely to facilitate the growth of multi-stakeholder cooperative services.

A few multi-stakeholder cooperatives were included in the Swedish study of social enterprises providing social services. One multi-stakeholder cooperative day care facility was found in two major urban areas, Gothenburg and Stockholm. The Stockholm day care center, “Sitting Bull”, explicitly labeled itself as such, while the Gothenburg multi-stakeholder cooperative preferred to call itself a parental day-care center. Both the staff and the parents were represented on the board of the day care facility, although with some variation. In Gothenburg, the parents have four seats on the board and the staff three. In Stockholm the multi-stakeholder cooperative day-care center developed unintentionally during the reorganization and expansion of a problematic parent cooperative day care facility. Presently, all thirty of the families with a child enrolled are members in the day-care cooperative, as well as all nine employees. At the annual general meeting there are thirty parents and nine staff, and each of them has a vote, giving the parents a clear majority, if they voted as a group. This has occasionally happened in important questions. like moving to different premises. The parents out-voted the staff and decided to remain in their current closer, but cramped more expensive location. Both groups, however, elect four representatives each to the board, and the chairwoman lacks a deciding vote in case of a tie.

In the northern county of Jämtland, there are several multi-stakeholder cooperatives which provide various kinds of social services, including handicap care during the day and elderly care at rest homes or home care for senior citizens. Both the clients and the staff are members of such cooperatives, both have voting rights at the annual general meeting, that decides policy questions, and both elect representatives to the board. Clients are informed and consulted about all important decisions. However, either developmentally handicapped clients or clients handicapped by age and senility, lack the resources to pursue their own interests themselves when they differ with those of the staff. On the other hand, such multi-stakeholder cooperative social services are often the result of local community development cooperative projects. Moreover, in elderly care cooperatives, the staff are normally both a neighbor and relative or off-spring of the clients. Therefore, they share both family ties, neighbor ties and a common interest in promoting local community development (Wahlgren, 1996). While the clients lack the same kind of formal influence available to parents in the multi-stakeholder day-care cooperatives in the major urban areas, they have several additional informal channels of influence not usually found in urban areas.

5.E Membership in Multi-Stakeholder Cooperatives

The Canadian discussion of multi-stakeholder cooperatives points to the need for carefully considering why multi-stakeholder institutions are developed and then who should be represented on them. Both theoretical and practical aspects are important. One approach sees the potential contribution of cooperatives in terms of developing economic democracy. Here emphasis is on representation of "significant" stakeholders in enterprise decisions, as a way to promote the goal of economic democracy (Laycock, 1994, 4-5). Three, four, or at times five different groups or categories of stakeholders could/should be included in the decision-making of multi-stakeholder cooperatives. They include: 1) the members; 2) the firm's employees; 3) the management; 4) the local community; and 5) the state.

However, the larger the firm the greater the risk of management domination of decision-making, even in supposedly democratic organizations like cooperatives (*ibid.*, see also Pestoff, 1991 & 1996). Management is automatically a player in cooperatives, by virtue of its function. Therefore, it needs no separate representation, since its power on decisions exceeds that of all other "significant" stakeholders combined (Laycock, 1994). Even the Canadian multi-stakeholder cooperative, CDSL, introduced earlier, explicitly excludes managers from any form of representation on the board, in a firm with 750 employees (Jordan, 1989). The community where a firm operates should also be given representation, to avoid "social externalities" within the decision-making process. A final, and occasional stakeholder requiring representation, is the state, or some specialized state agency with responsibility for economic development, especially where it provides substantial financial assistance to the cooperative (Laycock, 1994).

It is interesting to note which "significant" group of stakeholders are not explicitly included in this proposal; i.e., the financiers, unless the state functions as a financier of a multi-stakeholder cooperative. Moreover, consumers are only included implicitly as members, since multi-stakeholder cooperatives are seen as a tool or method for reorganizing consumer cooperatives and expand the representation of those "significant" stakeholders groups excluded by today's principal user cooperatives, i.e., workers.

The Co-operators' Group was interested in developing legal structures that proved viable in terms of uniting the diverse and often conflicting interests of various stakeholders in other cooperative enterprises. At the outset of the CDSL experiment with multi-stakeholding, it was necessary to answer several questions about membership and stakeholder influence in great detail. Thus, the Canadian discussion of multi-stakeholder cooperatives is very illustrative of numerous practical considerations necessary for moving beyond ideas and proposals. A different concept of the corporation was necessary at the outset of their experiment. A corporation may be a legal person - but should not be seen as a person that is independent or autonomous in its interests. Its interests are those of its stakeholders and it has, or should have, none of its own. (See Section 5.A above for similar ideas). Accordingly:

> the stakeholder logic is designed to empower defined interests; this means that a stakeholder is defined by the organization's importance to the stakeholder - and not vice-versa... Therefore, we must go beyond a generic definition of stakeholder as an organized interest which is significantly affected by the action or inaction of [*sic*] an organization. The breadth of this definition also poses difficulties; it is so broad that it would include, for example, competitors whom one would not want empower. This definition also suggests the stakeholders are passive parties who are simply recipients of the organization's actions. Instead, we want a definition that sees the organization as the product of the stakeholder's purposes and activity. For these reasons, a more appropriate definition of stakeholder is: those organized interests who co-produce the results of the organization. (Jordan, 1989, 157, emphasis in the original)

An analysis of the operating companies within the Co-operators' Group revealed that several interests were significant - the users of service, the providers of services (staff) and the Co-operators' Group, as the financier of the new multi-stakeholder cooperative. They also looked at broader interests such as the community, but concluded that it was difficult to define the appropriate relationship. As a result they began with relationships that were clearest, while keeping open the possibility of extending the model at a later point (*ibid.*, 158).

However, in the new data cooperative, the *user* was not an obvious stakeholder. The cooperative may not matter significantly to some users of its services. Whether it did or not depended both on the nature of the business relationship and on the value the user put on being part of a cooperative. Users were, therefore, designated as a category which should have the option of becoming stakeholders, but the likelihood of that happening would vary considerably from case to case. Thus, criteria was established for user or client stakeholders, including a minimum amount of business per year and a commitment not to compete with the multi-stakeholder cooperative (*ibid.*, 160).

The *staff* seemed to be a more clear-cut category, but they did not always see it that way. Younger, more mobile staff may not necessarily see themselves as having a long-term interest in the organization that was implied in the stakeholder model. Thus, only those employees who voluntarily joined were included as members in the new multi-stakeholder cooperative. The Cooperators' Group provided the entrepreneurial initiative and supplied the initial *capital* for new multi-stakeholder cooperative. It also provided a link with the broader cooperative community, and saw to it that there was a desirable co-ordination among cooperative companies (*ibid.*, 160).

5.F Conclusions

Not only the owners of capital and their direct agents have legitimate interests in a firm, several other stakeholder groups also do, including the workers, consumers, suppliers, local community and government, etc. Various stakeholders have divergent interests that may come in conflict. Structures need to be developed for an alignment of the divergent interests of various stakeholder groups. Multi-stakeholder organizations provide one method for resolving some of these differences of interests. Certain significant stakeholder groups could be given representation on the board of such organizations. It is often argued that firms owned by heterogeneous groups will have significantly higher transaction costs for decision-making. These potentially higher costs are off-set by greater staff engagement, lower contacting costs, higher quality services, consumers as co-producers, etc. Multi-stakeholding organizations promote a dialogue between consumers and producers of goods and services and help to eliminate information asymmetries normal to single stakeholder organizations.

The interests of and intensity of involvement by different actors in the production of goods and services vary greatly with their production function. At the most basic level there are three primary functions in the production process, i.e. as owners of the capital, or financiers; as producers of the goods or providers of services, or workers and employees, and as consumers of the goods or clients of the services. Each of these functions is related to different property rights.

Private firms in market economies most clearly distinguish these functions in relation to property rights. The owners of capital are guaranteed the right to dispose of the profits accrued from a firm's production, workers and most other employees are provided hourly remuneration for the sale of their labor, while the customers or clients have the right to dispose of the goods or services acquired through their purchase. Traditionally, cooperatives differ from private firms in that they normally attempt to fuse at least two of these functions of production, and the interests associated with them. Ownership in cooperatives is either combined with the function of the producers or the consumers of the goods or services. Thus, in a worker cooperative, the majority of the workers control the majority of the stocks or shares in the firm and seats on the board. In a consumer cooperative, the majority of the members control the majority of the stocks or shares in the firm and seats on the board.

Cooperative organizations are supposedly governed by democratic rules and decisions are based on the principle of one member/one vote. Here, conflicts of interests might theoretically be simpler, since the interests of two groups are fused and decision-making is democratic. Thus, the interest of the owners/financiers corresponds with those of the member/workers or member/consumers. There may, however, be a latent conflict between the owners of the cooperative and other groups in the production process. It is, moreover, rare to find a cooperative that fuses all three functions, ownership, production and consumption in the same organization. The latter are referred to as multi-stakeholder cooperatives. In such organizations potential conflicts of interest are institutionalized into the governing board of the cooperatives. The governing bodies, thus, become a forum for discussing and debating the quality of the social services provided.

Returning to the empirical focus of our study, we note that social services are primarily financed by public funds in Sweden. Thus, we are mainly concerned with representing the interests of clients and personnel of social services. But, there are two main ways of organizing co-operative social services in Sweden, based on the consumer cooperative and the worker cooperative models. Each of these models institutionalizes the interests of a single group, either the consumers or producers of social services. A single group is normally represented on the board of such service providers, either the clients or the personnel. A hybrid of these two is the mixed social enterprise, which institutionally combines the interests of both the consumers and producers of social services. An additional model is found in some types of nonprofit organizations that function like quasi-multi-stakeholder organizations, but that nevertheless have different ways of institutionalizing the interests of the clients, staff and perhaps other interested groups, like volunteers and sponsors.

The Canadian, Italian, Spanish and Swedish experience point to a number of important issues surrounding multi-stakeholder organizations.

Are there some limits in terms of size of an organization or its complexity that render it less suitable for the multi-stakeholder model? Will (con-) federative models, like that found in Barcelona, work best when the divergent interests of various stakeholders are great? Which significant group should be included as members and given a vote in the running of a multi-stakeholder organization? Are multi-stakeholder organizations able to develop rules that help to reduce the collective decision-making costs, i.e., about the composition of membership and decision-making rules, etc.? Can the transaction costs of decision-making be reduced in multi-stakeholder organizations by including only those groups or persons who are clearly identified as co-producers, as seen in the Canadian experience? Does the information asymmetry between managers and other stakeholders preclude the inclusion of the former, at least in organizations over a certain size? Should the decision to become a member in a multi-stakeholder organization be individual, thereby only giving the committed users, staff members financiers and/or local communities voting rights, etc.? Can some stakeholders be indirectly represented, like children by their parents, handicapped by their relatives or someone from a local handicap organization or the elderly by a neighbor and/or off-spring? Are multi-stakeholder organizations inherently unstable and do they degenerate into single stakeholder organizations controlled by the dominant stakeholder, e.g., financiers in Canada and worker in Italy? Answers to these questions are important for the future development of multi-stakeholder organizations and social enterprises.

We agree that multi-stakeholder organizations offer various advantages compared with traditional nonprofit organizations and for-profit firms (Borzaga & Mittone, 1997). In particular when market or contract costs are notably greater than ownership costs, or the costs of collective decision-making (Hansmann, 1996; Borzaga, 1998). In the presence of information asymmetries, they provide consumers with more reliable guarantees of the services provided than either traditional nonprofit organizations or for-profit firms. They prove equally as efficient as for-profit firms. They can also help to generate greater trust between the producers and consumers of personal social services than for-profit firms. Experimentation with the development of the multi-stakeholder organization model could help social enterprises to evolve into a unique institution of grass-root economic democracy and thereby help to change the provision of publicly financed social services. Multi-stakeholder organizations can help to transform the welfare state into a welfare society in Sweden and elsewhere in Europe.

6. Accounting for the Activities of Social Enterprises

Epistemology helps social actors frame their reality and act upon it. In particular, "the market epistemology relies heavily on the numerical descriptions and coding of economic activities, on the background of the ethical - and often implicit - standpoint that utility is the only thing that counts", while organizations and networks make greater use of verbal representation. Epistemology has far-reaching effects, not only on *how* effectively something is done, but also on *what* is done (Kallinikos, 1995; 119-120). "The market epistemology directs attention to the notion of*price* and the implications stemming from the conversion of human accomplishments into *numerical values*" (*ibid.*, p. 123). But, such a description of human activity and social goals in terms of numbers is achieved at the expense of variety; i.e., rights, preferences and obligations are dissolved into the least common denominator (*ibid.*). Not only do words and numbers differ greatly, but there are important trade-offs between the informational richness of qualitative messages of words compared with the precise and standardized messages of numbers (*ibid.*).

The traditional economic balance sheet provides social enterprises, cooperatives and nonprofit organizations with feedback about their economic performance. However, the need to consider social, and often philosophical, objectives makes the overall assessment of their success more elusive (Bold, 1991, 95-97). This ambiguity had continually plagued researchers studying the behavior of such organizations. Their members have different sets of expectation and any attempt to capture all of the expectations of their stakeholders demands the use of a model and methods of performance evaluation that are designed to consider multiple objectives. Such models and methods are rare, but social accounting and the social audit movement can provide some encouragement and guidance. "(C)onvential accountability attempts to reduce the social to the economic and the economic to the cash nexus. The importance of the social audit movement lies in its commitment to the restoration of social and political control over the economy" (Geddes, 1992 as quoted in Gray *et al.*, 1996, 237).

Compared with for-profit organizations or private commercial firms, cooperatives have several goals rather than a single one that they must attempt to maximize. The owners of a cooperative are its members and each member has an equal number of shares, usually just one. Thus, a cooperative's internal decision-making is based on the democratic principle of "one member - one vote". After investments, the surplus generated from a cooperative's commercial transactions is returned to its members as a rebate or in some other form in accordance with their patronage or purchases, rather than resulting in profits dispensed in accordance with the number of stocks held. Cooperatives and nonprofit organizations have social as well as economic goals. Management is more complex in multiple goal organizations than in single goal organizations. Profit, sales or market share fail to provide adequate or sufficient guidance for such multiple goal organizations. This is both a challenge to and an opportunity for the managers and members of multiple goal organizations. Swedish consumer cooperatives, however, provide a good illustration of the pitfalls of merely evaluating the performance of cooperative and nonprofit organizations in financial terms, i.e. in terms of a single goal.

This chapter addresses differences between the financial and social responsibilities of social enterprises, cooperatives and nonprofit organizations. The transformation of the welfare state and contracting out of the production of publicly financed personal social services to social enterprises, cooperatives and nonprofit organizations results in a growing need to develop systematic and comprehensive social reporting and auditing. Social accounting is still a young and underdeveloped field in business administration and the social sciences. Yet it is very important, if not crucial for the development and future of the social enterprises, cooperatives and nonprofit organizations providing personal social services, as well as for many of those providing other types of goods and services. Social accounting can and should serve several different purposes. Four main ones are introduced briefly here, and two of them are discussed at greater length. First, social accounting provides a powerful tool for evaluating the performance of an organization, in particular the non-monetary aspects of its activities. Second, social accounting is a basic and essential means of guarding against goal deflection and voluntary failure. Third, social accounting is an important means of promoting and marketing an organization and its goals, and can, thus, contribute to increasing a firm's or organization's legitimacy, both in the market and in politics. Finally, social accounting also provides a new tool for greater member influence and control, and thus promotes organizational democracy. It goes hand-in-hand with multi-stakeholding in promoting greater grass-roots economic democracy (see Chapter 5 and Pestoff, 1995c). After considering the first tow of these reasons for developing social accounting procedures, we move on to discuss what type of accounting is necessary for organizations in the third sector. Then we turn our attention to various proposals for social reporting and accounting and finally to examples for cooperative social accounting in Canada and Italy.

6.A Performance Evaluation: How and for Whom?

A good illustration of the need for social reporting is seen in the different perspectives on the evaluation of a publicly supported employment creation projects. One such project promoted the creation of cooperative farms by former farm workers in California. A major pitfall in evaluation research is setting the criteria for assessment that reflect the full range of the consequences; i.e. who decides the terms of success. When evaluation criteria are established outside the targeted population, e.g., by funding agencies, evaluation consults, or the staff of public programs, there is a grave risk that it may mask and undervalue the accomplishments as seen through the eyes of the participants themselves (Wells, 1981).

Public sponsors and private agencies providing supporting funds have tended to evaluate farm worker cooperatives as they would a standard enterprise, that is in terms of their attainment of levels of profits and economic self-sufficiency comparable to those in the private sector, thus, resulting in a disappointing record in their eyes. Cooperative members, on the other hand, take a broader view of cooperative accomplishments, emphasizing its impact on the quality of their social, political and economic life (*ibid.*, 239). They mention not only access to higher income and more employment stability in the cooperative; but also greater independence and more control over their working conditions, as well as more influence in their communities and an improved relationship with their families as the major advantages of membership and employment in the cooperative farm (*ibid.*, 241). All of the latter belong to the social rather than the financial sphere.

Performance evaluation is an important, yet often ignored, part of operating cooperatives and nonprofit organizations, if for no other reason than all organizations must balance their resources in such a fashion that their income exceed expenses. Organizations which fail to do so cannot survive in the long run. Neither cooperatives nor nonprofit organizations are exceptions to this. They may choose to call the surplus in operations something other than profits, but they must produce a surplus. In a narrow perspective, it could be argued that a financial statement would be sufficient to evaluate the performance of a cooperative or nonprofit organization. However, this fails to take into account the other goals of cooperatives and nonprofit organizations, in particular their social goals. Methods must be developed for evaluating the performance of cooperatives and nonprofit organizations in terms other than the narrow financial ones uses for judging profit maximizing firms.

A number of key definitions have been developed to evaluate the performance of social care programs in England (Hoyes, *et al.*, 1992), including efficiency and equity in the delivery of social services. Concerning *efficiency*, a myriad of different and conflicting definitions exist. However, two basic concepts appear to underlie most of these different interpretations.

The first refers simply to the cost of service provision irrespective of *quantity* or *quality*. It is known as *crude efficiency*, where an efficient service is one that minimizes the cost of service delivery and results in "cost-cutting" as the main way of improving efficiency. This is the kind of efficiency most often used in the public debate. The second concept is known as *allocative efficiency*, which explicitly relates the benefits derived from services to the costs. More specifically, a service is allocatively efficient if it *maximizes the difference between the benefits and the costs of the service* (*ibid.*, 12). Allocative efficiency is very broad and can include most anything of positive value, but should not be equated with *effectiveness*.

Equity is also a term that can be interpreted in many ways, but once again there appear to be two main alternatives, *equity of care* and *equity of access*. Equity of care is usually related to need. It has two aspects: equal treatment for equal need (horizontal equity) and the corollary of unequal treatment for unequal need (vertical equity). Equity of access on the other hand, refers to the *availability* of services, not their level of take-up or the actual amount of care received (*ibid.*, p. 15). Thus, the important point here is that both efficiency and equity can mean quite different things, depending on how they are defined.

The issue of evaluating the effectiveness of voluntary nonprofit organizations has recently become the focus of an academic exchange between Osborne & Tricker (1995) and Herman & Heimovics (1995). The former criticize the methods developed by the latter. Rather they recommend the framework developed by Knapp (1984), which makes it is possible to arrive at an operational definition of effectiveness and other key concepts of service delivery (*op. cit.*, 88). Effectiveness, according to them is about relating the outcomes achieved by an organization to its policy framework and objectives and is open to contention and debate from a range of stakeholders (*ibid.*, 89). Thus, the social constructionalist method proposed by Osborne & Tricker is both organizational specific and relative to the organization in question.

Herman & Heimovics (1995) point out in their rejoinder that: "[T]aking a social constructionalist perspective seriously requires that researchers avoid, to the extent possible, the assumption that they know what criteria real stakeholders use in making judgments of organizational effectiveness" (*ibid.*, 93-94). Instead, they propose a "focus group" method, which tries to identify criteria or indicators that persons in their study agreed upon and actually used in making assessments of the effectiveness of nonprofit organizations. Thus, they conclude that different stakeholders may have different ways of evaluating an organization. Some stakeholders in nonprofit organizations do evaluate its effectiveness in terms of a few output or outcome criteria, while other stakeholders manifest greater concern with using the correct processes and procedures (*ibid.*, 95). However, they continue with a recommendation that only quantifiable information or data be employed, for the sake of comparison. Many stakeholders, especially donors and contractors, are often interested in effectiveness of one organization compared to another (*ibid.*, 97).

Note, however, that this is very similar to the typical "stake" of the researcher(s) in his/her study object(s) - they would also like to be able to compare them. However, we need to ask for whom performance evaluations and studies of effectiveness are undertaken. Are we developing methods of evaluating performance for outside stakeholders who finance some or much of the actives of a nonprofit organization, for researchers or for the members? Clearly, this does not need to be conceived as an "either/or" question. It depends largely on whether we are concerned with a nonprofit organization providing social services mostly to non-members on a contracting-out basis, or with a social service cooperative mainly for members. Herman & Heimovics appear more interested in the former, while our focus is primarily on the latter. But their focus also seems prejudiced in favor of providing methods for those with stakes outside an organization to gain greater influence on the running of the nonprofit organization. We are more interested here in developing methods for providing members with greater insight into and control over their own social enterprise, cooperatives and/or nonprofit organizations.

6.B Goal Displacement and Voluntary Failure

Goal deflection is an important phenomenon in all types of organizations, e.g. public, private and nonprofit. Organizations are started for one purpose or goal, but often fail to fulfill them, either because they are inefficient and unable to do so, or because they start pursuing other, and sometimes conflicting goals. This can be phrased in terms of "permanently failing organizations". Such organizations fail to provide a surplus on their operations for long periods of time, and yet somehow continue to exist and maintain their operations, at a constant loss (Meyer & Zucker, 1989). The cause of their inefficiency is that they pursue some other goals in addition to the economic ones that contribute to their failure. They may, however, successfully pursue other goals, e.g., power for their owners or social aims. Permanent failure is not restricted to any single type of firm, and they provide in depth examples from the public, private and nonprofit sectors (*ibid.*).

Michels (1911 & 1962) classical work on oligarchic tendencies of modern democracy, *Political Parties*, focuses on the problem of goal deflection in the German labor movement shortly before the outbreak of W.W.I. He decries the embourgeoisment of the German trade unions and socialist party of the time, and relates this to goal deflection in voluntary organizations. Due to the division of labor in complex organizations, an organization soon changes from a means for its members, to an end for its leaders. Thus, the special interests of organizational leaders come into conflict with those of the members. Michels concludes his work by formulating his famous Iron Law of Oligarchy: "he who says organization also says oligarchy".

A more recent and relevant example of goal displacement and voluntary failure is found in the Swedish consumer cooperatives, once the pride of the International Cooperative Alliance (ICA). The unsuccessful attempts during the 1970s to develop a multi-dimensional evaluation of the performance of the Swedish consumer cooperatives illustrate the fallacy of merely focusing on commercial activities of a cooperative or social enterprise, and ignoring the members and the democratic aspects of such organizations (Pestoff, 1991 & 1996).

During the 1960s and 1970s there was a lively discussion within Swedish consumer cooperatives concerning their goals, basic principles, organizational structures, democratic problems and the efficiency and effectivity of cooperatives. Various internal committees were given responsibility for analyzing and developing ideas and making proposals concerning such matters. The concept of "*cooperative effectivity*" was discussed explicitly for the first time, in *Swedish Consumer Cooperatives Facing the 1980s* (1979). It was argued that cooperatives need to develop a different efficiency or effectivity concept because of their multiple goals. Private business could afford to rely on purely business criteria, but "*cooperative effectivity*" should have a more composite character. Member participation should not be conceived merely as a means to an end, but rather as a goal in itself. "Our organization is effective first when we can unite a functioning member democracy and our other non-material goals, with success in business" (1979, 22). "Cooperative effectivity" was defined here as being composed of consumer political effectivity, business-like efficiency, and democratic effectivity. It should provide an overall guide the activities of consumer cooperatives. This report goes on, however, to lament the "...lack of methods which, in an objective way, can measure our 'cooperative effectivity' in relation to non-economic areas" (*ibid.*). Thus, we were left with the traditional financial balance sheet and/or market shares as the sole indicator(s) of the success or failure of the Swedish consumer cooperative movement.

A decade later a new "*Program of Action*", called *Working Together for Mutual Gain*, was adopted by KF's Congress in 1989. It presented the purpose and guidelines of the Swedish consumer cooperatives in an eight point program. The concept of "*cooperative effectivity*" is, however, conspicuously absent. The 1989 *Program of Action* provides little practical benefit for arriving at a suitable measure that takes into account the whole range of activities included in this eight point program.

Furthermore the Membership Committee's report on "*Members' Involvement in the Consumer Cooperatives in the 1990s*" (1990) to the same congress provides nothing to rectify the failure to develop an operational concept for evaluating the performance of the multiple goals of cooperatives. On the contrary, it appears to justify the further diminution of the importance and necessity of active members. It maintains that members play three different roles, as a customer, as a member and as an owner, which must be kept separate in the running of consumer cooperatives. The customer role is an entirely sufficient form of involvement for most members (*ibid.*), but, it notes, rather pathetically, that the consumer cooperative's customers should have the same or even greater influence in cooperative as in their competitors (*ibid.*, 6). It states that most members have little or no knowledge of how to influence their local cooperative society (*ibid.*, 7), and assumes, therefore that they are only interested in the economic benefits provided by cooperatives.

Moreover, elected officers are no longer to be seen as the representatives of the interests and wishes of members and should not be considered as surrogate owners in the management of Swedish consumer cooperatives (*ibid.*, 6). Officers must be more carefully selected in the future (by a Selections Committee) and educated in order to assume executive responsibilities on the boards where they serve. It also refers to the idea of a more member related accounting and economic statement, but it quickly rejects this under present economic circumstances.

A new wave of structural rationalizations in the 1990s, separated most of the local membership organizations from the commercial activities of the consumer cooperatives in Sweden. Their commercial activities are now amalgamated into a nation-wide concern and run as a limited company; i.e., without any further membership influence nor interference what-so-ever. These developments in the 1990s in the *Kooperativa förbundet & Konsum* provide a recipe for "making membership meaning*less*", to paraphrase the title of a recent ICA publication.

Some authors clearly associate voluntary failure with goal deflection. A few provide recommendations for avoiding these twin ills. Michels (*op cit.*) discusses several techniques for attempting to restrict the influence of leaders of voluntary organizations, including the membership referendum. Lipset argues that only competitive leadership elections can maintain union democracy. Ben-Ner & v. Hooissem (1994) contend that a deficient body of law and policy in the USA has fostered a situation characterized by a marked depreciation of the good will associated with the term "nonprofit". This is due to increasingly frequent reports of fraud and unethical behavior in the nonprofit sector, found in daily newspapers. As a remedy, they call for changes in the law in support of the governance of NPOs by enhancing the rights of their "owners", demand-side stakeholders, i.e., the consumers, donors or sponsors who have an economic demand for the good or service provided by a NPO. In essence, their proposal calls for transforming NPOs into something more like membership organizations or consumer cooperatives.

While agreeing with much of their analysis of the situation of NPOs in the USA, we feel that it falls short of the mark in certain respects. First, neither membership organizations nor consumer cooperatives are immune from opportunism and self-engrandizment by managers nor from permanent failure. Second, although calling for greater transparency in NPOs, their suggestions for such legal changes fail to recognize the need for external social accounting. Rather they propose to establish a formal status for stakeholders, to grant them legal standing in courts of law and to provide them with the right to elect a Board of Trustees (*ibid.*). But stakeholders who lack a social account of a NPO's activities will have insufficient information to prevent the very goal deflection that they are interested in preventing. While their proposals might seem appropriate in an American context we suggest that they should be supplemented by legal requirements for mandatory social accounting, both of the monetary and non-monetary activities and goal of social enterprises, cooperatives and NPOs.

Thus, we propose the development of a new and different technique for attempting to avoid goal deflection and voluntary failure, namely social accounting. It could provide an early warning system for unwanted changes in the management of social enterprises, cooperatives and nonprofit organizations. But social accounting needs to be further developed and adopted to the constraints of social enterprises, cooperatives and nonprofits before it can become a widely used method in the third sector.

6.C What Type of Accounting - Financial and/or Social?

Until the early 1990s there were very few books devoted to external social accounting. One of the earliest books on this subject is *Social Redovisning (Social Accounting)* (Gröjer & Stark, 1978). Nearly ten years later *Corporate social reporting - accounting and accountability* (Gray, *et al.*, 1987) appeared, and more recently *Accounting & Accountability. Changes and challenges in social and environmental reporting* (Gray, *et al.*, 1996). Another recent contribution is *Auditing the Market: a Practical Approach to Social Auditing* (Zadek & Evens, 1993).

Gröjer & Stark note the discrepancy between external financial accounting and the evolution of social values. Conventional financial reports fail to take into account new values reflecting concerns with quality of life, environmental protection, consumerism, unemployment, co-determination and numerous other prevailing social values. They propose a new social accounting model, one which provides a description, both in monetary and non-monetary terms, of the positive and negative effects to individuals or groups of humans stemming from a company's operations. They also propose to integrate financial accounting into social accounting, arguing that the former is a sub-set of the latter. It is neither possible nor desirable to separate economic from social factors, nor a firm from its environment.

"[Corporate] social reporting, according to Gray *et al.*, is the process of communicating the social and environmental effects of organizations' economic actions to particular interest groups within the society and to society at-large". This involves extending the accountability of an organization or firm beyond the normal role of providing annual financial reports to its shareholders. Such an extension is based on the assumption that companies *do* in fact have wider responsibilities than simply to make money for their shareholders (*ibid.*, p. ix).

The essence of social accountability is captured by the "principal/agent" perspective. "Accountability" means the requirement or responsibility to provide an account, but not necessarily only in financial terms, for certain actions. According to the law of contract, one party (an agent) acts on the behalf of some other party (the principal). A contract, which is not necessarily written nor explicit, determines the rights and duties of these two parties vis-à-vis each other. Under the contract, the principal typically gives instructions to an agent on what actions are expected of him and what rewards and powers, etc. the latter has. There are two main types of responsibilities which the principal places on an agent, responsibility for his actions and responsibility to regularly and systematically account for those actions (Gray, *et al.*, 1987).

"Principal/agent" relations are usually codified in a "Company Act" of sorts, the details of which vary from one country to another, and also from one type of organization to another, i.e. limited stock company, economic association or nonprofit organization. The responsibilities of an agent are expressed in financial terms and an agent is required to discharge his accountability through regular financial reports. Here the contract between the shareholders and agents can be viewed as primarily a financial one; as too is an agent's responsibility for accountability.

But few "contracts" or relations are strictly financial, and the relationship between other stakeholders all involve different degrees of non-financial or social responsibility and accountability. The responsibility of accountability arising from such actions cannot be completely discharged through financial measures of performance alone. Once the existence of a responsibility for accountability has been determined, we must then determine the extent to which that responsibility is being met. How this responsibility is expressed is important, if not crucial for the development of an organization. If we state that a company primarily has the responsibility to create wealth, then we must find a way of measuring the wealth created, i.e. via a financial report. But, if as in cooperatives and nonprofit organizations, the principal places a responsibility on an agent to fulfill actions which are partially financial and partially non-financial, then other types of reporting are called for. If the responsibility of an organization is to generate improvements in the social welfare of its members and well-being of society, then we must devote our energy to identify and measure these types of improvements. Unfortunately, this is something that is rarely done.

Moreover, an annual report is designed to provide information on the performance of an organization, but it should be useful for the parties for whom it is intended. Financial reports are designed for stockholders, bankers and other financial interests. A social report should primarily be designed for other stakeholders, whereby those persons or groups with a "social" interest or "stake" in an organization are provided with relevant information for evaluating the social performance of an organization. Thus, social accounting is particularly relevant for cooperatives and other nonprofit organizations, which normally have clear social goals in addition to those of economic survival.

Financial accounting, annual financial statements and balance sheets by private for-profit firms in Sweden serves two purposes, both of which are intended to prevent fraud and are stipulated by law. First, corporate bookkeeping law and the annual financial accounts it stipulates are designed to protect private persons. Financial accounting informs presumptive or existing stockholders about the factual economic activity and therefore value of the assets of the firm in question, so as to avoid an exaggeration or over-reporting of its value. They are thereby spared from investing in something worthless or of little value. If over-reporting is a threat to private persons who could be persuaded to invest in a company that lacks sufficient assets, then the opposite is a threat to public authorities who attempt to collect taxes based on an evaluation of a company's assets, turn-over and profits. It is necessary to avoid under-reporting of a company's assets, turn-over and profits if taxes are to be accurately assigned and collected by public authorities. Furthermore, under-reporting by one company has consequences for other companies, as it would distort competition in favor of the company under-reporting its income and the taxes due on that amount. Thus, financial accounting and annual balance sheets in the private for-profit sector serve the double purpose of preventing over-reporting and under-reporting of a company's economic activities and assets in any given year. This allows for a factual evaluation of their performance and changes in it over time.

Financial accounting and balance sheets also provide necessary techniques of economic control and fraud prevention both in the public and private nonprofit sectors. But neither the public nor the private nonprofit sectors have as their main purpose to maximize the volume of nor the returns on their economic activities, however important such activities may be to their survival. They also have other purposes, usually several of them.

Thus, some means of evaluating their performance in the pursuit of these other goals must be established. Financial accounting and the annual balance sheet provide insufficient information about such non-economic activities of public and private nonprofit actors.

It is common to speak of the political accountability of the public service, i.e. the fact that civil servants are supposed to carry out the will of the elected officials and can be replaced if they fail to do so, or if they in some other fashion distort the public will, as expressed in elections and interpreted by elected politicians. Here, it is normal to assume that the opposition and the mass media keep a watching eye on the public service, informing or exposing willful distortions by politicians or civil servants and efforts of personal and/or organizational self-aggrandizement.

Figure 6.1 Different Types of Control in the State, Market and Third Sector

	State	Market	Third Sector
-main value:	equality	liberty	fraternity
-associated values:	general provision	profit maximization	self-help and benevolence
-control functions:	political accountability	financial accountability	social accountability
-purpose of control:	insure goal fulfillment, equal treatment of citizens, prevent bureaucratic engrossment and avoid fraud	insure stockholders/ government against inflated/deflated company value and avoid fraud	insure goal fulfillment, prevent management engrossment and avoid fraud

Source: V. Pestoff, 1996a.

Further to the discussion in section 6.B, there is no reason to assume that cooperatives or NPOs in general, nor social enterprises in particular, are in any way better or superior by definition or in performance to private for-profit or public organizations, nor to markets or governments. Just as there are numerous examples of market failure and government failure, so too we can find examples of voluntary failure. The third sector is less systematically surveyed by mass media, and management self-engrossment and self-aggrandizement therefore normally receive less public attention. Yet, it is equally important to insure the fulfillment of organizational goals, to avoid goal deflection and fraud in the third sector as in the private for-profit and public sectors. But, unlike both of the latter sectors, no established techniques exist for the continuous systematic control of the third sector. Thus, some new techniques for systematically and regularly evaluating the performance of third sector actors must be developed. Social reporting and social accounting are proposed as one possible set of techniques for evaluating the performance of third sector actors and organizations. Figure 6.1 summarizes different types of control of state, market and third sector actors. We will now turn to developments in social reporting and accounting.

6.D Different Types of Social Accounting

We will discuss developments in social accounting below, beginning with human resource accounting, then corporate social reporting and finally the social auditing movement. Developments in human resource accounting show some parallels with social accounting, in particular when it comes to methodological hurdles. Corporate social reporting emphasizes the social responsibility of all firms, regardless of type. It compares developments in several countries. The social audit movement of the 1990s demonstrates a promising new and vital approach to social accounting.

6.D.1 Human Resource Accounting

Conventional accounting treats employees as an expense rather than as resource (Belkaoui, 1984). Human resource accounting (HRA) is the process of identifying and measuring data about human resources and communicating this information to interested parties. The concept of human value is derived from the general economic value theory, because individual employees' ability to render future economic service to their employer (*ibid.*; Gröjer & Johanson, 1991). HRA is designed to provide relevant information to managers of human resources by giving them estimates of acquisition costs, replacement costs, opportunity costs, etc. for the personnel under their control and to fulfill the basic information needs concerning management's control of physical, financial and human resources, both internal and external to the organization. Thus, it aims at the continuing cooperation of qualified and motivated employees with the purpose of achieving the organization's objectives, financial or otherwise (Filios, 1991, 270).

While many authors express an awareness of the limitations of human resource accounting (see for example Filios, 1991; Belkaoui, 1984;

Gröjer & Johanson, 1991), some pay much greater attention to three particular measurement problems facing attempts to operationalize HRA (Scarpello & Theeke, 1989). They include a) a grave error of the substitution of unmeasurable surrogates for unmeasurable original constructs, like "personnel replacement costs" being substituted for human resource value; b) the lack of accepted reliability of standards for the proposed measurement instruments; and c) the lack of validity of the surrogates employed. All these problems were recognized by Flamholtz more than 20 years earlier, but little effort has been made to rectify them (*ibid.*, 275). Thus, these critics call for abandoning any further consideration of the possible benefits from HRA, until such time as these problems have been resolved (*ibid.*, 276).

Although human resource accounting came into in vogue almost 20 years ago, "it still has not got past first base" (Turner, 1995), mostly because of two main problems; i.e., managers' unwillingness to consider people as assets and problems of measuring human resources. While HRA, undoubtedly, faces certain measurement problems, its apologists argue that it nevertheless is more precise than current profit/loss reports. But, it also faces implementation problems, not the least of which are related to the internal politics of an organization. These often stem from the misconceptions of managers, usually personnel managers and chief accountants, about the impact of such an information systems. If they see HRA as potential threat to their established authority and/or as a jeopardy to their promotion prospects, they will fight it. The same may well hold true performance evaluations of social enterprises, cooperatives and nonprofit organizations they may be opposed by managers.

6.D.2 CORPORATE SOCIAL REPORTING, CSR

Since the turn of the century it has been recognized that corporations have some degree of social responsibility that exceeds maximizing economic performance and profits (Bold, 1991). One of the earliest attempts to measure the social performance of firms was undertaken by Kreps (1940), who developed the *social audit*, which relied heavily on economic indicators of performance, chosen for the ease of measurement. Later work with the *social audit* continued as a method for an independent appraisal of a business enterprise that could make valuable recommendations for management about areas of social concern for corporations (Bowen, 1953). Eight areas were suggested for appraisal: prices, wages, research and development, advertising, public relations, human relations, community relations and employment stabilization. Although this broadened the area of social responsibilities, such work remained purely conceptual, and did not include any methods of measurement or application.

In the 1970s the social audit or social accounting or social performance reporting began to receive some more attention. There are several international developments of relevance for the spread of social reporting, including:

United Nations *Draft Code of Conduct on Transitional Corporations* (1982), which includes requirements for information on: employment levels, working conditions, health and safety, education and training, industrial relations, wages and employment benefits, all of which concern the relationship between the enterprise and the work-force; plus the distribution of value added, impact on the environment and the enterprise and external parties, including shareholders, other providers of capital, local and national government, customers and suppliers, all of which concern the relationship between the enterprise and society (Gray *et al.*, 1987).

In France social reporting is primarily external reporting, based on a legislative approach. A bill was passed in 1977 requiring companies with more than 750 employees to publish annually a social balance sheet, and it was extended to all companies with more than 300 employees in 1982. They must include: number of employees, wages and fringe benefits, heath and safety conditions, other working conditions, education and training, industrial relations, and other matters relating to the quality of working life (*ibid.*).

In the Federal Republic of Germany social reporting is also external reporting, but in contrast to France, it is based on a voluntary approach. There are three different kinds of social reports in Germany, i.e., a) primarily a verbal description of goals, etc. in areas of social concerns; b) a value added statement indicating a company's contribution to GDP and its distribution among various stakeholders; and c) a social account, with quantitative accounts in financial terms (*ibid.*).

In Sweden internal social reporting dominates, with the exception of the work done by Gröjer & Stark (1978). Here the importance of social information for internal decision-making has been recognized and used by management. It consists mainly of financial estimates of recruitment, training, overtime, quality and production losses costs for lowering personnel turnover and lowering absenteeism (*ibid.*).

Numerous conceptual approaches to social auditing were developed as a result of renewed attention in social reporting in North America during the 1970s (Bold, 1991). Various types of social reporting are grouped into six categories (Blake *et al.*, 1976). Social audit procedures basically cover a spectrum that includes statistical measures, judgments by internal or external experts, comparisons across industries or countries, consultation with stakeholders, and reporting to the general public. The various types of social audit are: 1) the Social Balance Sheet and Income Statement, 2) the Social Performance Audit, 3) the Macro-Micro Social Indicator Audit, 4) the Constituency Group Attitudes Audit, 5) a Social Program Management Audit, and 6) the Government-Mandated Audit (*ibid.*).

Regardless of the type of approach, serious problems were experienced with the selection of appropriate criteria, with the reliability of indicators selected, and with identifying and isolating the actual impacts of particular programs in the community (*ibid.*). Largely because of the technical difficulties that plagued social auditing, limited progress in the assessment of corporate social performance occurred from the mid-1970s to the mid-1980s. Thus, we can note certain similarities in the methodological problems facing human resource accounting.

The Canadian Society of Management Accountants (Bold, 1991) suggests that issues related to corporate social responsibilities fall into three groups. First are regular business activities, such as occupational health and safety and quality of working life, i.e., typically human resource management concerns. Second are concerns that fall slightly outside regular business operations, i.e., such as pollution, product safety and social effects of plant locations and layoffs. Third are things are clearly external to the firm and comprise social problem of the larger society but which business is, or arguably should be, interested in alleviating (*ibid.*, 93).

6.D.3 THE SOCIAL AUDITING MOVEMENT

According to spokespersons for the social audit movement, "*social auditing is understood as a process of defining, observing and reporting measures of an organization's ethical behavior and social impact against its objectives*, with the participation of its stakeholders, and the wider community" (Zadek & Evens, 1993, 7). The "fair trading" organization, Traidcraft plc, in collaboration with the New Economics Foundation, has recently initiated a social accounting process of its own activities.

> The objective of promoting and applying social auditing practice is to provide for those involved in the business and affected by its products and activities information that is relevant to the range of their interests and concerns. Social audit will enable stakeholders, consumers, and the public to make informed judgments about whether the organisation is using their money, labour, environment and community responsibly. (Zadek & Evens, 1993, 7)

A key feature of the approach developed is that the accounting process both takes account of social aspects of the organizations activities and is itself socialized through the participation of relevant individuals and groups in defining the basis on which the organization should be assessed (Zadek, 1993). It involves several steps or stages, starting with defining key "stakeholder" groups, then initiating a process of consultation with each stakeholder group in relation to the company's own stated social and ethical aims. This is followed by drafting the social accounts, auditing them and then publishing the social audit (ibid.).

The main features of a social audit are:

-*a stakeholder perspective* in terms of defining what performance indicators should be used, as well as providing views of the organization's performance;

-*comparative* over time and groups of stakeholders

-*comprehensive* and reflect all the company's activities or stakeholder groups,

-*polyvocal* and reflect the views of stakeholders, managers, auditors, etc.,

-*learning* can potentially increase the capacity of all stakeholders,

-*regular* should take place annually,

-*externally validated* by independent auditors who must decide if it is "fair & reasonable" and

-*disclosure* should be made available to all stakeholders, in advance of the General Meeting (Zadek & Evens, 1993).

Thus, social auditing has several features that appear to be crucial for the future development of social enterprises, co-ops and nonprofit organizations in the 21st Century, in particular to increase their transparency and responsiveness to members' needs:

1) it is comparable to a statutory financial audit in that it involves *external verification, publishing of findings* and *is repeated annually*;

2) it takes a *comprehensive, inclusive view* of the scope of the market relationships to be accounted for in the social audit;

3) assessment criteria are *chosen by stakeholders* on the basis of their own agendas and values; and

4) it *allows for analysis of behavior* as well as impact or effects.

Similarly, corporate social reporting is very relevant for social enterprises, cooperatives and nonprofit organizations because it combines the following features:

a) accounting for different things (i.e., other than accounting strictly for economic events);

b) accounting in different media (i.e., other than accounting in strictly financial terms);

c) accounting to different individuals or groups (i.e., not necessarily only accounting to the providers of finance), and

d) accounting for different purposes (i.e., not necessarily accounting only to enable the making of decisions whose success would be judged in financial or even cash flow terms). (Gray *et al.*, 1996, pp. 3-11).

Moreover, social auditing is closely related to the concept of stakeholding (See Chapter 5 above & Pestoff, 1995c). A stakeholder is any body or group that can be influenced by, or can itself influence, the activities of the organization in question. Most organization have many stakeholders (Gröjer & Stark, 1978; Gray, et al., 1996), including their employees, communities, society, the State, customers - but also suppliers, competitors, local government, stock markets, industrial bodies, foreign governments, future generations, the environment, etc. The organization-stakeholder relation and interaction involves both rights, responsibility and accountability. Thus, the organization owes accountability to all its stakeholders, not merely its stockholders. The nature of that accountability is determined by the relationship(s) of that stakeholder with the organization (Gray, 1996).

Social auditing is also important for the development of democracy, in particular participative democracy. In participative democracy there must be information in which those controlling the resources of a society account to it their use of such resources. The development of this type of accountability carries the major potential of CSR (*ibid.*, p.37).

6.E The Need for External Social Accounting by Social Enterprises

The model of external social accounting presented by Gröjer & Stark (1978) conceives of conventional financial accounting as a part of social accounting. They employ a normative model based on both in monetary and non-monetary expressions of the positive and negative effects to individuals or groups of humans stemming from a firm's operations. They proceed from an interest or participant model of the firm, where the firm is considered a social institution for the benefit of several groups or constituencies. Furthermore, they employ a goal oriented approach, in which the management will have to consider the fulfillment of multiple goals, where the goals of various groups can and do come into conflict with each other (*ibid.*). Such conflicts raise questions about power within a firm and should be dealt with explicitly, rather than hidden by some "neutral" trade-off mechanisms for disguising power relations and differentials among various groups in a firm. Thus, they call for developing a separate "profit and loss" statement or report for each constituency or participant group within a firm. These separate "profit and loss" accounts show what each particular interest group has contributed to and derived from the firm, both in monetary and non-monetary terms (*ibid.*). Together they comprise a firm's social statement. Overall goal fulfillment can be broken down for the various sub-units of a firm, and goals can also be broken down into various sub-goals. Thus, they expect that external social accounting will have a spill-over effect on internal accounting (*ibid.*).

6.E.1 CANADIAN EXPERIENCE

Cooperatives' ability to provide services to individuals and groups at the community level and their potential for enhancing the quality of community life, can be inhibited by structural factors (Bold, 1991). One of the key inhibitions to success for cooperatives is the tendency noted in many countries for the atrophy of the democratic and community side of their activities in favor of the operational, economic side. But, there are two important considerations that need to be kept in mind, and also balanced against each other.

The first is what is referred to as the principal/agent problem, already mentioned above. In cooperatives, it means that boards of directors, once elected, do not necessarily do what members want done, and/or that paid managers, once appointed, do not necessarily do exactly what boards of directors want done. Evidence from established cooperative movements in Sweden (Pestoff, 1991 & 1996) and efforts at engaging cooperatives in community development in Canada (Fairbairn, *et al.*, 1991) suggest the need for a new management style and orientation in cooperatives - network-like rather than hierarchical, which would give a voice to and draw in various cooperative stakeholders, rather than imposing a one-dimensional, tops-down vision of a cooperative's objectives and activities.

The second is that cooperative managers also have legitimate concerns about the costs of cooperatives social goals and community-oriented initiatives. The costs are real, while the benefits are not typically quantifiable. It has to be possible to satisfy the legitimate concerns of managers, by find a process that identifies specifically what kinds of social goals and community-oriented activities to undertake, and to what degree. This process must both be selective and provide insurance that the social goals and community activities will nor deplete the reserves of a cooperative. What is needed is a process that can be internalized in cooperatives and tell its managers how much and what kind of resources to invest in social goals and community development.

A social audit process would help cooperatives to assess their effectiveness with respect to both economic and diverse social and democratic goals (Anderson, 1983). The social audit for cooperatives was defined as "a strategy and process which assists a corporation to define its mission and measure how well it is performing in line with community and societal expectations, while it achieves its own corporate purpose." In the early 1980s Canadian cooperators also recognized the importance of such a project, and under the auspices of the Cooperative Future Directions Project, the Social Audit Task Force was established, with the goal of examining the concept of social audit and how it should be applied to cooperatives.

The Social Audit Task Force published a handbook *Social Auditing: a Manual for Cooperative Organizations* (1985). It outlines a process by which an organization can begin to identify those decisions and objectives that are most closely related to the organization's social responsibilities. The task force suggests six categories of business decisions that might be considered in this identification process; including decision-making approach and structure, product or service performance, the use of human resources, community involvement, environmental impact and economic performance.

In order to develop a social report a firm or social enterprise must initially set the framework for it, i.e. it must make two decisions about its ambitions. The first is whether to integrate the social goals identified with the organization's economic goals or to monitor them separately. The second is whether to adopt a partial approach in a limited number of areas, or a comprehensive approach in most or all areas of likely social impact. Then, having decided to undertake a social report, it must implement this decision.

There are several steps in implementing social reporting (Bold 1991, 94). The first step is in identifying the corporate *social* goals from a wide variety of sources, including employees, customers, suppliers, etc. The next step is operationalizing social goals, which is defined as increasing management and employee awareness of and commitment to social goals. The third step is measuring corporate social performance, which can either be done by corporate personnel or by outside consultants. After measurement comes the need for some means of monitoring and reporting corporate social performance. The last step is designing ways of controlling corporate social performance.

It is obvious that the social reporting and a social audit is a *process* or a vehicle for giving a voice to diverse groups or stakeholders in a cooperative and their questions and concerns, rather than a report that can simply be written up by managers or outside experts. It might be argued that the ability of cooperatives to succeed in implementing a social audit is greater that ordinary firms for two reasons. First, they are democratic organizations and should encourage involvement and commitment at all levels, from members to managers. The second reason is that given their commitment to social as well as economic objectives, they should be uniquely amenable to social audit.

Ironically, few practical steps have been taken to implement social reporting in the Canadian consumer cooperatives. Perhaps this is an indication that social reporting, similar to human resource accounting, is perceived as a threat by the management or certain groups in it and has successfully opposed the implementation of social reporting. This could also explain why the Swedish consumer cooperatives' efforts in the 1980s to develop measures of "cooperative efficiency" proved abortive.

6.E.2 The Italian *Lega* Co-ops' experience

Cooperative movements in certain European countries have demonstrated a growing awareness of the necessity of providing members and managers with more information than is possible through an ordinary financial statement. In France the concept of a *balan social* expresses such intentions. In Switzerland, the *Migro* cooperatives have operated with a social statement for several years. In Italy the *Co-op Emilia-Veneto* in the Bologna region prepared its first *Biancio Sociale* in 1987. The latter provides an interesting example with regard to cooperatives' use of social accounting principles.

Co-op Emilia-Veneto's social statement includes an introduction to the members, consumers, employees and operations of the *Co-op Emilia-Veneto*. It presents the typical information about market share, evolution of sales, structures, investments and plans for development - all the traditional information for evaluating economic efficiency. But, it also provides information about labor and training, the social base of the cooperative, its democratic activities and its activities in terms of consumer policy vis-à-vis its own members, all in great detail.

The *Biancio Sociale* was presented at the International Cooperative Alliances' World Congress in Stockholm in 1988, in the following fashion:

> The *Biancio Sociale* is a formal document through which the cooperative tells society, its members and its employees what has been done in the last year. Our

> intention is, however, to promote a more ambitious use of it. We want to turn the social statement into a policy instrument which would force all the actors involved in the process to take into account the social impact of their activities (Zan, 1988).

But, "the *Biancio Sociale* was also perceived as an instrument to govern the relations among different policies, and to control the rate of achievement of specific goals" (*ibid.*).

In spite of the *Lega* leftist origins, that had not prevented cooperative companies in various parts of Italy from transforming themselves in an entrepreneurial direction, where many of them had become large and very developed, thus combining leftist values with those typical of industrial capitalism. The management had previously been trained in trade unions or the parties, but was increasingly recruited from purely entrepreneurial experience, mostly from private companies. This gave birth to an organizational culture that was full of contrasts, contradictions and inconsistencies. By the early 1990s, a deep revision was necessary. On top of that the *Tangentopoli* scandal broke out, and implicated some parts of the *Lega* co-ops (*ibid.*, 5). Thus, the process of strengthening cooperative identity of the Italian *Lega* cooperative movement and of specifying and rejuvenating cooperative values gained greater importance in the 1990s. This was expressed in three main documents: the *Carta dei Valori Guida* (Charter of Values), the *Codice Quardo per imprese cooperative* (Ethic Code), and the *Biancio Sociale Cooperativo* (Cooperative Social Balance-sheet) (Viviani, 1995).

Research was carried out with a panel of cooperative managers on their perception of cooperative values. It turned out that the original values still had great attraction, and by no means were replaced by entrepreneurial values. But many managers expressed a feeling of distrust, anomie, confusion and loss of the cooperative meaning. Some other non-cooperative organizations were investigated and it was shown that the most dynamic organizations were those which were able to most clearly express their own vision. This encouraged the further development of the *Carta dei Valori*, which was approved by the Board of Directors of the *Lega* in July, 1993.

However, the *Carta dei Valori*, is a programmatic document, and therefore it is necessary to have two other tools to implement it, an analytical system of rules and an instrument of control of their application. The *Codice Quadro* provides the system of rules for the relations between members, between the management and members, between the cooperative and its other stakeholders and the roles and tasks of the cooperative in the application of the code (*ibid.*, p. 9). One of the most important parts of this legal code is relations with external subjects: clients, suppliers, environment, communities. This underlines the necessity of real transparency, respecting consumers' rights, caring for the wealth of the community, applying the law precisely, etc. The *Codice Quadro* was approved by the 34th Congress of the *Lega* in March, 1995, and now all the main cooperative sectors are writing their own specific codes (*ibid.*, 9-10).

This Congress also made the adoption of the *Biancio Sociale Cooperativo* (BSC) by all *Lega* cooperatives compulsory. Many regional *Lega* cooperative societies had employed a BSC since the 1980s, as previously seen in the *Co-op Emilia-Veneto*, but none of them clearly reflected the cooperative nature of the enterprise. With the *Carta dei Valori* this was now possible. The main steps in developing the BSC are two: defining the mission and constructing the account scheme. First, each cooperative society must re-define the Charter, adapting it to its particular nature, production, etc. (*ibid.*, 10). Next, following the formal adoption of the mission by the members assembly, each article of it is divided into smaller parts, to be operationalized in the social accounting scheme. It identifies all the management acts which need to be checked so as to establish whether the cooperative - during any given year - is achieving its mission and to what extent.

These very complex processes are still in the developmental stage, and it is not possible to re-establish the identity of a cooperative in a short time (Viviani, 1995). The *Lega* considers the *Carta dei Valori* as a necessary, but not sufficient step to strengthen cooperative identity. But, it is also necessary to put it into practice in ordinary day-to-day activities, which is only possible through the ethical codes and a social balance account (*ibid.*, 12-13).

In spite of the attractiveness of social audit, the measurement problems that inhibited its progress in earlier years still remain. However, Guba & Lincoln (1988) describe an approach called naturalistic evaluation, which placed values at the center of the evaluation process and shifts emphasis from quantitative measurement to definitions and methods constructed by the stakeholders and evaluators, based on the goals and ideals they seek to achieve. This has the dual benefit of making the evaluation both less overwhelming and more meaningful to groups and organizations seeking reliable information about their performance. It would also permit cooperatives to benefit from new ideas from various stakeholders, which could have a potential commercial value.

6.F Conclusions

"What cannot thus be objectified and codified [*sic.* by numbers] does not exist, in the sense of being capable of being perceived and handled by the perceptual and information-processing apparatus of the market" (Kallinikos, 1995, 126). Numbers fail to convey organizational and network relationships into numerical messages. What can be done by means of administration or networks cannot be accomplished by the market, and *vice versa* (*ibid.*, 130). In particular, networks serve as counterbalancing forces to the alienating effects of markets and large centralized bureaucracies, reasserting the significance of economic action which is adjusted to local conditions and shifting relationships (*ibid.*, 132). Focusing on numbers, efficiency and utility functions only captures part of the considerations, values and social preferences of social actors (*ibid.*, 134).

Financial accounting provides a much too narrow and niggardly picture of the performance of cooperatives and, in particular, of social enterprises. External social accounting is a necessary complement to financial information systems, if we are to accurately and continually judge the goal fulfillment and performance of social cooperatives and other nonprofit organizations. This is a logical extension of the principal/agent relationship between the owners and managers of social cooperatives. Various efforts to specify a model for social reporting by cooperatives have been discussed and developed recently. Two of the more noteworthy are the report of the Social Audit Task Force of the Co-operative Union of Canada, *Social Auditing: a Manual for Co-operative Organizations* (1985) and the processes of the *Lega* Cooperatives in Italy (Viviani, 1995), both described above. The social accounting model proposed by Gröjer & Stark (1978) provides a goal specific description, both in monetary and non-monetary terms, of the positive and negative impact cooperatives and nonprofit organizations have on individuals and groups stemming from their activities. The social audit movement focuses both on the diverse interests of various stakeholders and the specific goals of a firm. The rejuvenation of the *Lega* Cooperatives focuses this goal specific process on cooperative values. By combining these approaches we can achieve a synthesis and find a starting point for our further efforts.

Few of the existing approaches, methods nor techniques for social accounting are completely adequate or suitable for social enterprises or new social service cooperatives. Most of the available approaches focus either on private or public sectors, and they fail to take into account the specific needs of social enterprises, cooperatives and the third sector. Cooperatives and NPOs/NGOs need to develop approaches which combine several aspects of the procedures outlined above. It should therefore be normative in its nature, goal-related, stakeholder focused, both financial and non-monetary and short- and medium-term.

The main purpose of social accounting in social enterprises, cooperatives and NPOs/NGOs should be to increase the legitimacy of such organizations among all their important stakeholders, not to merely report on their efficiency or effectiveness. Equally it should strive to prevent gross goal-deflection. The need for social accounting for cooperatives and NPOs/NGOs stems from the moral obligation of the agent to account systematically and continually for their actions to the principal. Quite simply the transparency of the relation between the principal and agent, or the managers and members, must be improved dramatically. This means that neither *ad hoc*, unaudited nor nonuniform social accounting would be appropriate. Regular systematic information should be provided to all the principal stakeholders in cooperatives and NPOs/NGOs. The experience of the *Lega* Cooperatives in Italy, may show the way to developing a more comprehensive and comparable principles of social auditing for cooperatives and nonprofit organizations in Europe.

7. Work Environment and Social Enterprises

Our theoretical emphasis until now has focused on several dimensions that are necessary for understanding the unique organizational potential of social enterprises to enriching the working life of the public sector, to empowering citizens as co-producers of important social services and to renewing the welfare state from within. Previously, we discussed various definitions of the third sector; and proposed our own definition of civil democracy, and then we explored the political and economic aspects of civil democracy. We also discussed the importance of developing multi-stakeholder organizations and social auditing as a means for promoting grass-root economic democracy in social enterprises.

We will now turn our attention to psychosocial work environment, and explore the relevance of these concepts for it. Many of these concepts are perhaps indirectly related to the psychosocial work environment of social enterprises, but we now want to consider if and how they might find a more concrete expression in social enterprises. Building on some of the most important literature we propose to extend existing models of psychosocial work environment to the social services by adding a new dimension to them, namely the staff's relations with their clients. We will also describe some general developments in the Swedish psychosocial work environment and examine the situation for the staff of day care services. We will conclude by contrasting "good" and "bad" work.

We clearly do not want to claim that social enterprises provide a universal solution to all or most of the problems of the poor psychosocial work environment found in many big, if not huge, public bureaucracies. They often apply Tayloristic solutions, taken from mass industrial production of goods, to the provision of public services. Nor do we want to suggest that our social enterprise model is applicable to the entire service sector. Rather we believe that social enterprises can contribute a model for providing small scale personal social services, where the relationship between the clients and the workers is a long-term or enduring one, and thus not as subject to the whims of market forces as are mass produced goods, services in general, nor less enduring social services (Pestoff, 1994a).

7.A Factors Contributing to Good Psychosocial Work Environment: the Demand/Control Model

There are two or three main perspectives on the development of work in modern societies, i.e., those of Bell (1973) *The coming of the post-industrial society*, Braverman (1974) *Work and monopoly capitalism* and Prior & Sabel (1984) *The second industrial divide.* Bell argued that in the post-industrial society work would be transformed from simple tasks done by persons in the lower ranks of a hierarchy to more qualified jobs done by independent persons. In manufacture and industry, automation and the technical revolution would replace drudgery with jobs in the service sector. Relations between persons would replace those between machines and people. Service is more demanding and in the post-industrial society work will be upgraded to a level of higher qualifications and autonomy than in industrial society (Szulkin & Tåhlin, 1994, 88-89). Braverman strongly disagreed and his polemic claimed that work would be deprofessionalized and prolitarianized. Capitalism's hardening competition guarantees Taylorism's relevance, and detailed control would increase, rather than decrease (*ibid.*, 89).

Prior & Sabel had a different perspective and referred to the growing *flexibility* of production, where *mass production* continues to pauperize work, but *flexible/specialized production* results in the growth of handicraft-like work conditions. However, Prior & Sabel concentrate on manufacture and industry, while ignoring the growth of the service sector, and fail therefore to take into account the most expansive sector of the economy (*ibid.*, 92). The consequences of this failure become evident in a subsequent examination of Swedish survey data on psychosocial work environment, in section 7.C below. Both the post-industrial society and the flexible specialization of production perspectives point to important social changes, but both have their short-comings, in particular when it comes to production and work environment in large public bureaucracies. But, these very short-comings help to underline the importance of research on the work environment for this category of workers.

There are two general perspectives on the psychosocial work environment (Wickman, 1989; Wickman, 1991). The *first* is based on in-built automatic reactions in the way humans function under stress. Their breathing increases, there is an increased transmission of blood to the muscles, etc. Such reactions are genetically controlled, and stress helps humans to survive in dangerous circumstances, but in the long run it also takes a heavy toll on human organs. Stress is produced by shifting conditions, when demands are too high or when there is too much to do, but also when demands are too low or there is too little to do. The *second* psychosocial perspective is historical in nature. In pre-industrial society most persons worked in agriculture, in small self-sufficient groups. Every small group did or made most of the things they needed themselves, food, clothes, repairing tools, etc. Thus, everyone had several different tasks to carry out and it was easy to see the results of her/his own work. However, urbanization, industrialism and, in particular, mass production or "Fordism" combined with Taylor's ideas about "scientific management" changed most of that. Both these perspectives make important contributions to theories of psychosocial work environment (*ibid.*).

There are two main theories about psychosocial work conditions, one that takes its starting point in the level of qualification of work, often pursued by German researchers; and another represented by stress researchers, mainly in Sweden and the USA (Tåhlin, 1989). Beginning with the former action structure research focuses on human cognitive function patterns. When an individual learns a certain action pattern, learning is stimulated on three different levels. At the lowest level thinking is absent and routinized behavioral patterns take over. The medium level is characterized by variation and flexibility based on previously learned patterns. Action requires the development of strategies for dealing with new tasks, but once a successful strategy has been achieved, thinking turns into routine variations of the strategy. Actions are planned at the highest level, where human capacity is used to the highest degree. Thus, good work combines and activates all three levels of cognitive capacity (*ibid.*, 3-4).

The second theory stems from an Swedish/American interest in stress research, where B. Gardell was a pioneer, followed by R. Karasek, an American sociologist, who developed a more comprehensive interactive model of psychosocial work environment. In high stress jobs an individual is prepared to deal with a challenging situation, without the possibility being able to do so; thus amassing unused/unusable energy, which can later expresses itself in diminished health, psychological well-being and heart and circulation difficulties. According to Karasek's model, it is not psychological demands at work *per se* that have negative consequences, but rather only if they are combined with low control or decision autonomy over the work situation (*ibid.*, 6).

After several decades of research in the USA and Sweden on psychosocial work environment, Karasek and Theorell summarize their own and others' findings in *Healthy Work: Stress, Productivity and the Reconstruction of Working Life* (1990). It provides an analytical model of the relationship between the various components of the psychosocial work environment. In particular they point to the importance of demand, control and support for the well-being of workers, and build a model on these three components. They also relate this model to the challenge of redesigning working life in order to promote the twin goals of healthy work and sustained or increased productivity. We have fashioned our empirical study of social enterprises on their model. However, we want to go further and extend it into new areas, apply it under new conditions, but equally important to add a new dimension to it, a fourth dimension of psychosocial work environment, i.e., the relationship between the staff and of personal social services and their clients.

The rich complexity of the Karasek/Theorell demand, control, support model of the psychosocial work environment points to the unintended consequences of modern industrialization and shows how they are related to lost productivity, the decline in the quality of goods, the impersonality of services, the emphasis on short-term profits, etc., as well as to illness resulting from job related stress. Their own demand, control, support model derives greater coherence and rigor from a critical examination of some of the central tenets of classical economic and business management philosophy, from a work environment perspective. They criticize A. Smith's division of labor or specialization of tasks (*ibid.*, 61); M. Weber's model of hierarchical bureaucracy as the most efficient organizational form in industrial societies (*ibid.*, 10); F. Taylor's "scientific management", where work tasks were to be simplified into the elementary skills required and reorganized into minute detail by engineers (*ibid.*, 23); and J. Bentham's utilitarian philosophy which claimed that all pain and pleasure could be measured in economic quantities and via cost-benefit analysis of individual choice (*ibid.*, 164). The unintended, but equally unavoidable results of this management philosophy are the degradation of work life, stress that results in physical illness and a loss of productivity.

Work life stress is related to physical illness:

> Our findings show that social and psychological aspects of the work situation are indeed significant risk factors for coronary heart disease.... [However,] work that is demanding (within limits) is not the major source of risk. The primary work-related risk factor appears to be the lack of control over how one meets the job's demands and how one uses one's skills. In many cases elevation of risk with a demanding job appears only when these demands occur in interaction with low control on the job.... Thus, in our research findings it is not the demands of work itself, but the organizational structure of work that plays the most consistent role in the development of stress-related illness. (*ibid.*, 9)

Moreover, it is also clearly related to lower productivity:

> [I]ncreased demands lead to productivity increases only when the demands are combined with high decision latitude. When possibilities to control were perceived to be small, high levels of demand were associated with low productivity and stress symptoms. (*ibid.*, 11)

In the empirical part of their study of psychosocial work environment, using US national survey data (QES), they describe decision latitude as being composed of a combination of decision autonomy and skill discretion questions. Typical questions read: "Do you have a lot to say on your job?" or "Do you have freedom to make decisions?" (decision authority); "Do you keep learning new things?" or "Is there variety in your tasks?" (skill discretion). Psychological demand is measured by questions such as "Is there excessive work?" or "Must you work fast (or hard)?" (*ibid.*, 41).

Figure 7.1 Psychological Demand/Decision Latitude Model

psychological demands/ decision latitude:	**low**	**high**
high	*low strain*	*active*
low	*passive*	*high-strain*

Source: Karasek & Theorell, 1990, 32.

However, they note that: "[i]ndeed, psychological demands on the job remain difficult to conceptualize and measure because of the diversity of subcomponents and because of some theoretical problems that are as yet unresolved" (*ibid.*, 63). The first two dimensions of their model, and result in a four fold classification of jobs: high-strain, active, low-strain and passive jobs. The main characteristics of these four job types are:

1.) *high-strain jobs:*

> the most adverse reactions of psychological strain (fatigue, anxiety, depression and physical illness) occur when the psychological demands of the job are high and the worker's decision latitude in the task is low... The implied model of high-strain situation is that the arousal of energy is transformed into damaging, unused residual strain because of an environmentally based constraint on the person's optimal response process. (*ibid.*, 32-33)

2.) *active jobs:*

> some of the most challenging situations, typical of professional work, call for the highest levels of performance, but without negative psychological strain, like surgeons performing a difficult operation, rock-climbers scaling an unmastered peak,...professional basketball players, etc... Such situations, while

> intensely demanding, involve workers in activities over which they feel a large measure of control, the freedom to use all available skills... Because much of the energy aroused by the active job's many stressors are translated into action through effective problem solving, there is little residual strain to cause disturbance... This conversion of energy into action is also one necessary prerequisite of an effective learning process. Given the freedom to decide what is the most effective course of action in response to a stressor, the individual can test the efficacy of the chosen course of action, reinforcing it if it has worked or modifying it if it has failed (*ibid.*, 35-6).

3.) *low-strain jobs:* are characterized by few psychological demands and high levels of control, such as a repairman, which comprise a low-stress utopia (*ibid.*, 36).
4.) *passive jobs:*

> here low demand and low control result in gradual atrophying of learned skills and abilities, can only mean an extremely unmotivated jobs setting and result in long-term loss of work motivation and productivity, such as the trained machinist who have become machine tenders in automated computer-based manufacturing firms, which also lead to less than average levels of leisure and political activity outside the job. (*ibid.*, 37)

The focus of our own empirical study is on both types of jobs subject to high demands, i.e., on the first two. We also want to know if and how social enterprises can transform high-strain jobs into active ones. Simply lowering demands clearly could not and would not provide an optimal solution to high strain jobs. Rather, increasing employee control and freedom to use and develop their skills offers a more realistic and viable solution to the stress of high-strain jobs. We explore how social enterprises can promote greater staff control on the job and if they could provide a successful example of job redesign, in particular for civil servants providing social services.

7.B Additional Dimensions: Social Support, Consumer Contacts, etc.

After introducing the two basic elements of their model Karasek & Theorell expand it by adding a third dimension, social support. They note, however, that changes in social relations between workers and changes in decision latitude become almost inseparable in job redesign strategies, leading them elsewhere to refer to "participatory work design processes" (*ibid.*, 69). "Social support at work refers to overall levels of helpful social interaction available on the job from both co-workers and supervisors". Social support appears to provide buffering mechanisms between psychological stressors at work and adverse health outcomes. Thus, social contacts and social structure affect the basic physiological processes important to both maintenance of long-term health as well as the acquisition of new knowledge. Several types of social support in the workplace have been identified including the degree of social and emotional integration and trust between co-workers, supervisors and other. The relation between demand and support are envisioned below.

Figure 7.2 The Social Support Dimension of the Karasek/Theorell Model

Demand/support:	**low**	**high**
high	*obedient worker*	*participatory worker*
low	*isolated worker*	*"maverick" worker*

Source: modified from Karasek & Theorell, 1990, 70.

Together, these three dimensions of work activity - demand, control and social support - are capable of predicting much of the range of total variation in depression symptoms in the US population, which increases from a likelihood of 6% to a 41%, given the right/wrong combination of these factors (*ibid.*, 72). However, while the demand/control classification resulted in four types of jobs, inclusion of the third dimension now results in four types of workers: an obedient comrade, an isolated prisoner, a participatory leader and a cowboy hero. Somewhat less flamboyant terms might help to focus more on different type of workers and less on presumed individual attributes. Thus, we suggest replacing the nouns chosen by them with the word "worker" in all cases and the term "cowboy hero" with "maverick" worker. Similarly, they also note that:

> Jobs labeled "participatory leaders" reflect that both decision participation and social support are important for work environment change. Of course not all workers in these occupations are leaders in the conventional sense, but in general they share power, have influence, or at least some chance of affecting collective decisions. The occupations we find in this quadrant are professions: scientists, teachers, therapist, manager - even barber. (*ibid.*, 72)

We maintain that social enterprises provide for greater control by and support between workers, thus facilitating greater worker participation. Moreover, the worker cooperative model in particular builds on worker "ownership" or ultimate worker responsibility for the decisions of the firm. This not only facilitates, but in fact requires much greater worker participation. Thus, participatory workers require a minimum of influence on important decisions or some form for co-determination, and perhaps also some recognized their stakeholder claims, or maybe even ownership rights. Certain types of social enterprises facilitate greater worker participation than others, as will be seen in Chapters 8 and 9.

Furthermore, Karasek & Theorell argue that job security, risks in the physical work environment and social support by persons outside the work group, like consumers, family and friends, are important aspects of work environment and they deserve closely study. They also provide some examples of job redesign leading to greater interaction between workers and customers, particularly in the social service sector. There were positive benefits both for the workers and customers in activating the clients. We agree that their demand, control, support model could benefit from an extension that included interaction with clients. Such interaction can be divided into high and low categories, similar to the other three dimensions. Previously we discussed and analyzed client reactions to social services in terms of whether such services were enduring or non-enduring (See Chapter 4). Here we want to focus on the relations between the staff and clients. We will therefore use the categories of sporadic and enduring to describe differences in their relationship.

The figure below presents our proposal of how client relations could be included as an additional or fourth dimension to this model. Since we are mainly interested in the implications of client relations for social services, where job demands are high, we will thus take the two high psychological demand categories, active work and high-stress work, as our starting point.

Figure 7.3 Client Relations - a Fourth Dimension in the Psychosocial Work Environment Model

High demand work/ client relations:	**sporadic**	**enduring**
active	*sympathetic professional*	*co-producer*
high-strain	*bureaucrat*	*semi-personal*

Source: Pestoff, 1996a.

Staff members with active jobs, but only sporadic contacts with their clients can be expected to behave sympathetically but professionally toward clients, i.e., they will have a sympathetic professional relation with them. Staff with high-strain jobs, but only sporadic relations with numerous clients will probably display the typically bureaucratic distance to their clients, i.e., remaining impersonal, if not short or at times even hostile. Staff with an active job and enduring relation with their clients will most likely involve them in the design and implementation of the services being provided, thus turning them into co-producers. Finally staff members with high-strain jobs, but enduring contacts with their clients will most likely develop a semi-personal relation to them, but may experience more stress from such interaction.

Thus, we are now able to introduce a valuable new dimension for understanding stress and the psycho-social work environment, one that extends the basic demand, control, support model. This new dimension is particularly important to the development of the service sector in general and to the redesign of public service and developing the potential of social enterprises in particular.

Karasek & Theorell also underline the importance of two additional aspects of job redesign. The first is the necessity of getting support both from the service workers directly involved and from the upper levels of the city administration in the public services (*ibid.*, 321-32) or from the top management and trade unions in the case of a private company, like Volvo. Then they ask rhetorically if change should start from the top and move downward or from the bottom and move upward. It comes as no great surprise that their answer is "both are necessary". Both a bottoms-up and a tops-down process are needed to support job redesign and to overcome the forces of inertia against change (*ibid.*, 245). The second aspect is the need to develop "...altogether new methods of assessing industrial output, in which health, developmental capabilities of the employees appear as goals in their own rights" (*ibid.*, 164) or what they call "New Value" measures of productivity. While their concrete proposal for the essential elements of "New Value" measures differ in detail from the type of social auditing proposed earlier in Chapters 6, we feel that both they and we are calling attention to similar problems and proposing similar solutions to them. We will now turn our attention to general developments in Swedish work environment the past 25-30 years and to conditions in day care service in the 1990s.

7.C General Developments in Swedish Work Environment and in Day Care Services in the 1990s

There were two overall tendencies among employees in Sweden concerning the psychosocial work conditions and health situation in the early 1980s, (Tåhlin, 1989). First, workers had worse conditions than salaried employees and, second, women had worse conditions than men. In general salaried employees were exposed to higher psychological demands, but at the same they had time more decision discretion (*ibid.*, 24). Development of work during the period 1968-91, shows that a structural change took place, which meant that the total qualification level of the work force increased during the past quarter century (Szulkin & Tåhlin, 1994). Work that was both diverse and psychologically demanding increased during the same period, while the proportion with the lowest requirements has remained constant (*ibid.*, 97). During 1968-74 20 per cent of the population changed jobs from unqualified jobs to qualified ones, while between 1981-91, an additional 28 per cent did so. Thus, there is an extensive individual mobility between types of jobs with different quality demands, where the direction is upward. This is explained by structural changes in the education system and economy, leading to an overall improvement of qualifications among employees (*ibid.*, 102-3).

However, in terms of work environment this has led to a polarized development, with both better and worse jobs increasing at the same time. Perhaps the most important result is that stress-filled jobs increased significantly for women, but hardly at all for men (*ibid.*, 106). The increase of stressed jobs can almost entirely be explained by changes of work dominated by women, where there is a clear increase of stressful or demanding jobs, while decision latitude has hardly changed at all (*ibid.*, 110). At the beginning of the 1990s, negative stress was more frequent in the service sector than in industry and manufacturing (*ibid.*, 37), and active work was more typical of qualified white-collar employees, especially at small work places, in the public sector with day-time working hours and in the care sector, including child care workers (Tåhlin, 1995, 39).

In general women have worse psychosocial work conditions than men. In 1992/93 12 per cent of all women, compared with eight per cent of men, had stressed work. But occupation is very important, and it explains most of these gender differences (*ibid.*, 39). With the growth of the service sector and demands for a more rational work organization, combined with dramatic cuts in municipal budgets for social services, average demands will not decrease, probably the opposite. The development of decision latitude will be decisive for the psychosocial work environment in Sweden. If it is permitted to increase, growing demands can lead to more active work, but if not, more demands will lead to more high-stress jobs (*ibid.*, 40).

Work environment statistics from the Swedish Central Bureau of Statistics (SCB) provide more detailed information about work environment in the 1990s for various occupations and the entire work force. A sample of 10,466 persons were persons were chosen for SCB's Work Life

Investigation in 1989; while 15,158 were included in 1991; 14,061 in 1993; and 14,500 persons in 1995. Overall refusal to participate in these SCB studies was 26 per cent during the entire period (*ibid.*, 10-13). Our focus is on the staff of day care centers and we combined SCB's data on pre-school teachers (*förskollärare*), recreation instructors (*fritidspedagog*) and pre-school assistant teachers (*barnskötare*). Three comparative sets of data exist for the entire work force and the staff of day care services: data from 1991 & 1993; from 1991, 1993 & 1995 and from 1995 compared to the average for 1989-95. In addition SCB provides some retrospective data in 1995 for persons with the same occupation during the past five years. We will compare the working conditions, ailments and/or problems, work conditions, control at work and increased demands during the past years for the staff of day care centers with that of the entire work force.

Starting with work conditions, seven indicators were included in both the 1991 and 1993 studies, but not all of them were available in the 1995 study. There are only marginal changes between 1991 and 1993 for the staff of day care centers on these seven indicators of work conditions. The average for the staff of day care services is similar to that of the entire work force for a few of these indicators, but there are some notable deviations. The staff of day care centers and the entire work force show similar positive rates to the questions about responsibilities being so difficult that they need help or advise (42.0% compared to 46.6%), or not being able to get help with difficult responsibilities (7.5% compared to 9.1%). Fewer staff of day care services compared to the entire work force are exposed to violence in their work (4.1% compared to 7.7%), fewer claim low formal knowledge requirements for getting a job in day care services (16.9% compared to 28.9%) and many more of them claim possibilities for getting education/training during work (65.2% compared to 45.2%). Yet, more of them claim that they can not influence the planning of their work (54.8% compared to 42.7%); while fewer also claim that they can not decide about their own work (12.0% compared to 24.7%).

Next, indicators of standard work-related ailments and problems included the upper back; lower back; shoulders or arms; hands or wrists; hips, legs, knees or feet; feeling exhausted all over; difficulty getting to sleep; difficulty relaxing and anxiety due to job-related difficulties. The proportion of the staff of day care centers claiming one or more of these aliments and/or problems increased marginally between 1991 and 1993 for seven of the nine indicators included here. The proportion of the staff of day care centers with such aliments and/or problems was similar in 1993 to the average for the entire work force for most of these indicators. However, the proportion of the staff of day care centers with "difficulties relaxing due to thoughts about work" was higher than the national average for the entire work force, (46.0% compared to 39.6%). This was at the beginning of major municipal budget cuts for social services.

The 1995 study provided additional information about control at work between 1989-95. First it demonstrates that job related demands have increased in many respects for the staff of day care centers, in recent years, when comparing their 1995 figures with the average for the period 1989-95. In addition, it shows that a greater proportion of the staff of day care centers than the average for the entire population can decide their own work pace at least half of the time (61.1% respective 44.8%), a greater proportion of the former can take short rests, leave their work and talk with other persons at least half of the time (64.7% respective 50.2%), yet a greater proportion of them can not decide when different tasks are done (60.0% respective 43.9%). The staff of day care centers appear to have more control in some respects, but less in others.

SCB also documents changes in work tempo, expressed here as the proportion of staff agreeing with certain statements about work demand. The proportion of the staff of day care services agreeing completely or partially increased between 1991 and 1995 on four of the five statements included here and remained unchanged on the other. It was similar to that of average for the entire population on three of these five statements. The most notable difference for the staff of day care centers concerned psychologically demanding work, which had increased considerable for the staff of day care services between 1991 and 1995 (from 48.2% to 62.7% positive answers) and was much higher in 1995 than for the entire work force (42.0%). In addition, a much smaller proportion of the staff of day care centers claimed that their work was monotone throughout the 1991-95 period (3.0%) than the average for the entire work force in 1995 (17.4%). Finally, a similar proportion of the staff of day care centers and the entire work force express dissatisfaction with their work (5.8% compared to 6.6%).

The 1995 SCB study also includes some comparative question concerning job demands, to persons with the same occupation during the past five years, i.e., only to those persons who are able to make personal comparisons of developments. On four of five counts the staff of day care centers has experienced a greater increase in job related demands than the entire work force. More than three-fourths of the staff of day care centers with five years experience claim that the pace of work has increased, compared with less than three-fifths of the entire work force. Increased unemployment during the 1990s has driven up the tempo of work in general. In addition, major reductions in recent years in the child care budgets of most municipalities have resulted in lower staff to children ratios. This is coupled with growing difficulties in getting sick relief or temporary replacement help in municipal day care centers. Fewer staff having more children to care for clearly increases the tempo of work at most day care centers.

Nearly half of the staff of day care centers also claim that heavy work tasks have increased, compared with just over one-eighth of the entire work force. The recent reorganization of child care in terms of letting/requiring children to start school preparation classes (sometimes called the "zero class"[1]) resulted in clear changes in the age composition of the children enrolled in day care services. Six year olds have gone over to zero classes in most municipalities and there are relatively more younger diaper children per day care center. Diaper children not only require more attention than older children, but they also need to be lifted more often, resulting in an increase of heavy work tasks.

Table 7.1 Proportion of Employees in 1995 Claiming an Increase in Job Demands During the Past Five Years

increasing job demands over past 5 years:	**pre-school teachers, etc.**	**entire work force**
-the pace of work	77.7	58.6
-heavy work tasks	45.0	14.2
-dirty air & premises	25.3	8.8
-monotone work tasks	15.7	10.3
-risk of violence at work	6.9	11.3

Source: ASS/SCB, *Arbetsmiljon 1995*, Table 8.3, 126.

In addition, one-fourth of the staff of day care centers claim that dirty air and premises have increased, compared with less than one of ten for the entire work force. This suggests that municipal authorities may also be reducing their budgets for the maintenance and cleaning of the premises of day care centers. Thus, we can note a clear and dramatic increase in several negative aspects of the work environment of day care services in Sweden in recent years. This makes it all the more urgent to find ways and means of improving the work environment of the personnel in this category. This also

---

[1] See footnote 1 on page 172 for details.

makes it more important to explore new models for organizing work, in particular ones that permit greater participation and engagement of the staff and clients of day care services. Social enterprises and cooperative day care services provide one clear alternative to the general deterioration in the working conditions of today's municipal services.

7.D Conclusions: Social Enterprises Should Provide Good Jobs

Karasek and Theorell (1990) argue that it is possible to distinguish between good and bad jobs:

> The bad job in the future industrialized world, although it pays well and has decent physical working conditions, is still a horror of modern debilitation: no opportunities to learn, computerized monitoring, boredom interspersed with crises, unexpected layoffs, no rights, social isolation, inter-worker competition, loss of contact with the real world of customers, etc... The good jobs are good because they offer the potential for human development: learning, user-friendly tools, responsibility, negotiable demands, stimulating challenges, co-workers as teachers, pride of accomplishment in creative achievement, customers whose growth restimulates the workers. We cannot change bad jobs into good ones by increasing wages, decreasing working hours or remove physical hazards... (*ibid.*, 314, underlining in the original)

In particular, concerning social services and health care, they note that:

> the principles of service-like goods production [or flexible specialization] as opposed to mass production, are needed to save the service industries from the increasing use of old-mass-production-like models to reorganize health care [and social services]. Positive examples found in Enskededalen [in Sweden] and at the Martland Clinic [in the US] are small health care units, where the staff was reorganized to treat the patient as an equal partner in the process of creating a joint patient/institution care strategy. It involved an active customer who was willing to learn how to manage his or her own diabetes or to organize his or her own activities in the elderly center (but with assistance)... These workers had to facilitate a broad range of activities in patients with unknown needs. This approach may have been feasible only within small-scale non-bureaucratic units, where close communications could mediate unrealistic demands and summon uncatalogued resources. These were new job demands, to be sure, but the challenge made these medical workers feel alive and purposeful... The models we have described are more relevant for chronic illnesses that for acute, life-threatening situations. (*ibid.*, 323)

"Good" jobs are intellectually demanding, they provide chances for development, they are challenging and provide room for independent choice. The categories of workers with good working conditions has increased most in Sweden during 1968-91, while those with the worst conditions have decreased most during the same period (Szulkin & Tåhlin, 1994). Changes in the economic structure have made a clear positive contribution to improving the character of work during the past quarter of a century (*ibid.*, 114). Thus, the content of existing jobs remained relative stable over the period under study, but structural changes contributed to improvements in the average qualification of jobs. However, changes in the 1990s in the working conditions of the staff of day care services, and perhaps of other personnel intensive public services also subject to dramatic budget cuts, like elderly care, etc., deviate clearly from their general findings. Perhaps these increased work demands can also be interpreted as the first signs of a change in the trend toward improved work environment. Balancing the budget and the retrenchment of the welfare state may be at the expense of the work environment of civil servants providing social services.

In the empirical part of our study that now follows we will demonstrate that social enterprises in Sweden provide good jobs in the fullest meaning of Karasek and Theorell. In addition to being psychologically demanding, they provide high decision latitude to the workers, high social support for the workers and enduring interaction with the clients. These work-life attributes, however, stand in sharp contrast with those found in the services provided by the large hierarchical bureaucratic organizations often associated with the public sector services in Sweden, including municipal day care services, judging from the data presented here. Thus, in this sense the social enterprise model can not only help to transform social services jobs into active, participative and interactive jobs. The social enterprise model can also help to enrich work-life of the employees and transform to the welfare state into a welfare society, one where citizens can become co-producers.

Part 2
Empirical Aspects

8. Social Enterprises and their Work Environment in Sweden

This chapter provides a brief introduction to some of the main findings of the Swedish Project on Work Environment and Cooperative Social Services, WECSS. First we will present a brief summary of the growth and development of social enterprises providing day care services. Next we will discuss the planning of the three WECSS studies: the Organization Study, the Staff Study and the Parent Study. Following that, we will present a brief summary of the WECSS Organizational Study that sets the parameters for social enterprises providing day care services in Sweden. Finally, we will briefly introduce the WECSS Staff Study and present and compare the work environment of the three types of social enterprises included here. These materials are presented and discussed at greater length in the WECSS report *Social Enterprises in Sweden: Enriching Work Environment, Empowering Citizens as Co-Producers and Transforming the Welfare State* (forthcoming, 1998).

Here we can only to provide a brief overview of the materials included in the WECSS Project. In subsequent chapters we will, however, analyze the two main themes of our project in greater detail. Chapter 9 is deals with enriching the work environment of Swedish civil servants and is based on a comparison of the work environment in social enterprises and municipal day care services. Chapter 10 addresses the empowerment of consumers as co-producers of the social services they demand.

8.A The Growth and Development of Social Enterprises Providing Day Care Services in Sweden

Perhaps a few words are in store at the outset about the main forms for providing child care in Sweden. (See Exhibit 7 in the Appendix for an English explanation of some important Swedish terms.) Both pre-school activities for children between 0 - 6 years old and child care (*barnomsorg*) for children between 0-12 years old refer to publicly financed, institutionalized care now made available in theory to all working parents and students with children below a given age. Until recently publicly financed pre-school activities took one of two forms. Either children were enrolled in a *daghem*, a day care center, or they went to a *dagmamma*, a "day-care mother". Then, in the early 1990s a major institutional reform[1] took place, when the age for starting school was reduced from seven to six years old. Many local school authorities responded by initiating a *zero class* or type of kindergarten, at special school related recreation facilities or *fritidshem*.

Today municipal day care services are the main form for providing pre-school activities, usually in premises housing one to four groups of 15 to 20 children. Most day care centers are open from the early morning until the late afternoon, five days a week. Day care mothers are approved by the municipal authorities and provide day care services in their own homes to between two and five pre-school children. They often have young children of their own, and may receive compensation for caring for them too. Many parents enroll their child in the services provided by a day care mother while waiting for a place in a nearby day care center. However, some parents prefer keeping their child(ren) at day care mothers until they start school because of the small size and family-like atmosphere.

Child care developed as one of the main features of the Swedish welfare state, starting in the late 1930s and early 1940s. Prior to that child care was only available on a very limited scale. It was provided various non-governmental organizations, foundations, and diverse societies, and was financed mainly by charities, donations, etc. In 1941 there were 347 child care institutions, that looked after 13,700 children. More than half of them were located in municipal areas, but less than one of ten were run by municipal authorities. By 1946 the number of children in child care facilities reached 18,250. Child care developed slowly after that.

In the early 1970s the *Riksdag* passed the first Pre-School Law, which set ambitious goals for the expansion of day care services during the

---

[1] These changes make comparisons between various forms of child care and their development over time more difficult. In 1996 58 per cent of all children between the age of 0-12 were enrolled in child care activities of one type or another, and seven per cent of them attended non-municipal services (SoS & SCB, 1997). Only one-third of the children between 7-12 years old were enrolled in school related after-school recreational facilities, or *fritidshem*. Three-fourths of the children between 0-6 attended some kind of pre-school activity. Nearly all (97%) six year olds attended some kind pre-school activity (*ibid.*). But, our focus is on day care centers and 43 per cent of children between 0-6 years old were enrolled in this form of pre-school activity in 1996, while one of eight attended non-municipal services.

coming five years. Although the idea of expanding municipal day care facilities was widely approved by both the national and municipal authorities, fiscal constraints prevented this from taking place at a pace that could keep up with the increase in demand for new services. By 1974 there were nearly 62,000 children enrolled in day care services, and approximately 30 parent cooperative day care facilities, providing service for nearly 300 children. Public efforts fell short by two-fifths of the target goal of 100,000 new child care places by 1980. Under these circumstances new actors were encouraged to enter the "market". By 1985, 266,000 children were enrolled in day care facilities, including 1,300 in nearly 100 "parent cooperative" day care centers.

The (re-)appearance of cooperative day care caused a lively debate at the time. Many of the parent cooperative day care services, started in the late 1970s and early 1980s, practiced a special pedagogical philosophy, e.g., Montessori, Regio-Emilia, Walldorf, etc., not available at municipal day care facilities. They often attracted parents who were not satisfied with the pedagogical philosophy of municipal services, or what they perhaps considered as a lack of a pedagogical philosophy. This first wave of parent cooperatives took the legal status of voluntary associations, as they were the only non-municipal day care services that could qualify for public financial support prior to 1985.

Parents also began to consider access to day care a social right, rather than a dearly sought municipal privilege. In 1985 a second wave of parent cooperatives started, when a change in the law made it possible for parents to form economic associations and receive public financial support on terms similar to those enjoyed by municipal day care services. By 1987 the number of parent cooperatives had nearly doubled and three years later it reached 500. This dramatic growth was hotly debated at the time. It was, and still often is, claimed that only "privileged" parents with higher education who articulated their needs could participate in such day care arrangements. The trade union movement in general, and unions of municipal employees in particular, were reluctant to accept parent cooperatives as legitimate actors in the provision of day care services.

A parliamentary committee on reforming child care presented its conclusions in *Förskola för alla barn 1991 - Hur blir det?*/Pre-school [activities] for all children by 1991 - How will it turn out? (SOU 1990:80). It recommended that the Social Service Law be amended to include the legal right for all children between 18 months and school age (7 years old) to a place in a day care facility by 1993. The number of children seven years old or less enrolled in pre-school services grew rapidly between 1975 and 1994, increased from less than 250,000 to nearly 560,000. As a proportion of children between the age of 0 - 6 years, it nearly quadrupled during this period, going from 14 to 51 per cent[2]. The number of children seven years old or younger enrolled in day care services increased from nearly 66,000 in 1975 to nearly 340,000 in 1995, growing by more than five-fold during the past 20 years. Expressed as a proportion of the of 0 - 6 year olds, it increased during the same period, going from eight to 39 per cent. An additional 11 per cent of all pre-school aged children attend services provided by a day care mother.

The bourgeois government, which won the general election in 1991, introduced several new features in day care. They removed most of the previous restrictions on the "free establishment" of day care, and from 1992 onward private commercial firms could also receive public funds for running day care services. From 1993 municipal authorities were given even freer hands to arrange social services. They are given lump sum funding by the central government for all types of social services. Now they are free to decide how best to spend it, without any national standards or regulations about allocation for specific activities or needs. This, in effect, removed the national government's possibilities to directly influence and guide the development of the availability and quality of child care through public funds. After-school activities are also available to the children of working parents, both before and after school hours until the age of 10 or 12.

Non-municipal day care services, usually known as "alternative" or "private" services in the Swedish debate, expanded dramatically after 1985. In 1988 there were just over 500 non-municipal day care centers that met public requirements for state support, but they reached nearly 1,900 at the end of 1995; an increase of three and a half times. The number of children enrolled in these non-municipal day care services increased from 8,500 in 1988 to 39,000 at the end of 1995[3]; an increase of nearly five fold. On average in 1995 nearly one of eight children enrolled in day care facilities attended non-municipal services. However, large variations can be noted for different parts of the country: in Uppsala County nearly one fourth of the children attended non-municipal facilities, while in Västerbotten in the north only about one of twenty did so (SoS, 1996).

---

[2] This is unusually high compared with the average of five per cent in many countries of the European Union (Esping-Andersen, 1996).

[3] This figure was reported at 57,000 in 1996 (SoS & SCB, 1997).

A closer look at non-municipal day care services shows that a variety of forms are employed for organizing and running such activities; including parent co-ops, voluntary organization, worker co-ops, organizations with special pedagogics, a combination of these or "other" forms, etc. Nearly two-thirds of the "private" or non-municipal day care facilities in 1995 were either provided by parent and worker cooperatives or voluntary organizations. More than half of the non-municipal day care services were organized as parent co-ops in 1995, or 1016 of them. Worker cooperative day care was a new form at the end of 1991, and between then and 1995 the number of worker co-ops increased from 13 to 157. In 1995 there were 250 non-municipal day care centers and after-school homes with a special pedagogics, e.g., Montessori, Regio-Emilia or Walldorf. They call themselves "parent co-ops", but usually organize themselves as a voluntary organization or foundation. The parishes of the Swedish Church ran 47 day care centers in 1992, and in addition there were several "parent co-ops" affiliated with the Swedish Church, which took the legal form of a voluntary organization.

The legal form of non-municipal day care facilities is manifest at the time of their registration. More than half of them were registered as economic associations in 1995. Three-fourths of the cooperative day care facilities chose to register their services as economic associations, which is the preferred form for cooperative firms[4]. The number of voluntary organizations providing day care services decreased during the 1990s, and their proportion of all non-municipal facilities dropped from one-third to one-fourth. Some have re-registered themselves as economic associations in recent years, however, many of the oldest ones are still run as voluntary associations. The new form of "ecumenical foundations" has rapidly become the preferred form of the Swedish Church in recent years and 115 of them were registered in 1995. It first became possible to register private for-profit or commercial day care in 1992. During the period 1992-95 the number of commercial firms increased by more than three-fold, from 41 to 215, mostly in southern Sweden.

The average size of municipal child care facilities is twice the size of parent cooperative day care services, 42 respective 20 children. Worker co-ops are about 50 per cent larger than parent cooperative day care services,

[4] Until recently, this required a minimum of five persons to register an economic associations, but in 1993 it was reduced to only three.

while the size of private for-profit firms providing day care services approaches that of municipal services. Municipal day care services require more personnel than non-municipal, but parental participation partially makes up for the lower staff intensity in parent co-ops.

Looking at Stockholm, research shows that in 1995 there are about 200 parent cooperatives in Stockholm. During 1989 and 1990 parent co-ops represented most of the growth of day care in Stockholm. Parents choose parent co-ops because of the lack of nearby municipal day care services. It was often the only chance for parents to obtain a day care place. The reasons for this were municipal rules about sibling preference and an "over-heated" labor market, making it often hard to get a day care place for a first child in Stockholm. (Sundell, m. fl., 1991). A total study of co-op day care in Stockholm in 1990 and 1991 (*ibid.*) showed that parent co-ops were often small organizations (one & two sections or units), they arranged their own recruitment of children and they had shorter opening hours than municipal day care. Our study confirms this for other parts of Sweden. Parent co-ops in Stockholm had more parents with higher socio-economic status, more two parent families and fewer with foreign background than municipal day care. (See Chapter 10 for the social background of parents in our study).

Municipal budget cuts in the 1990s led to a rapid deterioration in the quality of municipal day care services, a sharp decline in the staff to children ratio, and the near disappearance of temporary sick relief, etc. This change in the quality of municipal services did not go unnoticed nor unanswered by parents, as materials from the WECSS Parent Study presented in Chapter 10 demonstrate. Parents began to look elsewhere for better alternatives. Thus, it is not a question of "queue-jumpers" who want to get ahead of the municipal waiting-lines nor parents who are unsolidaristic with municipal services (Antman, 1996). Rather, it is a reaction to the lack of municipal services, budget cuts and a decline in quality of the municipal services that threatens to ghettoize the same municipal services. There is a serious risk when the quality of the service deteriorates, that only those parents who lack other alternatives will continue to use the services provided by municipal authorities. Other parents will find/create alternative services elsewhere, often together with each other. Thus, the emergence of non-municipal day care services is more a symptom or result of budget cuts and the decline in the quality of service, than the cause of them.

By the end of 1995 the difference between the costs of municipal day care facilities and non-municipal services was about 10 to 15 per cent. The average municipal funding to non-municipal day care services came to

51,420 SEK per child/year in 1995, while the total costs for running municipal day care services were 70,309 SEK per child/year. Part of this difference is due to parent fees, which are included in the latter figure, but not the former. They were 12-15 per cent of the total costs of all kinds of day care services. Another part is due to the work obligation found is some types of non-municipal services. Nearly all (98%) parent co-ops stipulate some kind of work obligation or parental participation, e.g., administration (94%), temporary relief for the staff's leaves of absence (91%), cleaning (74%), preparing food (31%). However, less than one-fifth (17%) of the other types of "private" day care services require any parental responsibilities. Where they exist, parental responsibilities on the average each month are 4.5 hours per child in parent co-ops, 0.8 hour/child in worker co-ops and 0.3 hour/child in other "private" day care services. For each day care facility this means an annual average of 61 hours in parent co-ops, 13 hours for worker co-ops and seven hours for other types of non-municipal day care services (*Socialstyrelsen*, 1995). Other differences in the provision of non-municipal day care services, like a more engaged staff, can in part explain differences between the costs of municipal and non-municipal day care services. (See Chapter 9 for more details.)

8.B The Project on Work Environment and Social Enterprises

In order to study work environment of social enterprises providing social services, we planned and carried out an empirical investigation, primarily with survey methods. We originally intended to study several different types of social services, but for practical reasons we concentrated our efforts in the beginning on day care services. We wanted to have a broad geographical base and we chose to study social enterprises providing day care services in six different parts of Sweden, i.e., the counties of Gothenburg & Bohus, Jämtland, Malmöhus, Stockholm, Uppsala and Västerbotten. As a first step, we drew a simple random sample in each of these counties, approximately every third "cooperative" day care center in these six regions, or a total of 278 social enterprises providing such services. Three of five, or 166 of them, indicated a willingness to participate in our study. As a second step, we then complied a quasi-random sample of 57 day care services. It comprised 29 day care centers drawn from a second simple random sample among those willing to participate; 21 interesting cases, chosen on the basis of additional information provided in the first round of contacts; and seven worker cooperatives in Stockholm, chosen on the basis of a reputational study. (See Exhibit 1 in the appendix and also Pestoff & Gullström, 1994, for more details.)

Our sample included three different types of social enterprises providing day care services: 24 parent cooperatives, 16 voluntary organizations and 17 worker cooperatives. Our project design was multiple in nature, and called for studying the social enterprises themselves, as well as both their staff and clients. Thus, we undertook three different but parallel studies, an Organization Study of these 57 cooperative day care centers, a Staff Study of 244 members of the staff at these same cooperatives and a Parent Study of 580 parents to the children at these 57 day care centers. We interviewed the managers of these 57 day care centers, most of them during a personal visit to their premises. A few in Jämtland and Västerbotten, were, however, interviewed by phone for practical reasons. We collected written materials during and after these visits, in the form of statutes, budgets, their contract with the municipality, etc. The questionnaires for the Staff Study and the Parent Study were distributed and collected by the managers of these day care centers. The response rate to the staff questionnaire was 81.7%, while that of the parents questionnaire was 70.4%. Most of the data in the three WECSS data sets was collected in 1994.

Our intention of continuing to study social enterprises providing other types of social services in the second phase of our research ran into several serious practical constraints, including time, funds and the availability of an overview or register from which to select them. However, a pre-study was undertaken of cooperative handicap care, elderly care and primary health care in the northern county of Jämtland to adapt our questionnaires. But, in the end we had to abandon a more complete study of them, at that time.

In designing our project our efforts were based on the idea of extending existing research, as far as possible. Thus, we contacted the nationally and internationally known centers in Sweden for studying work environment, to find out what aspects they normally included in their studies. We hoped in this way to facilitate the comparability of our work with theirs. The measurement instruments in three studies undertaken here focused on the following aspects:

a) *The Organization Study:* measured both the physical and organizational aspects of different work places, and contained questions about the physical character of their work places, the workers degree of presence/absence, the organizational structure and interaction within the organization, the economic aspects as well as questions about the interaction with the concerned public authorities. Different versions were prepared for different types of social enterprises.

b) *The Staff Study:* measured the workers' experienced degree of well-being with the physical and psycho-social work conditions, and also highlighted the workers' degree of participation in the decision-making process. Two versions of the questionnaires (one for worker cooperatives and another for parent cooperatives and voluntary organizations) intended to measure the staff's evaluation of their physical and psycho-social work conditions in these social enterprises. Retrospective questions permitting a comparison, when relevant with the psycho-social work environment in municipal day care facilities were also included.

c) *The Parent Study:* measured the conditions from the clients' perspective, focusing on the interaction between clients and staff in the social enterprise providing day care service, as well as their reason for choosing a particular type of day care social enterprise. Retrospective questions permitting a comparison with municipal day care services were also included. Different versions of the questionnaire were prepared for workers and consumer cooperatives.

8.C The Parameters of Social Enterprises Providing Day Care Services

This part of our study draws on interviews with the managers of the 57 day care cooperatives making up the Organizational Study of the WECSS Project, plus the written materials collected. On the basis of the latter, we undertook a separate Budget Study and a Municipal Contract Study. Here we will begin by discussing the when, where, why and how of starting these new social enterprises. We documented some of the clear differences in terms of the start of the three types of cooperative day care services. Just one-tenth of our sample of cooperative day care services were started prior to 1985, when it first became possible for parents themselves to run day care services as an economic association. More than two-fifths of our sample has its origin in the period between 1985 and 1990. Nearly half of our sample was started after 1990. Taking organization type into account, we find that more than four-fifths of the voluntary organizations were started before 1991, two-thirds of the parent cooperatives were started between 1985 and 1990, while nearly nine-tenths of the worker cooperatives were started after 1990.

Social enterprises providing day care services are primarily a urban phenomenon[5] , and nearly three-fifths of our sample is drawn from the three major metropolitan areas of Stockholm, Gothenburg and Malmö. But, there is a clear difference between these three types of social enterprises in terms of urbanization. Three-fifths of the parent cooperatives and two-thirds of the voluntary organizations are located in one of the three major cities or their suburbs, while only two-fifths of the worker cooperatives are found there. The worker cooperative form has a more pronounced rural profile than the other two forms of social enterprises providing day care services.

Relations between the local municipal authorities and these social enterprises are an important aspect of the development of non-municipal services. Two aspects of this relationship are of particular interest here, the extent of municipal assistance at the start of the new services and the nature of that relationship today. We found a pattern of extensive collaboration between the municipal authorities and social enterprises during the start phase. First, it was only after a change in the law regulating public support for day care services, that economic associations of parents and later employees could qualify for public funds to provide day care services. This led to a dramatic increase in the number of social enterprise day care facilities. More than nine of ten social enterprise day care facilities were started by the parents and/or employees. Three-fourths of them were complimentary to municipal services; i.e. they were designed to provide services and to meet needs that municipal authorities could not[6] , while only one-eighth were started as employee "take-overs" of existing municipal services. This was a defensive move by employees to protect their jobs[7] but they could also "compete" with existing municipal services.

Negative aspects of municipal services, such as the simple lack of them or wanting to avoid (the rigidities or bureaucracy of) municipal services

---

[5] 83% of the Swedish population lives in the metropolitan areas of greater Stockholm, Gothenburg or Malmö.

[6] Often in newly built suburban areas where no municipal services existed.

[7] Municipal service plans often called for shutting down existing day care services in rural areas or urban areas with a decreasing number of children under 7 years old, or for combining several local services into larger facilities. The staff of such facilities often opposed such plans, and decided to continue providing such services in the same place, but under different leadership. One third of the worker co-ops were started as worker take-overs of municipal services.

were often given as the reason for starting social enterprises providing day care services. Positive motives of wanting to develop a special pedagogics or to increase parental influence were provided as the reasons for starting these new day care centers, by many of these new social enterprises. Thus, it was the failure of municipal authorities to meet citizens' needs, combined with the positive attributes of the cooperative day care, that lead to the growth of this new form for satisfying the needs of the parents to very young children.

Social enterprises providing day care services normally received the active support of their local municipal authorities when starting. Three-fourths of them received direct financial support from municipal authorities in starting, and four-fifths received special "start-money". In addition, half of them received advice on how to start and additional help from municipal authorities and nearly one-third received such help from regional cooperative advisors, while only one-quarter received no such help. Three-fifths of them either took over existing premises or received new ones from municipal authorities. Two-thirds claim that their premises were in good condition when they started operations. Finally, more than half of these social enterprises followed the pedagogical guidelines for day care services set by municipal authorities.

From the information above we can get a profile of the three types of social enterprises providing day care services in terms of their starting conditions. *Parent cooperative* day care services were mainly established in one of the three metropolitan areas between 1985 - 1990. They were often started by the parents themselves to provide new services, due to a lack of municipal day care facilities and to increase parental influence. They received help in getting started from municipal authorities and a regional cooperative development agency. They are mostly small facilities, normally with only one group of between 12-18 children. Their small size is one of the attractions for parents. *Voluntary organizations* were mainly started in one of the three metropolitan areas, but earlier that the other types of social enterprises providing day care services, many of them already in the 1970s. They provided new services and were started by the parents and staff to promote special pedagogics and because of a lack of municipal services. They received no help getting started and they range from small to large facilities. *Worker cooperative* day care services were all started after 1990, often in rural areas, usually by the staff. They mainly provided new services, but a few took over existing municipal services. They were started by the staff to avoid the bureaucracy of municipal day care services and to promote special pedagogics. They received assistance from municipal authorities and local cooperative development agencies in getting started. They range from small to large facilities, or one to four/five groups of 12 to 15 children each.

However, when we shift our attention to the nature of their relationship with municipal authorities in 1994 quite another picture emerges. First, we found a great deal of diversity in the municipal operating contracts. In brief, no two municipalities offer social enterprises providing day care services the same conditions of operation, e.g., parental fees, municipal grants, recruitment of children, etc. This complicates any attempts at making meaningful comparisons of operating conditions with municipal or non-municipal day care facilities, as no two social enterprises providing day care services have the same operating contracts (Hansson, 1995).

Second, we found the following pattern concerning the day-to-day relations between these social enterprises and municipal authorities. One-third claim neither to have an operational relationship with municipal authorities nor with other municipal day care centers, nearly half claim only to have working relations with the municipal authorities, but not with municipal day care services, while a few claim working relations with both municipal authorities and municipal day care facilities. Note, however, that information is missing for one-quarter of our sample, indicating perhaps a reluctance to make "critical" statements.

Thus, aside from sporadic meetings at courses and seminars, there are few chances for the staff of these social enterprises to regularly meet their counter-parts in municipal day care facilities. Informal meeting are sometimes arranged in some municipalities. However, in the smaller municipalities in particular, where few alternative day care facilities exist, social enterprises appear to be isolated. In the metropolitan areas some of them stated that they regularly attended meetings of local organizations devoted to their special pedagogics; i.e., Montessori, etc. or of local interest associations for non-municipal day care centers.

Needless to say the exclusion of social enterprises providing day care services from these regular meeting not only makes it much more difficult for them to get the information necessary to fulfill their contract with and responsibilities to the municipal authorities or to guarantee high quality day care services. This makes it hard for them to keep abreast of professional developments, changes in the law, etc. On the other side of the coin, it also makes it much harder for the municipalities to follow the development of non-municipal services, to monitor their activities and to insure a good quality of service. These day care services are often provided by small, single unit facilities, which also puts them in a difficult situation when specialists are required, as they lack the necessary resources.

The managers suggestions for improving their contacts and relations with municipal authorities, included finding forms for more systematic and regular opportunities for exchanging information and greater understanding for the cooperative form or the special pedagogic employed. They read: "better information", "a well functioning network", "a network for everybody", "we should be invited to the monthly information meetings for day care center managers", "more education opportunities", etc.

Moreover, more than half of the social enterprises providing day care services claim that they are not subject to any type of inspection or control from responsible authorities in their municipality, while the remainder claim they are occasionally collected. But, once again more than one-quarter failed to answer this question. Most social enterprises sent their annual general report and their economic report to relevant municipal authorities, often as the only form of municipal control. Some mention occasionally filling in and returning questionnaires to municipal authorities. Several of them lament this minimalist approach to control and inspection by the municipal authorities. Thus, we found that the quality of municipal monitoring and overseeing clearly comes in to question under present circumstances. Sending in an annual general report and/or returning a questionnaire once a year to municipal authorities is a far cry from on-the-spot visits and regular face-to-face meetings with a responsible municipal authority.

More than two-thirds of these social enterprises administer their own waiting list for their day care services, more than one-eighth depend entirely on the municipal authorities to provide them with the names of children who are next in turn to be admitted, while a similar proportion have their own waiting line, but also take children from the public waiting list in their municipality.

Turning to other aspects of the Organizational Study, we found that parental participation and work responsibilities were normally limited to administrative, manual and social matters. They clearly did *not* include pedagogical activities, except in a very marginal fashion. Parents, or some of them, sit on the executive board of the parent cooperative day care facility, and are formally responsible for running the cooperative. Thus, much of the administrative burden is born by those parents who are elected to the board. Nearly two-fifths of the parent cooperatives and voluntary organizations regularly scheduled parents to clean and/or repair the day care premises and/or contribute in other ways to the management and maintenance of the day care facility. Most worker co-ops lack any form of parental participation.

Cooperatives are normally democratically run organizations that attribute members voting rights at the annual general meeting and the right to elect and be elected to the board. However, who becomes a member of a cooperative depends in part on which type of cooperative comes in question. Employees could sometimes become members of parent cooperative day care facilities, particularly if they had their own child enrolled in the day care service facility. However, the statutes of some social enterprises rule out this solution. Two-thirds of the voluntary organizations excluded employees as members, while half of the parent cooperatives did so. The staff is automatically represented on the board of worker cooperatives, since they comprise the members and are both eligible to vote and be elected. A few of the parent cooperative plus some of those voluntary organizations both permitted staff representation and gave them a vote. Staff representation was, however, often limited to the manager of the day care center, but without necessarily giving her the right to vote. More than half of the parent cooperative and voluntary organizations allowed for some kind of staff representation, but only a minority gave the staff voting rights.

Our own Budget Study for the year 1993 showed that average annual government support for cooperative day care centers in 1993 was 57,260 SEK, and average annual parent fees are 10,910 SEK. The municipal authority grants pay 84 per cent of the operation costs of cooperative day care and parent fees pay for 16 per cent (Onn, 1995). This is comparable with the proportion 85/15 per cent noted for all day care facilities (*Konkurrensverket*, 1993, p. 37). The amount paid by municipal authorities, and to a lesser extent that paid by parents, was strongly influenced by the amount of rent paid for the premises, which were much higher in urban areas that rural ones. Municipal authorities normally paid nominal rent costs for day care services.

Finally, in terms setting the parameters of our further study of work environment, we also noted that two-fifths of the social enterprises providing day care services claim "very low" absenteeism and one-third claimed a "rather low" rate of absenteeism; making for three-fourths with low absenteeism. This brings us closer to one of the main topics of this research, work environment, in particular the social-psychological work environment of social enterprises providing day care services, which is the focus of the next section.

8.D The Psychosocial Work Environment of Social Enterprises Providing Day Care Services

This section briefly summarizes the main empirical results of the Staff Study of the WECSS Project. It presents the most important information from the questionnaires of 244 staff members of 57 social enterprises providing day care services, quasi-randomly chosen from six different parts of Sweden. These day care facilities were divided into three different categories, based on their ownership; i.e., consumer co-ops, voluntary organizations and worker co-ops, and their answers were compared with each other.

The basis of this study of work environment and social enterprises in Sweden is the demand/control/support model of psycho-social work environment (Karasek & Theorell, 1990), presented in greater detail in Chapter 7. This model includes several components or dimensions and each of them is important for understanding work life. A two dimensional demand/control model provides the starting point for analyzing psychosocial work environment. Then social support is added to the model. Other aspects, like client interaction, job security, etc., provide added complexity to the model. Psychological demands consist of excessive work, having to work fast or hard, etc., while worker control concerns decision autonomy and skill discretion, e.g., having a lot to say about the job, having the freedom to make decisions, keep on learning new things, variety in the tasks, etc.

In the model both psychological demands and staff control or decision autonomy ranges from low to high, resulting, as we saw earlier, in four different types of jobs: 1) high strain jobs, 2) active jobs, 3) low strain jobs and 4) passive jobs. We are primarily interested in the first two categories, and in exploring if and how social enterprises can turn high-strain jobs into active ones. *High strain jobs* are high in terms of demands, but low in terms of control, and they result in adverse reactions to psychological strain such as fatigue, anxiety, depression and physical illness. *Active jobs* involve high levels of performance without negative psychological strain, since they provide high degrees of control. Such jobs result in learning and growth that is conducive both to health and productivity. Given the freedom to decide what is the best course of action, the individual can discover the most effective course. S/he can reinforce it if it works or modify it if it fails. Many women are traditionally found in high strain jobs, while men clearly dominate active occupations and have the highest income and job satisfaction.

Social enterprises and cooperatives, by virtue of their internal social and political processes, extend decision autonomy or control of work and facilitate the participation of employees in decision-making. They, therefore, have the potential of turning high strain jobs into active jobs. Day care services are typically psychologically demanding jobs, since they require working with many small children, but a change in the organizational model, i.e., going from municipal facilities to provision by social enterprises implies greater control of work by the staff over what is done, how it is done and when it is done.

In the presentation below, we will consider each of the variables in the demand/control/support model separately, i.e., psychological job demands, skill discretion, decision authority or co-determination, and social support at work. Then, we will turn to employer/employee relationships and client interaction, aspects not given equal attention by the model. After that we will look at the other side of the coin and turn our attention to some of the potential effects of these factors on the health of the staff, on service quality, on staff discussions of their work environment and on their view of the future of their social enterprise and the overall job satisfaction. Our comparison of three different types of social enterprises was rhapsodic. However, it provided the basis for several contrasts between the three types of social enterprises studied herein, and led to some conclusions concerning their differences in terms of their psychosocial work environment.

First, we noted that few of the staff members of any social enterprise providing day care services previously had any direct personal experience with cooperatives of any type. Some notable differences existed concerning the staff's motives for choosing work for the three types of social enterprises. The staff of all three of them indicated that "wanting a meaningful job" was most important in their decision, and the staff of both parent and worker co-ops stated that "increased staff influence" was next most important, while the staff of voluntary organizations gave preference to "a special (pedagogical) profile" as their second most important motive for choosing to work for a social enterprise providing day care services.

Summarizing their self-evaluation concerning *psychological demands*,[2] there were some points of similarity between the staff of these three types of social enterprises. They express similar levels of psychological demands and similar levels of conflicts. There were, however, several other areas where we found differences between these three groups. The staff of worker co-ops had less varied work and greater responsibility. They were more tied and had unfree work, they had more to do, had more heavy and demanding work. But they also had better contact with the management, and got more praise for their work and experienced more agreement within their social enterprise than the staff of the other two types day care services.

The psychological demand profile of the staff of worker cooperatives clearly reflected the fact that they were their own employers and they alone were responsible for the success or failure of their day care services. By contrast, the psychological demand profile of the staff of parent co-ops also reflected their organizational characteristics, where parents are both the employers and clients. Fewer members of the staff of parent co-ops had good contact with the management, i.e., the parents, and more of them complained that they got too little praise. A larger proportion of the staff of voluntary organizations claimed they had varied work, untied and free work, but too much responsibility, while fewer of them claimed that they had too much to do or physically heavy and demanding work. Thus, the work situation for the staff of worker co-ops may be more demanding, but it also involved fewer conflicts or more agreement within the social enterprise itself.

We then considered several indicators of *personal development, decision authority* and *participation in important decisions*, and both *collective and individual influence*, in more that a dozen areas of importance for day care services. The staff of worker cooperatives had higher or more positive scores on most of the indicators studied here. They had greater possibilities for personal development, greater possibilities for decision authority and they participated in important decisions more often than the staff of the other two types of cooperative day care services. They also had the highest scores in terms of collective and individual influence on most of the items considered. This is both an expected and fairly non-controversial finding, due to the unique nature of their organization, which promotes worker empowerment and combines the roles of workers with those of managers or owners. Thus, the staff of worker cooperatives seemed to have better opportunities for turning high-strain jobs into active jobs, by virtue of the greater skill discretion, decision authority and co-determination normally associated with the worker cooperative model.

The staff parent co-ops often had the lowest scores in terms of collective or group influence, while the staff of both parent co-ops and voluntary organizations reported lower individual influence. The general impression was that staff influence was greater in worker co-ops, mid-range in voluntary organizations and lowest in parent co-ops.

In terms of *social support* we found no major difference between the three types of day care services. The staff of all three types of cooperative day care services attributed themselves similar levels of social support from their boss and fellow workers. So, there appear to be equally good possibilities for the development of "participating workers" in all three types of social enterprises. (See Chapter 7 for more details).

Turning our attention to the additional dimension of *employer/employee relations* and *client interaction* or *staff collaboration with parents*, it should be kept in mind that a special feature of the cooperative model is the radically changed relationship between the employers, the staff and the clients. The normal tripartite model of employer, employee and client is replaced by a bipartite one, where two of these roles are combined. The two clearest examples are found in the consumer and the worker co-ops. In the former, the consumers or clients become an employer, while the staff's position by-and-large remains unchanged. In the latter, the staff become their own employer, while the clients role by-and-large remain unchanged. Voluntary organizations fall somewhere in between these two, since both the staff and clients can become members of the association and, thus, sit on, or elect representatives to the board, which in turn is now an employer. Thus, relations between the staff and their employer in cooperatives includes aspects not normally found in employer/employee relations in the public nor private sectors. Not unexpectedly, the staff of worker co-ops were the most positive to their relations with their employers, i.e., themselves, and fewer of the staff of parent co-ops and voluntary organizations were very satisfied.

We found that worker cooperatives were subject to less parent participation, but the parents more often showed respect and recognition, combined with fewer parent demands and less interference, while the staff of voluntary organizations experienced more parent participation, demands and interference than the other two types of day care services. Voluntary organizations and parent cooperatives more readily promoted an active and positive interface between producers and clients, or the staff and parents, and voluntary organizations also more readily facilitated communication between the parents and staff. The staff of parent co-ops expressed the least positive attitudes, in terms of the effects of their collaboration with parents. In terms of potential changes in the day care services brought about by parent participation, the staff of the voluntary organizations was often most positive, while that of the worker co-ops was usually least positive.

Turning to some of the potential outcomes of the psychosocial work environment, in terms of indicators of *physical aches and pains*, *stress* and *psychosomatic symptoms*, we noted that the proportion of the staff of worker co-ops claiming such symptoms was greater than that of the other two types of day care services on most items, while the proportion of the staff of parent co-ops or alternatively that of voluntary organizations was usually smaller than the two other types of day care facilities on half of these items each. Thus, the staff of worker co-ops showed more stress symptoms and had more aches and pains and more psychosomatic problems that the staff of the other two types of day care services, although differences were not always large. On the one hand, this could be interpreted as a reflection of a greater staff responsibility inherent in the worker cooperative model, compared with the other two models, where the staff share these responsibilities with the parents to a greater or lesser degree. On the other hand, it might also reflect the fact that the staff of worker co-ops most recently worked for municipal day care services, where a rapid deterioration of the psychosocial work environment took place in the first half of the 1990s, due to dramatic cuts in municipal budgets for social services. Thus, many of these symptoms may be "inherited" from their previous work place. (See Chapter 7 for more details on changes in the work environment of day care workers in the 1990s).

Focusing on the *staffs' discussion of their work environment*, we saw that in general there appears to be more discussion about it among the staff of worker cooperatives, a greater willingness to improve the children's play environment, fewer conflicts among them concerning trade-off with other values and a greater willingness to accept lower wages, if necessary to improve their work environment. The staff of parent cooperatives and voluntary organizations had similar, but lower scores on most of these items, but at the same time the staff of parent co-ops was less willing to make a trade-off between their own wages and work environment for improving the children's play environment. They also had somewhat more conflicts over such matters, and were less willing to accept lower wages for making improvements in their own work environment. Thus, the staff of parent co-ops appeared least satisfied with their present work environment.

Finally we examined the staffs' *plans for the future*, *overall job satisfaction* and a few *general statements about work*, but we found that no clear pattern existed. The staff of one type of social enterprise was more positive on some indicators and the staff of another on other indicators. Thus, is not possible to state that the staff of one type of social enterprise is generally more satisfied than the staff of other two.

Some more general conclusions can be reached from the WECSS Staff Study about the work environment of social enterprises providing day care services. First, the worker cooperatives are consistently rated higher by their staff on most of the over 200 items employed in our study of psychosocial work environment. This should not be simply interpreted as worker cooperatives provide a superior model for worker empowerment. Rather the worker cooperative model is based on organizational structures that facilitate group processes that are positive for promoting the interest of workers/employees. But, on the other hand, it meant greater responsibilities and was often accompanied by more signs of stress. Moreover, greater worker influence was achieved at the expense of parent involvement and engagement. We also saw one or two examples in the comments of a worker cooperative where the manager was repeatedly criticized by one or more staff members for treating the worker cooperative and her fellow workers as if they were employees in her private firm. Voluntary organizations appeared often to function like mixed or multi-stakeholder organizations, with the big difference that they had a common ideology or pedagogical perspective which united the interests of various stakeholders. Parent cooperatives often demonstrated several signs of dysfunctional parent/staff relations, which detracted from their psychosocial work environment.

The organizational logic of these different types of social enterprises are clearly played out in their answers on employer/employee relations. The staff of worker cooperatives were their own employers, the staff of parent cooperatives were the employees of their clients, while the staff of voluntary organizations were jointly members and employees of the day care service. It is obvious from the materials in the WECSS Staff Study that the staff of parent cooperatives allowed for too little staff influence in relation to their qualifications and responsibility. (The parents' perspective of this relationship is presented in Chapter 10). One suggestion for improving this situation that comes to mind on the basis of the discussion in Chapter 5, is for extending membership to employees and turning parent cooperatives into multi-stakeholder organizations. Here both the parents and staff are members and, therefore, represented in the management and governance of the day care cooperative, similar to the situation found in many voluntary organizations.

What also needs closer attention are some of the other problems vented by the staff of parent cooperatives. In particular, the lack of professionalism of the managers of parent cooperatives in their relationship to the staff needs to be taken seriously. Several solutions come to mind. One suggestion would be to provide training and education for the members of the board of parent cooperatives in matters relating to employer/employee relations. Members of the board need quite simply to learn how to become better employers, how to negotiate labor agreements, how to manage their staff in a professional fashion. However, the resources of these small social enterprises will not bear the costs of such training. So either the municipal authorities and/or their employer organization, *Kooperationens förhandlingsorganisationen*, KFO, will have to provide outside support for such efforts, if this form of cooperative day care is to survive and thrive.

Taken as a group, however, all three types of social enterprises were rated much better in term of their psychosocial work environment than municipal day care services, as we will see in the next chapter. Social enterprises appear to turn high-stress jobs into active jobs by promoting structures and processes for providing more decision authority and control, more social support, and often more client involvement. Thus, social enterprises taken together, and each of these three types in particular, should be given much closer and more serious consideration as a way of improving the psychosocial work environment, renewing and enriching working life, providing good jobs and reforming the public sector in advanced welfare states. They also promote the empowerment of citizens as co-producers of social services, as will be seen in Chapter 10, and they foster civil democracy, thus helping to turn the welfare state into a welfare society, as we will see in Chapter 11.

9. Enriching Swedish Women's Work Environment

Until the 1980s social services were provided almost exclusively by the local government. A variety of alternative models for providing social services were developed in Sweden during the late 1980s and 1990s. Contracting out to the third sector, purchaser-provider models, cooperative social services, volunteering and third party provision are but a few of the models now being tried in order to resolve the acute ideological and financial problems currently facing the Swedish welfare state. Privatization and contracting out has led to the growth of many new social enterprises, that have become an important alternative to the public provision of such social services.

In the current debate social enterprises are all too often discussed in terms of their potential contribution to reducing costs or creating new jobs. The fact that they promote other social values is normally overlooked. Social enterprises can enrich the working life of their staff, improve their work environment and provide them with greater influence in the decision-making of their social enterprises. Enrichment of working life and staff empowerment are considered in this chapter. Social enterprises can also empower the clients of such services as co-producers, which is the topic of the next chapter. Both the staff and the clients are typically women. Nearly all the staff of day care services in Sweden are women, while mothers often play a more active role in the care of their own small children, either getting them from or leaving them with day care facilities, fulfilling the work obligation, etc. So staff and/or client empowerment also means women's empowerment.

In Scandinavia today women rely to a greater extent on their own wage-work for economic survival and to a smaller extent on their husband's wages. Due to their responsibilities as mothers and their unequal position in the labor market, they have increasingly become dependent on the state, both as employees in the public sector and as consumers of social services, as well as clients of social welfare systems (Siim, 1990, 89). This growing dependency on the state is perhaps less of a problem than the historically economic dependency of a wife on her husband. So, it is wrong *per se* to equate a strong welfare state, like the Scandinavian one, with strong dependency on the state. Rather for many women it is the other way around: a strong public service sector seems to be a precondition for entry into the labor market, and thus avoiding being solely dependent on a husband as the breadwinner, on the state as clients, or on both.

In Denmark and Sweden women have come to rely on the state primarily as employees in and consumers of public services; and only to a small degree as clients of such services. The opposite is true in Britain and the United States, where women to a greater extent have to support themselves and their children by relying solely on family relationships or on the labor market, while turning to the state first when these efforts fail, and then only as clients (Siim., *op cit.*, 102). Thus, we can note considerable differences in terms of the role of women between countries. Britain has quite *explicitly* supported motherhood with a very low commitment to child care and has maintained a family orientation of policies in general. Norway has *implicitly* supported the breadwinner-homemaker family model by keeping public child care provision at a minimum. Sweden and Denmark have *actively* supported the integration of women in the labor force and have experienced a considerable shift from private to public child care in the post W.W.II period (Brochorst, 1990; 176).

Increased public control of and spending on matters that used to be left to the family, church or charity help to define central features of the welfare state and create a distinction between formal and informal care, paid and unpaid, private and public care-giving. For example, child care can be provided at home, unpaid, by parents or siblings, alternatively it can also provided by professionals in crèches, day care services and nursery schools. The dependence of women on the welfare state in Scandinavia makes them particularly concerned by changes in the provision of social welfare services, both as workers in and as consumers of such services. In particular, contracting out the provision of personal welfare services to social enterprises can have far going consequences for the dependency of women on the welfare state, but also for the enrichment of women's working life and their empowerment as consumers. The purpose of this chapter is to explore the enrichment of Swedish women's working life by examining the case of social enterprises in day care.

Earlier we saw in Chapter 7 that women's work environment in general was worse than that of men and that stress-filled jobs increased significantly for women between 1968 and 1991 (Szulkin & Tåhlin, 1994). We also found that the psychological work demand had increased considerably for the staff of day care services between 1991 and 1995 and that it was much higher than the average for the entire work force. Moreover, the SCB retrospective study among employees with five years in the same occupation, showed that job demands for the staff of day care services had increased more or much more than it did for the entire work force during the early 1990s. In particular, this was evident in the larger proportion of the staff of day care centers who experienced an increase in the pace of work and heavy work tasks (See Table 7.1 above for details). The dramatic deterioration in the work environment of the staff of day care services can be related to sharp reductions in the budgets of municipal authorities dealing with social services. This has resulted in lower staff to children ratios plus growing difficulty in getting sick relief or temporary replacement help in municipal day care centers. These growing negative aspects of work environment in day care services make it all the more urgent to find ways and means of improving the work environment for this category of personnel. They also make it more important to explore new models for (re-)organizing work, in particular ones that permit greater staff control, engagement and participation in the provision of day care services. Social enterprises and cooperative services provide one clear alterative to the general deterioration in the working conditions of today's municipal services, as is clearly seen in the WECSS Staff Study.

Our Staff Study divided social enterprises into the three different types of firms or organizations discussed above; i.e., parent cooperatives, voluntary organizations and worker cooperatives (Pestoff, 1996a and Pestoff, forthcoming). The overwhelming majority of the respondents in our study were women, 95 per cent of them. The worker cooperatives are consistently rated higher by the staff on most of the over 200 items employed in our study of psychosocial work environment. This should not be simply interpreted as worker cooperatives provide a superior model for worker empowerment. Rather the worker cooperative model is based on organizational structures that facilitate group processes that are positive for promoting the interest of workers/employees. This may, however, take place at the expense of parent involvement and engagement, as will be seen in Chapter 10. Moreover, we saw one or two examples in the comments of a worker cooperative where the manager was repeatedly criticized by staff members for treating the cooperative and her fellow workers as if they were employees in her private firm. Voluntary organizations appear often to function like mixed or multi-stakeholder cooperatives, with the big difference that they have a common ideology or pedagogical perspective which bridges over the divergent interests of various stakeholders. Parent cooperatives often demonstrate signs of dysfunctional parent/staff relations, which detracts from their psychosocial work environment. We called attention to such problems and made some suggestions for alleviating them elsewhere (Pestoff, 1996a and Pestoff, forthcoming), including the development of multi-stakeholder cooperatives and a social audit.

9.A Social Enterprises and Municipal Services

Social enterprises are a relative recent phenomenon in Sweden. Most of the staff of cooperative day care services, regardless of type, have previously worked in municipal day care service. The proportion of staff with personal work experience from municipal day care services was 56 per cent for voluntary organizations, 75.3 per cent for parent and 84.5 per cent for worker cooperatives, which reflects in part the length of operation of various types of cooperative day care service. Until 1975 only municipal day care services could qualify for public funds. Then voluntary organizations with special pedagogics qualified for public support to provide such services. Further changes came in 1985, when parent cooperatives first qualified for public support; and again in 1991, when most of the remaining restrictions for public financing were eliminated. Worker cooperatives and private for-profit firms could then commence to provide day care services with public funding.

In the continued discussion we will focus our attention on the staff's retrospective comparison of their present work life conditions with those of municipal day care services. By comparing their current situation with their experience as employees in municipal day care services we can undertake a retrospective comparison of the two. Although this is not the same as making a parallel study of these two/four types of day care facilities, it nevertheless helps to throw light on the differences experienced by the same persons with direct participation in and personal experience from both forms of day care services.

However, before presenting this retrospective comparison of work environment we will briefly explore whether the staff had previous experience with other types of cooperatives and the most important reasons for taking a job with a cooperative day care center. This is necessary as these two background factors might be related to the employees' initial expectations of social enterprises.

The staff were asked about their previous experience with the cooperative work form, in order to see if their present employment might represent positive selection, but very few had any such experience. Only between one-tenth and one-fifth of the staff of all three types of cooperative day care services had any previous personal experience of working for/with cooperatives, before taking employment in a cooperative day care facility. Very few were members, and even fewer had an elective office in a cooperative. The majority lacked any direct personal experience whatsoever, while a third or more only had indirect experience of it from reading or hearing about cooperatives from their friends. Staff comparisons with municipal day care services are, therefore, based in the overwhelming majority of cases on newly first hand experience, gained from working in both forms, public and social enterprise.

The staff of cooperative day care facilities were also asked to state their motives for taking employment with their present day care service, by indicating their stance on a seven point scale, ranging from "completely false" (1) to "completely true" (7), on several alternatives. Only the proportion of the staff agreeing completely (a score of 6 or 7) are indicated

Table 9.1 Why Did You Take Employment with Present Cooperative Day Care Center?

Agree Completely with following*:	Parent Co-ops	Vol. Orgs	Worker Co-ops
-wanted a meaningful job	67.1	71.9	78.4
-increased staff influence	44.7	28.5	65.6
-good working hours	44.1	38.6	34.1
-near home	40.9	35.7	38.6
-small organization	38.8	38.6	48.4
-possibility for parental participation	40.7	35.1	20.3
-specific (pedagogical) profile	28.2	49.2	44.2
-good job benefits	28.6	29.8	40.0
-had colleagues who worked here	20.2	12.3	40.0
-only way to get a job	8.4	9.9	9.6
-while waiting for another job	7.2	8.6	4.2
average	33.5	32.6	38.5

Source: WECSS Staff Study, 1996a; *only the proportion of respondents agreeing completely with the above statements, i.e., those with scores of 6 or 7, are included here.

here. On the average about one third of the staff of each type of social enterprise have a high score, but some notable differences exist among them on particular items. These differences clearly reflect their organizational base of each organization and its profile.

The staff of all three types of day care services rate "wanting a meaningful job" as the most important reason for taking employment with their current employer; and the staff of parent and worker co-ops, rank "increased staff influence" as the second most important reason; while the staff of voluntary organizations rate "a specific (pedagogical) profile" as their second most important motive for working at their current day care service. The staff of worker co-ops demonstrate more interest in questions like increased staff influence, small organizations, good job benefits and having a colleague who worked there, than does the staff of the other two daycare services. The staff of all three types of day care services paid roughly equal importance to nearness to home, and they also attributed the least importance to reasons like "the only way to get a job" and "while waiting for another job". The staff of parent co-ops gave some more weight to good working hours than did the staff of the other two types of day care services. Thus, job content combined with either more influence over work or a specific pedagogical profile provide the most important reasons for taking employment with social enterprise day care services. Rather than providing a solution to temporary employment or other practical problems, our material clearly shows that working in social enterprise day care service is considered a positive development in the work life by most employees, and not merely as a necessity.

9.B Work Life in Social Enterprises Compared with Municipal Day Care Services in General

Our retrospective study begins with a general comparison of work life in cooperative and municipal day care services. Respondents were encouraged to provide comments explaining their preference for cooperative or municipal day care services. They were also asked to compare 23 different

Table 9.2 How Do You Like Working for a Social Enterprise Compared to a Municipal Day Care Facility?

General Comparisons*	Parent Co-ops	Vol. Orgs	Worker Co-ops
-better	68.3	71.9	85.5
-no big difference	27.0	25.0	10.8
-worse	4.8	3.1	3.6
(md - %)**	(28.4)	(45.8)	(14.4)

Source: WECSS Staff Study, 1996a. *Adds to 100% column wise. **Proportion of the staff who lacked previous experience from municipal day care services.

aspects of work life in both forms of day care services. Answers to the general comparison of working for cooperative and municipal day care services show clearly that the overwhelming majority of the staff of all three types of social enterprises prefer working for cooperative day care services. Over two-thirds of the staff in parent co-ops and voluntary organizations and more than four-fifths in worker co-ops say it is better working for social enterprise. Only a tiny fraction of the staff of any type of cooperative state that working for it is worse than municipal day care.

Half of the staff of parent co-ops, nearly half of the staff of voluntary organizations and nearly three-quarters of the staff of worker co-ops provide comments on this question to explain their clear preference for the cooperative form. This was the second most commented upon question by the staff of parent co-ops and voluntary organizations, and the most commented upon by the staff of worker co-ops. The fact that this question came near the end of a long questionnaire did not hinder them from making comments. The number of comments elicited indicates the saliency and importance of this topic for the respondents - they felt quite strongly about it. (See Exhibit 2 in the appendix for some of their comments).

The overwhelming majority of the comments from the staff of *parent cooperatives* concerning their personal comparison with municipal day care services were positive to the social enterprise form, but there were also a few negative opinions. The comments include issues like greater influence and responsibility or freedom; better contacts with parents; quicker, shorter decision-making; everybody's involvement, direct contacts with their employers, smaller group size, etc. The two most frequently made comments concerned greater contact with parents and greater influence. The overwhelming majority of the comments from the staff of *voluntary organizations* concerning their personal comparison with municipal day care services were positive to the social enterprise form. The issues were nearness to their employer; better contacts with the parents and/or their involvement; closer, shorter or quicker decision-making; greater influence and/or responsibilities and greater freedom; being more motivated and engaged, praise from parents; smaller group size; or a combination of several of these motivations. Greater influence and/or responsibilities was mentioned slightly more frequently than the other alternatives. The overwhelming majority of the staff of *worker cooperatives* were very positive to the social enterprise form when compared with municipal day care services, but a few were also neutral or negative. Comments concerning increased influence and/or responsibilities or greater freedom stands head-and-shoulders above all the other alternatives mentioned in terms of the frequency with which they were employed by the staff of worker co-ops, while being able to make their own decisions came a second, and could conceivably be added to the former comments.

9.C Detailed Comparisons of Work Life in Social Enterprises and Municipal Day Care Services

We will now turn to more specific details making up the work-life of day care services, including the psychosocial work environment and co-determination, etc. The staff also answered a series of questions comparing their current work conditions with those in municipal day care services, in terms of improving, remaining the same or becoming worse. They were asked to state whether each of numerous items or aspects had "increased a lot", "increased somewhat", "remained unchanged", "decreased somewhat" or "decreased a lot", in the cooperative compared with municipal day care services. The twenty-three different aspects of work life in day care services

Table 9.3 Compared to Municipal Day Care, How are the Following Things Today?

possibilities increased a lot in the following areas*	Parent Co-ops	Vol. Orgs	Worker Co-ops
-to influence your own work	42.3	48.5	81.0
-to take your own responsibility	52.9	39.4	81.0
-of participating in decision-making	35.8	65.4	78.3
-of trying out your own ideas	48.5	36.4	62.2
-contact with parents	40.3	41.2	27.7
-satisfaction with work	25.4	35.3	60.2
-for personal development	28.4	23.5	45.8
-shared work values with work-mates	22.4	14.7	43.4
-to influence your work-environment	17.9	27.3	42.0
-contact with the management	20.6	40.6	43.5
-work status	12.2	15.6	24.1
-dirty air & dirty premises	18.2	15.6	1.2
-more flexible work hours	6.0	8.8	14.6
-fewer conflicts**	3.0	14.7	18.3
average for all 23 items:	20.6	20.9	31.5

Source: the WECSS Staff Study, 1996a, *alternatives were: increased a lot, increased somewhat, unchanged, decreased somewhat, and decreased a lot, only the proportion stating **increased a lot** are included here; **the proportion claiming a large decline are indicated here, while those claiming increased conflicts were 4.5%, 2.9% and 1.2% respectively.

included here permit a detailed comparison of the social enterprise and municipal forms, in terms of physical, social-psychological and organizational aspects of work environment and co-determination.

Table 9.3 presents only some of the major differences in the comparisons of the staff in these three types of cooperatives compared with municipal day care services. Only the proportion replying "increased a lot", i.e., those indicating a large improvement, are included in the table for reasons of simplicity. The aspects presented have been chosen for the large differences between various types of day care services and/or because they illustrate one or more of the theoretically expected differences discussed previously. Such differences between different types of cooperatives help to clarify the central characteristics of each type of cooperative day care services.

Various aspects of increased control over the work situation are among those showing a large improvement by the staff of all three types of day care cooperatives. They include: improved possibilities to influence their own work, improved possibilities of taking their own responsibility, improved possibilities for participating in decision-making, improved possibilities of trying their own ideas, improved contacts with the parents, greater work satisfaction, improved possibilities for personal development, greater shared values with colleagues, greater possibilities to improve their own work environment, and improved contacts with the management, all of which receive a sizable proportion of the staff replying "increased a lot" for most types of social services, compared with municipal day care services.

While these possibilities improved considerably for the staff of all three types of day care services, the improvement for the staff of worker co-ops is often greater or much greater than for the staff of either parent co-ops or voluntary organizations. A greater proportion of the staff of worker co-ops claimed a 'large improvement' on 15 of these 23 items than did the staff of the other two types of social enterprises. The improvement scores noted by the staff of parent co-ops and voluntary organizations are often rather similar, but lower than those of worker co-ops. One notable exception is contacts with parents, where the proportion of the staff of worker co-ops indicating great improvement is considerably *less* than that of the staff of the other two types of day care services. This is of course quite logical, since parents are also members of the other two types of day care services.

Also, the staff of parent co-ops report a smaller decrease in conflicts that the other two types of day care services. On the other hand, a smaller proportion of the staff of worker co-ops report increases in dirty air & premises. There are several other items where smaller improvements have taken place compared with municipal day care services. They include the risk of being exposed to violence, the length of vacations, the creation of new positions, the admission of children with special problems, psychological demands, more flexible working hours, salaries and physically demanding tasks.

9.D Personal Engagement: At the Start and Now

The staff all three types of cooperative day care were asked to provide an evaluation of their personal engagement at the time of starting work in their present employment and of their engagement today. Two-thirds or more were always involved at the beginning and another one-fifth to one-fourth were engaged "most of the time". Thus, we note similar levels of engagement for the staff of all three types of cooperative day care facilities at the start of their employment in cooperative day care facilities, but different degrees of engagement today.

Table 9.4 At the Start of Your Present Employment Were You Very Engaged in Your Work?

Engagement at the start?*	Parent Co-ops	Vol. Orgs.	Worker Co-ops
-Yes, always	70.9	65.9	72.2
-Yes, most of the time	23.3	24.1	20.6
n	88	59	97

Source: WECSS Staff Study, 1996a, *=doesn't add to 100% column wise, since the answers "Yes, once in a while" and "No, never" were so few and have therefore been excluded here.

More of the staff of worker co-ops show a higher degree of engagement today than either the staff of parent co-ops or voluntary organizations, while considerably more of the staff of parent co-ops claim a lower degree of engagement today than at the start[1] . This can also be expressed as an engagement differential, by subtracting those with a lower degree of engagement today from those with a higher degree. Here a positive score indicates a surplus and a negative score a deficit in terms of engagement.

---

[1] There is a notably lower degree of engagement today among the staff of parent co-ops in Stockholm (45.2%) and Uppsala (36.4%) than in Gothenburg (25.7%), while this decreased engagement is smallest in Malmö (10.0%).

The engagement differential for parent co-ops is -6.7, for voluntary organizations 8.6 and as much as 28.3 for worker co-ops. However, it should be kept in mind that the staff of worker co-ops have only worked at the present social enterprise a few years, compared with a longer or much longer average length of service in the other two types of cooperative day care services. Nearly two-fifths of the staff of parent co-ops, nearly half of the staff of voluntary organizations and nearly one-fourth of the staff of worker co-ops provided comments to this question.

Table 9.5 Do You Have the Same Engagement Today?

Engagement today?*	Parent Co-ops	Vol. Orgs.	Worker Co-ops
-higher degree than at start	31.0	32.8	43.3
-same as at start	31.0	43.1	41.2
-lower degree than at start	37.9	24.1	15.0
n	88	59	97

Source: WECSS Staff Study, 1996a, *=adds to 100% column wise.

These comments do not provide support nor criticism for the social enterprise form *per se*, but rather underline the importance of the spirit of working together in small organizations for the same goal, of being able to influence that goal and how it is achieved. However, too much work, conflicts with parents, worsening economic conditions, diminishing financial support from local authorities, or the threat of bankruptcy may diminish the positive aspects of employment in social enterprise day care compared with the relatively secure employment municipal day care services. (See Exhibit 3 in the appendix for some of their comments).

Our final comparison with municipal day care services concerned the hypothetical question of choosing to work in a cooperative organization again (rather than returning to municipal day care or doing something else). The table above provides the answers of the staff of the three types of social enterprises. Twice the proportion of the staff of worker co-ops state that they would definitely choose to work in a cooperative again as do the staff of parent co-ops or voluntary organizations. Only a few state that they would not consider working for a cooperative again, if they could choose freely. This can be interpreted as only a small minority would prefer to work for municipal day care services. The question about having a free choice to work in a cooperative day care center received very few comments from any staff group. Less than one-fourth of the staff of parent cooperatives and voluntary organizations provided comments to this question, while only five per cent of the staff of worker co-ops did so,

Table 9.6 If You Could Choose Freely, Would You Work for a Cooperative Again?

Would you choose to work for a co-op. again?	Parent Co-ops	Vol. Orgs	Worker Co-ops
-Yes, definitely	33.3	33.3	66.7
-Yes, perhaps	54.0	59.6	29.2
-No, hardly/ definitely not**	11.5	7.0	4.2
n	88	59	97

Source: WECSS Staff Study, 1996a, *=adds to 100% column wise,
**combines alternatives "No, hardly" and "No, definitely not".

indicating the unproblematic nature of their preference for working in cooperative day care services.

9.E Summary and Conclusions

Summary

A summary of our findings shows that the overwhelming majority of the staff had no previous experience personal of cooperatives before starting to work in social enterprise day care, but most of them had previously worked in municipal day care services. Thus, social enterprises and cooperative day care services can, therefore, become an important channel for spreading personal experience with and knowledge about the cooperative model (see Stryjan, 1989 for a discussion of the reproduction of cooperative ideas). The great majority clearly preferred working for a social enterprise compared with municipal day care services. In almost all respects of work life social enterprises were rated better or clearly better than municipal day care services by the staff of all three types of cooperative services. The average proportion claiming a "large improvement" for all 23 items of work life in social enterprises was one fifth for parent co-ops and voluntary organizations and nearly one-third for worker co-ops. The number of items where the proportion of the staff claiming a "large improvement" was 40 per cent or more came to four for parent co-ops, three for voluntary organizations and nine for worker co-ops. In general terms, the staff of worker cooperatives are clearly the most positive about improvements in their current work situation compared with municipal day care services. The staff of parent cooperatives and voluntary organizations demonstrate lower levels of improvement. Thus, the clearest improvement in most aspects of work life was noted by the staff of worker co-ops.

A large majority of the staff of all three types of social enterprises were always engaged in their work at the start of their current employment, while a greater proportion of the staff of worker co-ops retained the same engagement today. Finally, given the chance to do it all over again, two-thirds of staff of worker co-ops, while only one-third of the staff in parent co-ops and voluntary organizations would definitely choose the cooperative form. Only a tiny fraction of the respondents in any type of social enterprise would consider working in municipal day care services again.

The staff of worker co-ops have both the freedom and responsibility to make decisions on their own, both as independent day care facilities and their own employers. It comes, therefore, as no great surprise that they experience the most positive changes when comparing their current situation with that of working for municipal services. The positive changes between municipal day care and parent co-ops or voluntary organizations appear much smaller. This should not, however, detract from several areas, particularly those related to self-development and co-determination, where the staff of parent co-ops and voluntary organizations also note substantial improvements over their previous situation as employees in municipal day care.

Numerous comments to the questions illustrated both the positive as well as the negative side of work life in cooperative day care services. Again the overwhelming impression from these comments supports the picture provided by the figures and tables. Social enterprise day care services permit the staff much greater influence on their own work, much greater responsibility for and participation in decision-making, greater contacts with parents, greater possibilities for improvements in their work environment, greater work satisfaction, etc. than do municipal day care services.

Conclusions

The empirical part of our study demonstrated that social enterprises in Sweden provide good jobs in the fullest meaning of the word. In Karasek and Theorell's terms work in social enterprises is psychologically demanding, but it provides high decision latitude to, and high social support for the workers. These work-life attributes stand in sharp contrast with those found in the services provided by the large hierarchical bureaucratic organizations often associated with the public sector services in Sweden and elsewhere In this sense the social enterprise model can not only help to transform social services jobs into active, participative and interactive jobs, it can also help to enrich the work-life of the employees. This suggests that one of the quickest and most direct ways of enriching work life, redesigning work and promoting human resource management in the personal social service sector in Sweden would be to decentralize the provision of social services and to let social enterprises provide them.

Karasek and Theorell's contrasted good jobs with bad ones (1990). The former sound very much like work in social enterprises, whereas the latter sound like anything but. Thus, they characterize good jobs in the following way: *skill discretion:* the job offers possibilities to make the maximum use of one's skills and provides opportunities to increase skills on the job; *autonomy:* freedom from rigid worker-as-child factory discipline, workers have influence over selection of work routines and work colleagues can participate in long-term planning; *psychological demands:* the job has routine demands mixed with a liberal element of new learning challenges in a predictable manor; *social relations:* social contacts are encouraged as a basis for new learning and new contacts multiply the possibilities for self-realization through collaboration; *social rights:* there are democratic procedures at the workplace; *meaningfulness/customer/social feedback:* workers gain direct feedback from customers, and workers and customers work together, customizing the product to meet the customers' needs (*ibid.*, 316-7).

Moreover, we also noted that the women employed in worker cooperative day care services were more positive about these organizational changes than were their colleagues in parent co-ops. Parent co-ops, however, promote other values, such as greater parental influence, greater parental participation in the daily life of their child(ren). There are clearly two sides to the coin of organizational change, depending on which model of change is employed. Group interests and group conflicts are not completely resolved by greater participation of a single group in the decision making of social enterprises. Greater worker participation does empower the workers, but it does not necessarily promote the interests of the clients. Similarly, greater consumer participation does empower the clients, but not necessarily promote the interest of the workers.

This, in turn, suggests the limits of institutionalizing the interest of a single group in the decision-making structures of a social enterprise. Organizational changes of work environment that rely on social enterprises may improve the work environment, but nevertheless result in some trade-offs between the interest of workers and clients. However, organizational change relying on multi-stakeholder models can provide the supporting structures necessary for promoting the interests of more than a single stakeholder. Multi-stakeholder cooperatives recognize the legitimate interest of several groups contributing to the success of a social enterprise, and provide for the representation of their interests in the institutions of internal decision-making (Pestoff, 1995c; see also Chapter 5 above).

Voluntary organizations appear, in this context, to provide an alternative to both the worker and parent co-ops. They were often evaluated more positively by their staff in terms of improving the work environment, than are parent co-ops; but they are also rated more positively by the parents in terms of promoting the value of parent influence than by parents with children in worker co-ops. Voluntary organizations appear to be rudimentary form of multi-stakeholder organizations that are able to combine the interests of both groups in the pursuit of a common pedagogical program. Whether this is possible for other types of social services remains to be seen. More formal multi-stockholder institutions in other areas may provide the necessary basis for facilitating the trade-off between different and sometimes conflicting interest of various groups that contribute to the success of a social enterprise.

Social enterprises can, as our study clearly shows, enrich the working life of Swedish women and empower them in their work relations. Social enterprises can not resolve all the problems relating to women's unequal position in the labor market, but they can perhaps reduce their dependency on the state as workers and consumers, while augmenting their influence in both these areas at the same time. Women gain greater control over their jobs and/or the services provided through their greater participation and influence in the decision-making process of social enterprises. Which group stands to gain the most depends on who is a member and which model of social enterprise is employed.

Our study of Swedish women's work environment in social enterprises focused on one clearly delimited segment of personal social services, i.e., day care services. We hope that it can contribute to a greater understanding and pluralism of potential models for enriching work life and renewing the welfare state. No single model is universally applicable to *all* segments of work life nor *all* types of production, *all* types of services nor for *all* types of clients or consumers. Neither public, private nor cooperative models alone provide a panacea nor the model for producing all types of goods and services for everyone in modern societies. Solutions based simply on privatizing, on guaranteeing continued public provision or on running it as a cooperative, all fall short of the mark. Thus, we do not intend to propose *the* solution to the problems facing the welfare state at the turn of the century, but rather to propose *one* solution to *one* type of problem for *one* type of service in *one* welfare European state. It may have some relevance for other types of problems or for social services in some other countries. But, were it to be interpreted as *the* solution, we would have clearly failed in our endeavor. However, in combination with other solutions to other problems facing the public sector, it can contribute to enriching working life and, thereby to renewing the welfare state.

Enriching the work life of civil servants and improving their work environment are important and legitimate concerns of many tens of 1,000s of women and men working in the large bureaucracies of the public sector in Sweden and elsewhere. Given loss of productivity, the poor quality of services, the costs of treating stress related symptoms and absenteeism due to stress related sickness, etc.; improving the work environment is an important economic, social and political problem. Efforts to reform the welfare state should take improving the work environment into account. However, the public debate in Sweden seems only to focus on one thing at a time. Given the current historically high level of unemployment, the third sector and social enterprises are only conceived of in terms of their potential job creation. Jobs are, of course, necessary; but good jobs are preferable to bad ones. Why not try to get both at the same time?

Prior to that the potential contribution of social enterprises was framed in terms of providing cheaper services, and this was the major motive for enlisting their increased involvement in the production of personal social services. Cheaper services are of course desirable, but better quality services at the same price would be preferred by many, if not most Swedes. A more engaged staff is one of the best guarantees of good service quality. Social enterprises can contribute to greater staff engagement, but this varies with the organizational model chosen.

10. Empowering Citizens as Co-Producers

In this chapter we want to consider the implications of social enterprises and civil democracy in facilitating greater citizen participation in the production of local public services, in particular of personal social services. One way might be to encourage more market mechanisms or exit, while another would emphasize more direct involvement or voice by citizens (Hirschman, 1970). There are several other alternative approaches to the renewal of the public sector, including a "participatory state", where various groups excluded under more hierarchical models, are permitted greater organizational involvement (Peters, 1994). Such an approach concentrates on the lower echelons or front-line workers, as well as on the clients of organizations in an effort to enhance the role of the front-line workers and citizen and to attempt to induce democratic participation by means other than voting. (*ibid.*, 13).

The meaning of the public interest within the participatory state is dependent upon the workers and citizens themselves being involved in making some choices about policy. Thus, it too would give citizens more consumer choice and direct control over programs, similar to the market model. But the manner in which these consumer choices would be exercised in the participatory state would be more political. Rather than voting in the market place with their crowns, dollars or yen, citizens would vote through some sort of political process. This participation might be in referenda on policy or it may be in local structures, like parent involvement in school committees, etc. (*ibid.*, 15). In Chapter 1 we discussed and defined civil democracy in order to capture this new type of citizen participation, in term of cooperative citizen self-governance of the personal social services they demand.

We also refer readers to our earlier discussion of the concept of co-production (see Chapter 4) which is one of the main theoretical underpinnings of definition of *civil democracy*. Co-production bears particular importance for understanding changes in the role of clients or consumers of personal social services. This concept is also necessary for understanding the contribution of new social enterprises to empowering consumers as co-producers and to the role of the new social economy in renewing the welfare state. In particular we are interested here in exploring the value created for parents through the existence of possibilities for greater participation in some forms of cooperative day care services as opposed to the lack of such possibilities for participation in municipal and private day care facilities. Co-production therefore means greater consumer involvement in the production process in general and usually signifies greater consumer participation in one or more aspect or phases of the production process. For the purposes of this study, where we are particularly interested in the possibilities for consumer cooperatives and voluntary organizations to empower the clients of these services.

An alternative perspective can be found in the concept of "service democracy", proposed by the Swedish Power Investigation in the late 1980s. Most citizens were satisfied with the services provided by the public sector and did not want to engage themselves in such matters. A comparison of child care and elderly care in Uppsala County found "...several parents with children in a parent cooperative child care would have preferred municipal service, where they could avoid the responsibility they feel is too heavy.... Becoming engaged in the daily activities does not attract many" (Möller, 1996: 376). "Service democracy's passive consumption is attractive to many and parents do not experience activity as a value in itself" (*ibid.*, 383). In spite of differences in scope and method, we feel that the WECSS Parent Study challenges some of these conclusions, as will be shown below.

In Chapter 4 exit, voice and loyalty were introduced, and the costs of exit from enduring services were discussed. Exit can both be motivated by declining quality, as well as by the expectation of better quality services. Deterioration in the quality of municipal day care services during the 1990s, due to severe cuts and the continued reduction in the number of staff, may provide one reason why so many parents chose alternatively provided services in recent years. But many parents may also have chosen non-municipal services in expectation of being able to obtain improved services or to realize certain values not feasible in municipal services. Not only the reasons for choosing a particular type of service, but also the subsequent support for or trust in alternatively provided services may express different aspects or dimensions of the services provided.

Three kinds of loyalty were previously distinguished, i.e., instrumental loyalty, value loyalty and a combination of both (Cf. Möller, 1996), where the latter represents the strongest bonds between clients and a firm or organization. Parents who choose a particular type of day care service on the basis of specific values should demonstrate greater loyalty, if they are satisfied with the services, than those parents who merely choose services for instrumental reasons. This means that we expect parents with children in parent cooperatives or voluntary organizations providing day care services to be more loyal to their provider than parents with children in worker cooperatives care services. However, given the recent decline in the quality of municipal services, parents with children in any three types of social enterprises should be more satisfied than they were previously with the services provided by municipal day care centers. We examine parental satisfaction both with cooperative and municipal services in the empirical materials below.

The empirical materials and data presented here stem from the Project on Work Environment and Cooperative Social Services in Sweden, the WECSS Project. Nearly 600 client questionnaires were collected and analyzed in the Parent Study, the results of which are reported here. We are primarily interested in exploring the value created for parents through the existence of possibilities for greater participation in some forms of cooperative day care services as opposed to the lack of such possibilities for participation in municipal and private day care facilities. Three types of social enterprises are included in our study: parent cooperatives, voluntary organizations and worker cooperatives. The WECSS Parent Study sheds light on the motives parents have for choosing one particular type of social enterprise rather than another and for becoming involved as a co-producer or not.

10.A The Social Background of Parents to Children in Social Enterprises

We will begin our presentation of the WECSS Parent Study with a presentation of their social background and then turn to their attitudes in several relevant aspects of cooperative day care services. Nearly one-third of the parents with children in parent cooperative day care center participated in the start of the cooperative day care center, while less than one of ten parents with children in voluntary organizations or worker co-ops did so. This is a reflection of the fact that parent cooperative day care services often had their origin in a lack of municipal services in the 1980s and parents thus took these matters in their own hands by starting day care services of their own preferences. A brief survey of the socio-economic background of the parents to children in different types of cooperative social enterprises demonstrates that they do not comprise a homogeneous group of well-off parents.

Parents with children in day care services provided by voluntary organizations rate higher in most social respects, like mother's and father's education, mother's and father's occupation, type of housing and income, than parents with children in the two other types of cooperative day care services. Parents with children in worker cooperative day care services often come lower than the other two, except for type housing, where parents

Table 10.1 The Social Background of Parents to Children in Social Enterprises Providing Day Care Services

Social Background*	Parent Co-ops	Vol. Orgs	Worker Co-ops	Average
-married	91.5	94.1	87.4	90.9
-mother's education:				
gymnasium	34.7	28.9	44.8	36.9
university	57.7	68.1	46.6	57.4
-father's education:				
gymnasium	40.7	34.2	40.8	38.5
university	50.5	61.8	47.3	52.8
-mother's occupation:	47.3	54.6	47.9	49.9
white collar				
-father's occupation:	51.1	47.7	46.7	48.5
white collar	16.5	21.3	19.2	19.1
self-employed				
-housing:				
own home/row house	50.0	69.5	64.4	59.8
tenant owners	15.8	10.5	17.3	14.6
-av. monthly income:				
>25,000kr.	53.9	63.0	48.8	55.8
n	190	189	201	580

Source: WECSS Parent Study, Pestoff, 1996a, * in per cent.

with children in parent cooperatives come lowest. The average number of years that a child has spent in various types of cooperative day care services is similar among different types of cooperatives. It is 2.2 years for parent cooperatives, 2.3 years for children in voluntary organizations and 1.9 years for children in worker cooperatives.

Unfortunately, comparable data for parents with children attending municipal day care services is not available. We suspect that the averages shown above may be higher than the national average for adults with children under six or the average for parents with a child attending municipal day care services, but there is no way to determine the exact size of such differences.

10.B Parent Involvement, Motives and Satisfaction

Previously we saw that the institutional differences between these three types of cooperative day care services found a clear expression in the attitudes of the staff concerning their psycho-social work environment and possibilities for influencing their work (see Chapters 7 to 9, Pestoff, 1996a and Pestoff, forthcoming, for more details). The members of worker cooperatives were usually the most satisfied with their working conditions. Similarly, we should expect differences in attitudes between parents in different types of cooperative day care services, as the parents also have a different institutional base in them. Parents are members of the day care cooperative both in parent cooperatives and voluntary organizations, but not worker cooperatives. As members, they normally have a work obligation and possibilities for participating in the democratic structures of the cooperative. Does membership perhaps reflect parents' reasons for choosing one type of day care service and not another? Is it related to the main advantages and disadvantages parents associate with each type of day care cooperative? Does membership also affect the attitudes of the parents towards their collaboration with the staff and their satisfaction with the administration of the day care service? Finally, does it find expression in terms of parents' comparisons with municipal day care services? We will provide answers to these and other questions below. We will begin our inquiry by considering parents' attitudes about the work obligation and holding an elective office. Following that we will consider their reasons for choosing their cooperative child care and its advantages and disadvantages and then go on to discuss their collaboration with the staff and their satisfaction with the administration of the day care center.

10.B.1 Membership, the Work Obligations, Holding an Elective Office and Influence

The work obligation varies from one cooperative day care center to another. (See Exhibit 4.A in the appendix for two descriptions of the work obligation.) Work obligations primarily comprise tasks related to administration and maintenance and do not normally include pedagogical activities. But, parents often function as temporary relief or substitutes for staff on sick-leave or absent for a course, etc., in a rotating system of "jour" (daily) duty that eliminates the need for hiring temporary staff. The ownership structure and work obligation of parent cooperatives and voluntary organizations make for greater parent involvement in the running of such day care services. Worker cooperatives lack both parent representation on the board and an obligation to work in the day care center, although some of them have now established an advisory body to institutionalize their contacts with parents. Such advisory bodies meet a few times per year and mainly have information functions. Given the larger average size of worker cooperative day care services, 40 - 60 children compared with 15 - 20 children in parent co-ops and voluntary organizations, some form of parent representation in an advisory board is logical. Their size and structure seldom facilitate the informal exchange of information brought about by the work obligation in parent cooperatives and voluntary organizations, nor the formal representation of parents on the board. The table below presents data about parents' attitudes toward the work obligation.

Table 10.2 What Do You Think about the Work Obligation?

work obligation*	**Parent Co-ops**	**Vol. Orgs**
-gives a feeling of participation	88.0	81.8
-gives a feeling of belonging	68.0	62.3
-gives valuable insights	63.3	54.4
-provides possibilities for influencing the work here	45.3	29.2
average/(total) no. answers	2.7/(405)	2.4/(367)

Source: WECSS Parent Study, Pestoff, 1996a, *multiple options, add to more than 100% and based on eligible answers, i.e., only those who have a work obligation.

Just over one eighth of the parents in both these cooperative forms lack a work obligation. Negative aspects of the work obligation, such as being too demanding or unqualified, creating conflicts between parents or between parents and the staff, were seldom mentioned by parents, i.e., only between 1.3 and 5.2 per cent, and they are not show here for reasons of space. Moreover, only a small proportion of the parents lack an opinion altogether about the work obligation, seven and five per cent respectively. Those aspects of the work obligation given most positive support by parents include participation, belonging, valuable insights and influence.

The parents in both these types of cooperative day care services give similar priority to the rank order and magnitude of the positive aspects of the work obligation, except for possibilities for influence. More than four-fifths state that the work obligation gives a feeling of participation, and approximately two-thirds of them also name that it gives a feeling of belonging. In addition, the work obligation gives more than half of them valuable insights in the running of the cooperative day care services. Thus, the work obligation is not merely, nor mainly, perceived by the parents as a chore nor in a negative sense, but rather as a positive institution for facilitating their integration into the daily activities of their daughter's or son's day care center. The work obligation helps to eliminate uncertainty in the interaction between the parents and the staff of these two types of day care services, as well as between parents themselves. It also helps to promote greater trust between the parents and staff of such organizations.

The work obligation itself provides fewer parents with possibilities to influence the work. However, more parents with children in parent cooperatives see opportunities for gaining influence than parents with children in voluntary organizations. This probably reflects the fact that a greater proportion of parents also hold an elective office in parent cooperatives than in voluntary organizations. They can thus combine insights gained from the work obligation to bring about changes if necessary.

More than one of four parents with children in parent co-ops or voluntary organizations provide comments to their answering concerning the work obligation, holding an elective office, etc. Their comments include several diverse topics, including both positive and negative aspects and instrumental and expressive aspects. Positive aspects comprise the necessity of keeping the costs down, contacts with other children and their parents, contacts with their own child's daily life, belonging and participating, providing greater security for the children, providing greater influence and all parents having an active responsibility. More neutral expressions underline the division between parents' responsibilities for administration, maintenance and occasional temporary fill-in for staff on sick leave and the staff's responsibility for pedagogical matters. A few negative comments cover topics like only some of the parents hold an elective office, difficulties for new parents to get elected or conflicts between the parents on the board and the staff. (See Exhibit 4.B in the appendix for some illustrations of parent comments on the work obligation.)

The question about having an elective office included both parents at parent cooperatives and voluntary organizations, with a seat on the board of the cooperative, as well as parents at worker cooperatives, with a seat in a parental advisory body. More than three-fifths (62.6%) of the parents with children in parent cooperatives hold an elective office in the cooperative day care and more than two-fifths (43.2%) of parents with children in voluntary organizations do so, while only a few parents sit on advisory boards of worker co-ops. The latter will therefore be excluded in the table below. Once again the negative aspects of holding an elective office were excluded from this presentation, due to the low frequency of parents indicating negative experience with elective offices. Answers like too demanding or unqualified, creating conflicts between parents or between parents and the staff only ranged from 1.2 to 5.3 per cent.

Table 10.3 What Do You Think about Your Work on the Board?

Work on the board	Parent Co-ops	Vol. Orgs
-provides possibilities for influencing the work here	66.2	53.9
-gives a feeling of participation	62.4	48.6
-gives valuable insights	54.1	44.1
-gives a feeling of belonging	40.8	34.2
-no opinion	17.4	19.6
average/(total) no. answers	2.4/(400)	2.0/(328)

Source: WECSS Parent Study, Pestoff, 1996a, * multiple answers add to more than 100%.

Those aspects of holding an elective office most often named once again include influence, participation, insights and belonging, but now in another order of importance. Unlike parents' attitudes concerning the work obligation, elective office first and foremost provide parents with an opportunity to influence the work at their child(ren)'s cooperative day care centers. For the remaining aspects of holding an elective office, we find a similar ranking, if not magnitude, by the parents of both these types of cooperative day care services. Elective duties also provide a feeling of participation, give valuable insights and give a feeling of belonging. Nearly one-fifth of the parents do not indicate their attitude to holding an elective office, probably due to their lack of experience.

Parents also provided comments about holding an elective or honorary office. Most of their comments were positive, but some parents mentioned negative aspects. The positive comments emphasize the equality of everyone participating, while the negative aspects focus on the time demanded. (See Exhibit 4.C in the appendix for some illustrations of the their comments on holding an elective or honorary office.)

Through the work obligation and holding an elective office, parents in both these types of cooperative day care services quite simply become co-producers of their own child(ren)'s day care services. Holding an elective office provides greater influence, which helps to eliminate uncertainty in the interaction between the parents and the staff of these two types of day care services. It also help to promote greater trust between the parents and staff of such organizations. Few, if any, of these intangible integrative aspects are available to parents with children in worker cooperatives, since they are not members, very few of them have elective positions, and those who do mostly have an advisory position. Thus, their relationship with their child(ren)'s day care services is much more marginal than the parents of the other two types of day care cooperatives. (See Exhibit 4.D for some more general statements concerning the benefits of the cooperative form.)

Table 10.4 Can You Influence Things and Want to be More Active?

influence and activity (%)	Parent Co-ops	Vol. Orgs	Worker Co-ops
can you influence things*	84.2	81.4	51.0
want to be more active*	18.5	24.1	30.9
n	190	189	201

Source: WECSS Parent Study, Pestoff, 1996a, * only the positive answers are included here.

General questions about parental influence and activity also sheds more light on the differences between these three types of cooperative day care services. More than four-fifths of parents with children in parent cooperative and voluntary organizations claim that they can influence things in their child's day care cooperative, while only half of the parents in worker co-ops do so. This is a clear reflection of the differences in membership between these three types of cooperative day care services. However, a greater proportion of parents in worker cooperatives want to be more active. This can be expressed as a parent influence/activity index or surplus, which can be complied by subtracting the percentage giving a positive answers to question no. 7 from those answering positively to question no. 6. The influence/activity surplus is 65.7 for parent co-ops, 57.3 for voluntary organizations, but only 20.1 for worker cooperatives. Scores above 50 indicate the substantial parental influence and participation required for co-production.

10.B.2 Choice of, Advantages and Satisfaction with Cooperative Day Care Services

Parents were asked to motivate their choice of a particular type of cooperative day care service. If they have clear motives for putting their child(ren) in one type of cooperative or another, then it should be seen in their answers. Parents' motives should reflect the values they hope to promote by choosing one form of cooperative rather than another and

Table 10.5 Why Did You Choose this Form of Child Care?

reason for choosing co-op. day care*	Parent Co-ops	Vol. Orgs	Worker Co-ops
-possibilities for influence	52.6	42.3	**
-wanted to participate in my child's daily life	45.8	31.7	6.5
-wanted a special pedagogics	15.8	50.8	17.4
-possibilities for parent collaboration	25.8	24.3	**
-no other existing alternatives	31.1	14.3	18.4
-close to home	35.3	21.2	40.8
-dissatisfied with municipal day care	14.2	21.2	14.4
-recommended by relatives/ friends	19.5	20.6	22.9
-economic advantages	28.9	9.0	7.0
average (& total) no. of answers:	2.9/ (555)	2.5/ (465)	1.7/ (332)
n	190	189	201

Source: WECSS Parent Study, Pestoff, 1996a, *multiple answers, add to more than 100%, **these two alternatives were not available to parents with children in worker co-ops.

whether their motives were primarily value-based, instrumental or both. We should expect their answers to differ between these three types of social enterprises, and perhaps to provide us with a profile of each type of cooperative day care service and the particular client niche they serve.

Parents could choose from either 13 or 11 alternative motives and could provide more than one answer. Parents with children in parent co-ops provided nearly three answers each, parents with children in voluntary organizations two and a half, while parents with children in worker co-ops gave less that two answers each. The first four alternatives presented in

Table 10.5 express value judgments, while the remaining five are more instrumental in their nature.

A clear profile of each type of cooperative day care service can be seen in the motives provided by each group of parents. Parents with children in *parent cooperatives* give most importance to possibilities for influence, but they are also highly motivated by wanting to participate in their child(ren)'s daily life, as well as practical issues like closeness to home, a lack of other day-care alternatives and even economic advantages. Parents with children in *voluntary organizations* give greatest priority to special pedagogics, second priority to possibilities for influence and third priority to wanting to participate in their child(ren)'s daily life. They also refer to instrumental motives, like closeness to home, dissatisfaction with municipal services and recommendations by friends or relatives. In both these two types of cooperative day care parents share some values and they have value-based, as well as instrumental, motives. Parents with children in *worker cooperatives*, however, have a very different pattern of priorities and give greatest weight to practical issues like closeness to home, other unspecified motives (not shown here) and being recommended by friends. Parents with children in worker cooperatives are clearly motivated by instrumental attitudes in their choice of day care service.

Turning to the main advantages of each form of cooperative day care services, parents with children in parent cooperatives or voluntary organizations were provided 13 alternatives plus the option of suggesting other advantages, while those with children in worker cooperatives were only given 11 alternatives, plus an unspecified category. Once again multiple answers were possible.

The parents of children in *parent cooperatives* see the greatest advantages in more participation in their child(ren)'s daily life, the possibility to influence, an enjoyable atmosphere, an engaged staff and parent collaboration, all of which receive the support of half or more of the parents in this group. The parents of children in *voluntary organizations* find the greatest advantages in an engaged staff, a good pedagogical profile, an enjoyable atmosphere and the possibility of influence, all of which receive the support of half or more of the parents in this group. Parents with children in *worker cooperatives* give greatest priority to an engaged staff, an enjoyable atmosphere and a good pedagogical profile, which receive support from about three-fourths to one-third of the parents in this group.

Thus, once again we find different profiles for various cooperative day care services, in terms of their advantages. However, an engaged staff and an enjoyable atmosphere is given as an important advantage by parents of all three types of cooperative day care services. This provides support for evidence found earlier in Chapter 9. Our WECSS Staff Study showed a greater staff engagement among workers in all three types of cooperative day care services than municipal facilities where they were previously employed (Pestoff, 1998a).

Table 10.6 Main Advantages of this Form of Day Care?

main advantages*	Parent Co-ops	Vol. Orgs	Worker Co-ops
-possibility of influence	62.6	50.8	38.4
-more participation in my child's daily life	68.4	47.1	19.9
-enjoyable atmosphere	62.6	58.2	66.2
-engaged staff	59.5	73.5	75.6
-good pedagogical profile	35.8	64.9	38.8
-parent collaboration	50.0	37.6	**
-social network	30.0	23.8	6.5
-could keep my place during pregnancy	24.7	13.8	17.9
-economic advantages	32.6	10.6	10.4
-democratically run	21.1	15.9	3.5
average (& total) number of advantages:	4.8/(915)	4.2/(793)	1.6/(323)
n	190	189	201

Source: WECSS Parent Study, Pestoff, 1996a, *multiple answers, add to more than 100%, ** this alternative wasn't available to parents with children in worker co-ops.

The disadvantages associated with each type of day care service are also typical for their organizational profile. Most or many parents in all three types of cooperative day care services state that there is no disadvantage with their cooperative day care service. While not minding about the work obligation *per se*, parents in both parent cooperatives and voluntary organizations are nevertheless critical of the additional time required by the cooperative form and they are also concerned with the difficulty of combining their roles as parents and employers. Parents with children in worker cooperatives name few specific disadvantages.

Parents answered several questions about their collaboration with the staff. Two-thirds or more of the parents with children in all three types of cooperatives feel that their collaboration with the staff is very good in general. They are even more positive about the staffs attitudes toward the children and clearly feel that the staff promotes the general comfort of the children. The majority of them is also very positive about the staff's attitudes toward parents. Differences between the three types of cooperative day care services are small, suggesting that membership *per* se doesn't play an important role in forming their attitude about their collaboration with the staff. In fact, parents with children in worker co-ops are somewhat more positive about the staff's attitudes to parents.

About one in five parents with children in parent co-ops or worker co-ops provided comments to their answers about their collaboration with the staff, while more than one of eight parents with children in voluntary organizations did so. Their comments cover a wide range of topics including: having good relations, a division of labor between the parents and staff, difficulties of being both a parent and an employer or having both roles as a parent and staff member, as well as mentioning some problems. (See Exhibit 5.A in the appendix for examples of parent comments concerning their collaboration with the staff of cooperative day care services.)

Moreover, the overwhelming majority (between 94.4 - 97.7%) of parents in all three types of cooperative day care services feel that the staff is willing to discuss the suggestions for changes and improvements put forth by parents. About one in five parents with a child in all three kinds of cooperative day care services also provided additional written comments to this question. Most parent comments about the staff's openness and willingness to discuss changes fall into one of three categories, i.e., the staff's willingness to discuss changes, the staff is willing to discuss everything but pedagogics and the staff is not willing to discuss changes.(See Exhibit 5.B for some examples of parent comments on the openness of the staff of cooperative day care services.) This question was followed by another asking parents to provide examples of changes that had actually been implemented at the suggestion of parents. More than one-third of them provided concrete examples of such changes. (See Exhibit 5.C for some illustrations of the changes brought about by parents' suggestions.)

Parents were also asked to how satisfied they were with the running and administration of their daughter's and/or son's day care cooperative. More parents with children in worker cooperatives were "very satisfied" than parents in the two other types of cooperative day care, while fewer of the former were "somewhat satisfied". However, by combining these two categories, we find that more than four-fifths of the parents in all three types of cooperative day care services are satisfied with the running and administration of their child(ren)'s day care service. Parents' attitudes about their collaboration with the staff and their satisfaction with the running and administration of their child(ren)'s day care service show similar positive levels and they do not seem to reflect the major institutional differences between these three types of cooperative day care services, nor the possibilities they provide for parental participation. One conclusion might be that such possibilities make little difference to parents, however, we feel that it would be both hasty and wrong.

Table 10.7 How Satisfied are You with the Administration and Organization of the Day Care Center?

Satisfied with administration*(%)	Parent Co-ops	Vol. Orgs	Worker Co-ops
-Very satisfied	42.9	44.3	55.6
-Somewhat satisfied	46.7	42.2	25.8
n	190	189	201

Source: WECSS Parent Study, Pestoff, 1996a, * only those satisfied are included here.

Parents judge the performance of their child's day care service on its own merits, not on some general or absolute merits of "good pedagogics" or "good child care". If there is a relatively good match between their own values and motives for choosing a particular type of day care service and if the day care service can promote such values, then parents will be satisfied. This of course may even be true for parents with children in either municipal and private day care services. Thus, differences in work obligation and holding an elective office don't reflect these parents' satisfaction or dissatisfaction with the way the day care services are run. Rather, their attitudes toward the work obligation and holding an elective office may reflect more fundamental differences in the attitudes and values of different groups of parents.

Some of them are more engaged in the early years of their child(ren)'s life than others, some enjoy both the integrative aspects of the work obligation and/or the influence provided by holding an elective office, while others do not. Those parents who want to participate would, however, probably not be satisfied, or not nearly as satisfied, if such possibilities did not exist. Thus, it is not a question of *the* best form of day care services, but rather that what is good for one group of parents may not be so for another. So, greater welfare pluralism could promote numerous different forms for providing the day care services citizens want, including municipal and private day care services, parent cooperatives, voluntary organizations and worker cooperatives.

10.C Comparisons with Municipal Day Care Services

From a parent perspective there are two main ways of comparing cooperative day care services with those provided by municipal facilities. One is based on parallel studies of the parents in two or more types of day care services, and by comparing the evaluation of different groups of parents with each other. The averages of each type of day care service are obtained and compared with each other, similar to the parallel study undertaken here of the three types of cooperative day care services. Another way is based on letting parents with experience from both types of day care services to make such comparisons themselves. This is termed a retrospective comparison; and it is the method we chose. In the WECSS Parent Study, parents were asked if they previously had a child(ren) in municipal day care services. If so, they were then asked whether the staff of cooperative day care services were more open for and concerned about parents' wishes than municipal day care facilities and how they rate cooperative day care services in comparison with municipal day care facilities. The two tables below reporting the comparative questions only include those parents who have previously had a child in municipal services and can therefore make a meaningful comparative evaluation. More than one of three parents (35.0%) with children in parent co-ops had experience from both forms, more than two of five parents (42.6%) with children in voluntary organizations had such experience, while nearly half (47.6%) of the parents with children in worker co-ops did so.

Nearly three-fourths of the parents with children in all three kinds of cooperative day care services express an appreciation of the openness and concern of the co-op's staff compared with that of municipal day care services. Half or more of the parents with children in parent co-ops or voluntary organizations who were eligible also provided comments to their comparison of staff openness and concern, while three of five with children in worker co-ops did so. The overwhelming majority of their comments emphasize either their dissatisfaction with municipal day care services or the good relations they have at their present cooperative day care center, while some say that the openness and concern of the staff is the same at both types of day care. (See Exhibit 6.A for examples of parent comments comparing the staff of cooperative and municipal day care services.)

When asked which form they feel is better, parents with children in voluntary organizations are slightly more positive about cooperative day care services. More than three of four of the parents in all types of social enterprises express a clear preference for the cooperative form compared to municipal day care services. Nearly half of the parents (48.7%) with children in both parent co-ops and municipal services provided comments to this comparison, about three of four (76.9%) of the parents with children in voluntary organizations also made comments, while about three of five parents (61.9%) with children in worker co-ops did so. As such this was the question that received the most comments from parents, indicating its saliency for them, while comparisons of staff openness and concern received the next greatest proportion of parent comments. Parent comments can be divided into three main categories. Either they stress the advantages of their cooperative, as does the overwhelming majority, the disadvantages of the municipal services and other comments, including the importance of pedagogics, that there is little difference between co-op and municipal services, etc. (See Exhibit 6.B in the appendix for some illustrations of the parent comments comparing cooperative and municipal day care services.)

Table 10.8 Is Cooperative Day Care Better than Municipal Service?

Co-op. day care is better than municipal	Parent Co-ops	Vol. Orgs	Worker Co-ops
-Better	81.5	85.5	77.4
n*	65	76	84

Source: WECSS Parent Study, Pestoff, 1996a, *only eligible parents with experience from both forms of day care answered this question.

Finally, parents were also asked to state, if they could choose freely, whether they would choose cooperative day care services for their child(ren) again, given its possible disadvantages. Nearly three-fourths or

Table 10.9 If You Could Choose Freely Would You Choose a Parent/ Worker Cooperative Again?

Would choose a co-op. again?	Parent Co-ops	Vol. Orgs	Worker Co-ops
-Yes	89.5	81.0	72.1
(md*	4.7	14.8	23.9)
n	190	189	201

Source: WECSS Parent Study, Pestoff 1996a. *The figures given here are absolute percentages, i.e., they don't exclude missing data, due to the varying amounts of missing data for these three catgories of parents.

more of the parents in all three categories expressed a clear preference for cooperative day care over municipal day care facilities. Note, however, that there was much more missing data in the answers of parents with children in worker cooperative day care services. More than one of four parents with children in parent co-ops or voluntary organizations provided comments on their preference for cooperative day care even in the future, while more than one of five parents with children in worker co-op did so. Once again their answers either emphasize the advantages of the cooperative form, which most of their comments mention, the disadvantages of the municipal form, special pedagogics or occasionally some disadvantages of the cooperative form. (See Exhibit 6.C in the appendix for some expressions of parent preferences for the cooperative form for providing day care services.)

10.D Summary and Conclusions

Summary

In this chapter we were interested in exploring an extension and adaptation of the concept of co-production to the area of personal social services and social enterprises providing such services. We presented data on three different forms of social enterprises providing day care services in Sweden, i.e., parent cooperatives, voluntary organizations and worker cooperatives. However, both parent cooperatives and voluntary organizations have a work obligation associated with membership, while worker cooperatives lack this feature, as parents can not become members. The parents of both the first two types of social enterprises express similar attitudes to the positive aspects of the work obligation. It facilitates their participation, gives a feeling of belonging and valuable insights, i.e., it enables their integration into the organization and running of cooperative day care services. These two groups attribute less weight to gaining possibilities for influence through the work obligation. Turning to elected and honorary offices, many more parents held them in parent cooperatives than voluntary organizations, while few if any parents has such possibilities to become involved in worker cooperatives, and where so only in advisory bodies. In contrast to attitudes about the work obligation, parent attitudes about their work on the board emphasize first and foremost the political aspect of holding an elective office in cooperative day care services, i.e., it increases parental influence. The integrative aspects, already noted for the work obligation, are also rated high by both groups of parents in terms of holding elective or honorary offices. The higher rate of holding elective and honorary offices in parent cooperatives than in voluntary organizations, means that the parents have greater access to influence in the former than the latter type of cooperative day care services.

Turning to reasons for choosing their preferred form of social enterprise providing day care services we noted a clear profile for each type of day care service. Influence, wanting to participate more in their child(ren)'s daily life and closeness to home provide a clear profile for parents with children in parent cooperatives. Special pedagogics, wanting to influence and wanting to participate more in their child(ren)'s daily life clearly dominate the motives of parents with children in voluntary organizations. Both these sets of parents clearly motivate their choice of cooperative day care form more in terms of expressive values than in instrumental terms. Closeness to home, a recommendation by relatives or friends and the lack of other alternatives were the main motives of parents with children in worker cooperatives, which clearly express the more instrumental attitudes of these parents.

However, having made their choice, the differences between the advantages of three types of social enterprises allow for more room for instrumental values. An enjoyable atmosphere, an engaged staff and possibility of influence are given by the parents of all three types of cooperative day care services as one of the four main advantages, while participating the child's daily life and pedagogics are still important for parents from the first two types of day care services. Few disadvantages were mentioned.

Parents strongly appreciate the willingness of the staff to discuss parents' suggestions for changes and improvements Moreover, parents in all three types of social enterprises express a similar level of satisfaction with the running and administration of their child(ren)'s day care service. However, given the clearly articulated instrumental attitude of parents with children in worker cooperatives, as opposed to the more expressive attitude of parents with children in parent cooperatives and voluntary organizations, it is an open question if parents in the latter two types of social enterprises would be as satisfied with as little influence and chance to participate as parents with children in worker cooperatives. Thus, we are suggesting that no single type of social enterprise nor organizational formula can meet the needs and requirements of all parents for day care services. Rather a greater welfare mix and welfare pluralism requires a greater diversity of forms for providing personal social services.

Many parents have previously had a child(ren) in municipal day care services, and their comparisons between cooperative and municipal services are clearly to the advantage of social enterprises in terms of the openness of the staff. They also categorically feel that social enterprises providing day care service, regardless of the type, are better than municipal services. Finally, given a free choice, they state a clear preference for social enterprises as a form, regardless of the type of social enterprise.

Conclusions

Market failure and information asymmetries make personal social services well suited for provision by third sector and nonprofit organizations, since the latter mitigates some kinds of market failure and instills more trust in the relations between the consumers and providers of such services. The enduring nature of some personal social services renders them better suited for voice than exit. Moreover, the transaction costs of providing such services via markets are prohibitive for the consumers, producers and society. All these considerations argue for third sector alternatives to both markets and politics. Here citizens as co-producers, social enterprises and cooperative social services can provide an alternative to markets and quasi-markets. They also contribute to the development of civil democracy and local cooperative self-management of social services.

Our findings require a modification of the idea of a "service democracy", where parents preferred municipal services due to the burden of responsibility and few of them saw participation in the operation of their daughter's and/or son's day care center as a value in itself. The WECSS Parent Study clearly shows that parents with a child in a parent cooperative or voluntary organization value highly the integrative aspects of the work obligation and the possibilities for participation provided by holding an elective or honorary office. Furthermore, most parents state unequivocally that alternative or cooperative day care services are better than municipal services, and they provide several reasons to motivate their choice, including the deterioration of municipal services. A service democracy may be the ideal of many Swedes, but a growing number of them want to reduce the uncertainty in their relation to the providers of enduring services, as seen in the rapid growth of cooperative day care in recent decades.

Co-production is motivated by the degree of uncertainty in the exchange between the producer and consumer of goods and services and the potential benefit to the participants from eliminating such uncertainty (Wikström, 1996). Social enterprises and cooperative social services with clear social goals and nonprofit motives help to generate trust between producers and consumers of such services, by minimizing or eliminating possibilities for opportunistic behavior. In the case of child care, some types of cooperative services social eliminate uncertainty by promoting parental participation as co-producers, i.e. by the work obligation combined with their democratic procedures and parents holding honorary offices. The creation of benefits related to the values of the parents is made possible by some types of cooperative day care centers. In particular the values of parent influence, participation in their child(ren)'s daily life, special pedagogics, feelings of belonging are important values to the parents of children in parent cooperative and voluntary organizations. Co-production eliminates the uncertainty related to interaction between producers and consumers of such services since it involves parents in the production, and their participation is the best guarantee of quality, according to one parent. Co-production both enables the parents and empowers them in fulfilling their own values related to the institutional care of their children.

It is not as easy, if at all possible, to promote the same values in worker cooperatives, nor in municipal or private day care services, but worker cooperative day care services nevertheless promote the instrumental values of the parents. In this respect it can be argued that parent co-ops and voluntary organizations day care services are unique in promoting the creation of the values related to co-production. Without the existence of this form of day care for children and without the participation and involvement of parents in the production of the cooperative day care services such values would not be created for these parents. Thus, these special forms of day care service have created value for the parents by engaging them as co-producers. Both the lives and values of the parents with children in such day care services, and most likely of their children too, would not be enriched by the possibilities provided by co-production, if such alternatives no longer existed or were curtailed for political or financial reasons. None of these values associated with co-production are available in services provided by worker co-ops, municipal or private day care services, as parent participation and co-productions are not promoted by them. Without such forms of day care services, these parents would not be able to obtain such values. Thus, co-production promotes unique values for large groups of parents. It thereby enriches publicly financed personal social services and contributes to the renewal the welfare state by turning it into a more participatory welfare society.

By providing an opportunity for the realization of the expressive values of parents social enterprises promote civil democracy and facilitate the role of citizens as co-producers. In this fashion social enterprises not only help to eliminate uncertainty in the relations between parents and the staff of day care services, they also promote greater trust between the clients and their social enterprises.

Part 3
Conclusions

11. Vision for a New Millennium?

In the final chapter we will summarize our journey into the previously uncharted waters of social enterprises and civil democracy in Sweden. Here we want to consider whether social enterprise, in particular the social services they provided in Sweden, and civil democracy can provide a model for rejuvenating the welfare state in the New Millennium. What are some of the major advantages of this particular form of providing social welfare services compared with public or private provision? What are their drawbacks and are there remedies for them? Can social enterprise provide a vision for reforming the Swedish welfare state and for turning it into a welfare society? We will first summarize the main findings in this report before trying to answer these final questions.

We defined social enterprise in the introduction in terms of their multiple social goals, which set them apart from private for-profit firms in a number of ways. We examined more closely the specific social values associated with each of the three major types of social enterprises, worker cooperatives, consumer cooperatives and voluntary organizations. Worker cooperatives promote the empowerment of workers and the enrichment of working life, consumer cooperatives facilitate the empowerment of consumers and their participation in the production process, while voluntary organizations enhance other social goals. Civil democracy was defined in terms of cooperative self-management of small social firms providing enduring personal social services, and citizens as co-producers of the services they demand.

11.A Some Theoretical Reflections

In the theoretical background to the WECSS Project we discussed several major concepts necessary for understanding the importance of and connection between enriching work environment and empowering citizens as co-producers. Much of the current debate about the role of the third sector in providing personal social services, about the nature of civil society, and about the relationship between the third sector and civil society reflect a clear neo-liberal bias that is based on a distorted and misconstrued paradigm of competition and/or conflict between the third sector and the state or between civil society and the state. Not only is this perspective inaccurate and uninformed; the main aim appears to be to delegitimize, curtail, and eventually replace the universal welfare state in the Scandinavian countries with a means-tested minimal safety-net.

Then we discussed and delimited the concept of the third sector in relation to the welfare triangle and welfare mix. We expressed a clear preference for a relational rather than a principled definition of the third sector. Our definition of this concept does not rely on American tax law and the so-called first principle constraints. Rather, it is closer to European phenomena like *l'économie sociale* or *folkrörelser*, and, moreover, it retains an interest in the democratic side of social enterprises, rather than merely considering the economic aspects. We explained the major variations between three clearly different paths to privatization, i.e., via the market, the family or the third sector. Each alternative has its unique features and promotes distinct social values.

We then explored the political dimensions of civil democracy. We saw that it is related to the various roles citizens have in modern societies, to the concepts of citizens and citizenship rather than customers and to citizen empowerment in relation to the public sector. We discuss the citizens' various roles and the different channels of influence open to them, including political accountability. We considered the role of the third sector in renewing the welfare state, by promoting horizontal solidarity, expanding the area for citizen initiatives and their participation in the production of social services, thus, turning it into a welfare society. We emphasized the importance of retaining the concept of citizen as opposed to adopting the newer usage of consumer, given the implicit but often clear political ramifications of the latter, as well as the rights and responsibilities associated with the former term. And we found that some aspects of civil democracy could be observed in recent developments in neighboring Scandinavian and European countries. However, we saw that similar ideas have made little real progress in Sweden, except perhaps for social enterprises providing day care services.

We then proceeded to consider the economic aspects of civil democracy. Market failure and information asymmetries make personal social services well suited for provision by third sector and nonprofit organizations, since they instill more trust in the relations between the consumers and providers of such services. Quasi-markets are also constrained by possibilities for opportunistic behavior on the part of the producers of personal social services. The enduring nature of some types of personal social services renders them better suited for voice than exit.

Moreover, the transaction costs of providing such services via markets are prohibitive for the consumers, producers and society. All these considerations argue for third sector alternatives to both markets and politics. Here the negotiated economy at the local or micro level, citizens as co-producers and social enterprises provide an alternative to markets and quasi-markets. They also contribute to the development of civil democracy and local cooperative self-management of social services.

Private firms in market economies most clearly distinguish the functions of owners, workers and consumers in relation to their property rights. The owners of capital are guaranteed the right to dispose of the profits accrued from a firm's production, workers and most other employees are provided hourly remuneration for the sale of their labor, while the customers or clients have the right to dispose of the goods or services acquired through their purchase. Traditionally, cooperatives differ from private firms in that they normally combine two of these functions of production, and the interests associated with them. Ownership in co-ops is either combined with the function of the producers or the consumers of the goods or services. However, cooperatives operate under one or more major constraint or deficiency. One of the most important ones is that they only recognize the interest of one of the major stakeholders that contribute to their success or failure.

Moreover, social services are primarily financed by public funds in Sweden. So, here we are mainly concerned with representing the interests of clients, personnel and financiers of social services. But, there are different ways of organizing cooperative social services in Sweden. The two main ways, illustrated by parent and worker cooperative day care services, are based on the consumer cooperative and the worker cooperative models. Each of these models institutionalizes the interests of a single group, either the consumers or producers of social services. A single group is normally represented on the board of such service providers, either the clients or the personnel. A hybrid of these two is the multi-stakeholder or mixed social service organization, which institutionally combines the interests of both the consumers and producers of social services. An additional model is found in other types of nonprofit organizations which function like cooperatives, but which nevertheless have different ways of institutionalizing the interests of the clients, personnel and perhaps other interested groups, like volunteers and sponsors. Thus, the multi-stakeholder model could provide a major institutional innovation for promoting a dialogue between providers and clients of personal social services and for dispelling the asymmetry of information between them. Multi-stake holder organizations could also engage both the staff and clients as members of the organization. Examples of multi-stakeholder cooperatives from Canada, Spain and Sweden were introduced.

Turning to social accounting, we noted that financial accounting provides a much too narrow and niggardly picture of the performance of social enterprises. External social accounting is a necessary complement to financial information systems, if we are to accurately and continually judge the goal fulfillment and performance of social enterprises providing social services. This is a logical extension of the principal/agent relationship between the owners and managers of social enterprises. Various efforts to specify a model for social reporting by not-for-profit organizations have been discussed and developed recently. Few of the existing approaches, methods and techniques for social accounting are adequate or suitable for NPOs/NGOs and new social enterprises. Most of the available approaches focus either on private or public sectors, and they fail to take into account the specific nature of social enterprises. They need to develop their own approach to social accounting. It should be normative in its nature, goal-related, report both financial and non-monetary events and short- and medium-term. Examples of social auditing by cooperatives in Canada and Italy were discussed.

Finally, the model developed by Karasek & Thorell (1990) includes three components or dimensions, e.g., psychological demands, job control and social support, but they suggest several further dimensions, i.e., client interaction, job security, etc. Initially they propose a two dimensional model based on demands and control at work. They then develop and refine their model by including social support at work. However, we proposed a further extension of their model by including an addition dimension related to the regularity of contacts with clients. The rapid deterioration in the 1990s of the psychosocial work environment for women working in day care services in Sweden was also documented.

11.B Summary of our Empirical Findings

This summary of our empirical findings is based on a comparison of the three types of cooperative day care services, and sometimes comparisons with municipal day care services. It includes sections on the growth and development of cooperative day care in Sweden, the planning of our own study of work environment and social enterprises providing day care, the parameters of such day care services, the psychosocial work environment of social enterprises providing day care services, the enrichment of women's working life and the empowerment of citizens as co-producers of social services.

11.B.1 THE GROWTH OF COOPERATIVE DAY CARE SERVICES IN SWEDEN

The (re-)appearance of cooperative day care in the 1970s and 1980s and caused a lively debate at the time. Many of these parent cooperative day care services, started in the late 1970s and early 1980s, practiced a special pedagogical philosophy, e.g., Montessori, Regio-Emilia, Walldorf, etc., not found at municipal day care facilities. They often attracted parents who were not satisfied with the pedagogical philosophy of municipal services, or what was perhaps considered as a lack of a pedagogical philosophy. This first wave of parent cooperatives took the legal status of voluntary associations, as they were the only non-municipal day care services that could qualify for public financial support prior to 1985.

Parents also began to consider access to day care a social right, rather than a dearly sought municipal privilege. With the increasing demand for day care services and the growing shortage of municipal facilities a second wave of parent cooperatives started in 1985. A change in the law made it possible for parents to form economic associations and receive public financial support on terms similar to those enjoyed by municipal day care services. Non-municipal day care services, usually known as "alternative" or "private" services in the Swedish debate, expanded dramatically after 1985. In 1988 there were just over 500 non-municipal day care centers that met public requirements for state support, but they reached nearly 1,900 at the end of 1995; an increase by three and a half times. The number of children enrolled in these non-municipal services increased from 8,500 in 1988 to 39,000 at the end of 1995; an increase of nearly five fold. On the average in 1995 nearly one of eight children enrolled in day care facilities attended non-municipal services. However, large variations can be noted for different parts of the country: in Uppsala County nearly one fourth of the children attended non-municipal facilities, while in Västerbotten in the north only about one of twenty did so.

A closer look at non-municipal day care services shows that a variety of forms are employed for organizing and running such activities; including parent co-ops, voluntary organization, worker co-ops, organizations with special pedagogics, a combination of these or "other" forms, etc. Nearly two-thirds of the "private" or non-municipal day care facilities in 1995 were either provided by parent and worker cooperatives or voluntary organizations. More than half of the non-municipal day care services were organized as parent co-ops in 1995, or 1,016 of them. Worker cooperative day care was a new form at the end of 1991, and between then and 1995 the number of worker co-ops increased from 13 to 157. In 1995 there were 250 non-municipal day care centers and after-school homes with a special pedagogics, e.g., Montessori, Regio-Emilia or Walldorf. They call themselves "parent co-ops", but usually organize themselves as a voluntary organization or foundation.

The legal form of non-municipal day care facilities is manifest at the time of their incorporation or registration. More than half of them were registered as economic associations in 1995. Three-fourths of the cooperative day care facilities chose to register their services as economic associations, which is the preferred form for cooperative firms. However, the new form of "ecumenical foundations" has rapidly become the preferred form of the Swedish Church in recent years and 115 of them were registered in 1995. It first became possible to register private for-profit or commercial day care in 1992. During the period 1992-95 the number of commercial firms increased by more than three-fold, from 41 to 215, mostly in southern Sweden.

Concerning the development of day care services, starting in 1993 municipal authorities have a legal obligation to provide day care service to for the child(ren) of any resident requesting and qualifying for it. Public finance covers between 85-88% of the costs for such services, regardless of who provides them, while parent fees make up the remainder, or 12-15%. Public financed pre-school services grew dramatically after 1975, and more than half of all children between the ages of 0-6 years old now regularly attend them in one form or another in Sweden. Nearly 40 % of all pre-school children are enrolled in day care facilities of various types, and more than 12% of them regularly attend publicly supported non-municipal day-care services. Nearly 40,000 children regularly attend nearly 2,000 non-municipal day care service. Two-thirds of these non-municipal facilities are, in fact, social enterprises providing day care services.

Such day care services are publicly financed, but their services are produced by the members of the social enterprises themselves or the staff they employ. While the financing remains public, the actual provision of services is contracted out, resulting in a division between the financing and production of public services. What does the change in organizational form, going from public to social enterprise, mean for the work relations and work environment of the staff and for the influence of clients of cooperative day care services? Exploring these questions was the main purpose of the WECSS Project.

11.B.2 The Swedish Project on Work Environment and Cooperative Social Services

In order to study work environment of social enterprises providing social services, we planned and carried out an empirical investigation, primarily with survey methods. We wanted to have a broad geographical base and we chose to study social enterprises providing day care services in six different parts of Sweden, i.e., the counties of Gothenburg & Bohus, Jämtland, Malmöhus, Stockholm, Uppsala and Västerbotten. As a first step, we drew a simple random sample in each of these counties, of approximately every third "cooperative" day care center in these six regions. Three of five indicated a willing to participate in our study. As a second step, we then complied a quasi-random sample of 57 day care services. It comprised 29 day care centers drawn from a second simple random sample among those willing to participate; 21 interesting cases, chosen on the basis of additional information provided in the first round of contacts. Worker cooperatives in Stockholm were included on the basis of a reputational sample.

Our sample included three different types of social enterprises providing day care services: 24 parent cooperatives, 16 voluntary organizations and 17 worker cooperatives. Our project design was multiple in nature, and called for studying the social enterprises themselves, as well as both their staff and clients. Thus, we undertook three different but parallel studies, an Organization Study of these 57 cooperative day care centers, a Staff Study of 244 members of the staff at these same social enterprises and a Parent Study of 580 parents to the children at these 57 day care centers. We interviewed the managers of these 57 day care centers, collected written materials during and after these visits, and distributed questionnaires for the Staff Study and the Parent Study. The response rate to the staff questionnaire was 81.7%, while that of the parents questionnaire was 70.4%. Most of the data in the WECSS Project was collected in 1994.

11.B.3 The Parameters of Social Enterprises Providing Day Care

We began the WECSS Organization Study by exploring the reasons for starting "alternative" or non-municipal day care services, which either could be negative or positive. Negative aspects of municipal services, such as the simple lack of them or wanting to avoid (the rigidities or bureaucracy of) municipal services were often given as the reason for starting social enterprises providing day care services. Positive motives of wanting to develop a special pedagogics or to increase parental influence were provided by many of these new social enterprises. Thus, it was the failure of municipal authorities to meet citizens' needs, combined with the positive attributes of the alternative day care, that lead to the growth of this new form for satisfying the needs of the parents to very young children.

From the information in the WECSS Organization Study we can get a profile of the three types of social enterprises providing day care services in terms of their starting conditions. *Parent cooperative* day care services were mainly established in one of the three metropolitan areas between 1985 - 1990. They were often started by the parents themselves to provide new services, either due to a lack of municipal day care facilities and/or to increase parental influence. They received help in getting started from municipal authorities and a regional cooperative development agency. They are mostly small facilities, normally with only one group of between 12-18 children. Their small size is one of the attractions for parents. *Voluntary organizations* were mainly started in one of the three metropolitan areas, but earlier that the other types of social enterprises providing day care services, many of them already in the 1970s. They either provided new services and/or were started by the parents and staff to promote special pedagogics and because of a lack of municipal services. They received no help getting started and they range from small to large facilities. *Worker cooperative* day care services were all started after 1990, often in rural areas, usually by the staff, either to avoid the bureaucracy of municipal day care services and/or to promote special pedagogics. They mainly provided new services, but a few took over existing municipal services. They received assistance from municipal authorities and local cooperative development agencies in getting started. They range from small to large facilities, or one to four/five groups of 12 to 15 children each.

Turning to their circumstances today, we noted some significant shortcomings in their relationship with municipal authorities. First, there was a great deal of diversity in the municipal operating contracts, and no two municipalities offered alternative day care services the same conditions of operation, e.g., parental fees, municipal grants, recruitment of children, etc. This complicates any attempts at making meaningful comparisons of operating conditions with municipal or non-municipal day care facilities, as no two social enterprises providing day care services have the same operating contracts.

Second, we found the following pattern concerning the day-to-day relations between these social enterprises and municipal authorities. The managers of social enterprises are often excluded from meetings with pertinent municipal authorities and monthly meetings with their colleagues in municipal services. On the one hand, their exclusion from these regular meetings not only makes it much more difficult for them to get the information necessary to fulfill their contract with and responsibilities to the municipal authorities and to guarantee high quality day care services. This also makes it hard for them to keep abreast of professional developments, changes in the law, etc. On the other hand, it also makes it much harder for the municipalities to follow the development of non-municipal services, to monitor their activities and to insure a good quality of service. These day care services are often provided by small, single unit facilities, which also puts them in a difficult situation when specialists are required, as they lack the necessary resources.

11.B.4 The Psychosocial Work Environment of Social Enterprises

The basis of our study of work environment and social enterprises in Sweden is the demand/control/support model of psycho-social work environment (Karasek & Theorell, 1990). This model includes several components or dimensions and each of them is important for understanding work life. A two dimensional demand/control model provides the starting point for analyzing psychosocial work environment. Then social support is added to the model. In the model both psychological demands and staff control or decision autonomy ranges from low to high, resulting, as we saw earlier, in four different types of jobs: 1) high strain jobs, 2) active jobs, 3) low strain jobs and 4) passive jobs. We are primarily interested in the first two categories, and in exploring if and how social enterprises can turn high-strain jobs into active ones. The latter involve high levels of performance without negative psychological strain, since they provide high degrees of control. Such jobs result in learning and growth that is conductive both to health and productivity. Women are traditionally found in high strain jobs, while men clearly dominate active occupations and have the highest income and job satisfaction.

Social enterprises and cooperatives, by virtue of their internal social and political processes, extend decision autonomy or control of work and facilitate the participation of employees in decision-making. They, therefore, have the potential of turning high strain jobs into active jobs. Day care services are typically psychologically demanding jobs, since they require working with many small children, but a change in the organizational model, i.e., going from municipal facilities to provision by social enterprises implies greater control of work by the staff over what is done, how it is done and when it is done.

First, we noted that few of the staff members of any social enterprise providing day care services previously had any direct personal experience with cooperatives of any type. Some notable differences existed concerning the staff's motives for choosing work for the three types of social enterprises. The staff of all three of them indicated that "wanting a meaningful job" was most important in their decision, and the staff of both parent and worker co-ops stated that "increased staff influence" was next most important, while the staff of voluntary organizations gave preference to "a special (pedagogical) profile" as their second most important motive for choosing to work for a social enterprise providing day care services.

The psychological demand profile of the staff of worker cooperatives clearly reflected the fact that they were their own employers and they alone were responsible for the success or failure of their day care services. By contrast, the psychological demand profile of the staff of parent co-ops also reflected their organizational characteristics, where parents are both the employers and clients. Fewer members of the staff of parent co-ops had good contact with the management, i.e., the parents, and more of them complained that they got too little praise. A larger proportion of the staff of voluntary organizations claimed they had varied work, untied and free work, but too much responsibility, while fewer of them claimed that they had too much to do or physically heavy and demanding work. Thus, the work situation for the staff of worker co-ops may be more demanding, but it also involved fewer conflicts or more agreement within the social enterprise itself. The staff parent co-ops often had the lowest scores in terms of collective or group influence, while the staff of both parent co-ops and voluntary organizations reported lower individual influence. The general impression was that staff influence was greater in worker co-ops, mid-range in voluntary organizations and lowest in parent co-ops.

We found that worker cooperatives were subject to less parent participation, but the parents more often showed respect and recognition, combined with fewer parent demands and less interference, while the staff of voluntary organizations experienced more parent participation, demands and interference than the other two types of day care services. Voluntary organizations and parent cooperatives more readily promoted an active and positive interface between producers and clients, or the staff and parents, and voluntary organizations also more readily facilitated communication between the parents and staff. The staff of parent co-ops expressed the least positive attitudes, in terms of the effects of their collaboration with parents. In terms of potential changes in the day care services brought about by parent participation, the staff of the voluntary organizations was often most positive, while that of the worker co-ops was usually least positive.

The staff of worker cooperatives expressed a greater willingness to improve the children's play environment, fewer conflicts among them concerning trade-off with other values and a greater willingness to accept lower wages, if necessary, to improve their work environment. The staff of parent cooperatives and voluntary organizations had similar, but lower scores on most of these items, but at the same time the staff of parent co-ops was less willing to make a trade-off between their own wages and work environment for improving the children's play environment. They also had somewhat more conflicts over such matters, and were less willing to accept lower wages for making improvements in their own work environment. Thus, the staff of parent co-ops appeared less satisfied with their present work environment.

Some more general conclusions can be reached from the WECSS Staff Study about the work environment of social enterprises providing day care services. First, the worker cooperatives are consistently rated higher by their staff on most of the over 200 items employed in our study of psychosocial work environment. This should not be simply interpreted as worker cooperatives provide a superior model for worker empowerment. Rather the worker cooperative model is based on organizational structures that facilitate group processes that are positive for promoting the interest of workers/employees. But, on the other hand, it meant greater responsibilities and was often accompanied by more signs of stress. Voluntary organizations appeared often to function like mixed or multi-stakeholder organizations, with the big difference that they had a common ideology or pedagogical perspective which united the interests of various stakeholders. Parent cooperatives often demonstrated several signs of dysfunctional parent/staff relations, which detracted from their psychosocial work environment.

The organizational logic of these different types of social enterprises are clearly played out in their answers on employer/employee relations. The staff of worker cooperatives were their own employers, the staff of parent cooperatives were the employees of their clients, while the staff of voluntary organizations were jointly members and employees of the day care service. It is obvious from the materials in the WECSS Staff Study that parent cooperatives allowed for too little staff influence in relation to their qualifications and responsibility.

Taken as a group, however, all three types of social enterprises were rated much better in term of their psychosocial work environment than municipal day care services. Social enterprises appear to turn high-stress jobs into active jobs by promoting structures and processes for providing more decision authority and control, more social support, and often more client involvement. Thus, social enterprises taken together, as well as each of these three types, should be given much closer and more serious consideration as a way of improving the psychosocial work environment, renewing and enriching working life, providing good jobs and reforming the public sector in advanced welfare states.

11.B.5 The Enrichment of Women's Working Environment

The great majority the staff of all three types of social enterprises clearly preferred working for a social enterprise compared with municipal day care services. In almost all respects of work life social enterprises were rated better or clearly better than municipal day care services by the staff of all three types of cooperative services. In general terms, the staff of worker cooperatives was clearly the most positive about improvements in their current work situation compared with municipal day care services. The staff of parent cooperatives and voluntary organizations demonstrated lower levels of improvement. Finally, given the chance to do it all over again, two-thirds of staff of worker co-ops, but only one-third of the staff in parent co-ops and voluntary organizations would definitely choose the cooperative form again. However, only a small fraction of the respondents in any type of social enterprise would consider working in municipal day care services again.

The staff of worker co-ops have both the freedom and responsibility to make decisions on their own, not only as independent day care facilities, but also their own employers. It comes, therefore, as no great surprise that they experience the most positive changes when comparing their current situation with that of working for municipal services. The positive changes between municipal day care and parent co-ops or voluntary organizations appeared much smaller. This should not, however, detract from several areas, particularly those related to self-development and co-determination, where the staff of parent co-ops and voluntary organizations also noted substantial improvements over their previous situation as employees in municipal day care.

The comparison with municipal day care services, by those who had worked for both forms clearly demonstrated that social enterprises in Sweden provide good jobs in the fullest meaning of the word. In Karasek and Theorell's terms work in social enterprises is psychologically demanding, but it provides high decision latitude, and high social support for the workers. These work-life attributes stand in sharp contrast with those found in the services provided by the large hierarchical bureaucratic organizations often associated with the public sector services in Sweden and elsewhere. In this sense the social enterprise model can not only help to transform social services jobs into active, participative and interactive jobs, it can also help to enrich the work-life of the women employed there. This suggests that one of the quickest and most direct ways of enriching work life, redesigning work and promoting human resource management in the personal social service sector in Sweden would be to decentralize the provision of social services as far as possible and to let social enterprises provide them.

Moreover, we also noted that the women employed in worker cooperative day care services were more positive about these organizational changes than their colleagues were in parent co-ops. Parent co-ops, however, promote other values, such as greater parental influence, greater parental participation in the daily life of their child(ren). There are clearly two sides to the coin of organizational change, depending on which model of change is employed. Differing group interests and group conflicts are not completely resolved by greater participation of a single group in the decision making of social enterprises. Greater worker participation does empower the workers, but it does not necessarily promote the interests of the clients. Similarly, greater consumer participation does empower the clients, but does not necessarily promote the interest of the workers.

This, in turn, suggests the limits of institutionalizing the interest of a single group in the decision-making structures of a social enterprise. Organizational changes of work environment that rely on social enterprises may improve the work environment, but nevertheless result in some trade-offs between the interest of workers and clients. However, organizational changes based on multi-stakeholder models can provide the supporting structures necessary for promoting the interests of more than a single stake-holder. Multi-stakeholder organizations recognize the legitimate interest of several groups that contribute to the success of a social enterprise, and they provide for the representation of these interests in the institutions of internal decision-making.

Social enterprises can, as our study clearly shows, enrich the working life of Swedish women and empower them in their work relations. We do not suggest that social enterprises can resolve all the problems relating to women's unequal position in the labor market, but they can perhaps reduce their dependency on the state both as workers and consumers, while augmenting their influence in both these areas at the same time. Women gain greater control over their jobs and/or the services provided through their greater participation and influence in the decision-making process of social enterprises. Which group stands to gain the most depends on who is a member and which model of social enterprise is employed.

Enriching the work life of civil servants and improving their work environment are important and legitimate concerns of many tens of 1,000s of women and men working in the large bureaucracies of the public sector in Sweden and elsewhere. Given the loss of productivity, the poor quality of services, the high costs of treating stress related symptoms and absenteeism due to stress related sickness, etc.; improving the work environment is an important economic, social and political problem facing the welfare state in the New Millennium. Efforts to reform the welfare state should take improving the work environment into account. However, the public debate in Sweden seems only to focus on one thing at a time. Given the current historically high level of unemployment, the third sector and social enterprises are only conceived of in terms of their potential job creation. Jobs are, of course, necessary; but good jobs are clearly preferable to bad ones. Why not try to get both at the same time?

Prior to that the potential contribution of social enterprises was framed in terms of providing cheaper services, and this was the major motive for enlisting their increased involvement in the production of personal social services. Cheaper services are of course desirable, but better quality services at the same price would be preferred by many, if not most Swedes. A more engaged staff is one of the best guarantees of good service quality. Social enterprises can contribute to greater staff engagement, but this varies with the organizational model chosen.

11.B.6 The Empowerment of Citizens as Co-Producers

Parents were asked about their motives for choosing the present form of social enterprise providing day care services for their child(ren), and we noted a clear profile for each type of day care service. Influence, wanting to participate more in their child(ren)'s daily life and closeness to home provide a clear profile for parents with children in parent cooperatives. Special pedagogics, wanting to influence and wanting to participate more in their child(ren)'s daily life clearly dominate the motives of parents with children in voluntary organizations. Both these sets of parents clearly motivate their choice of a day care form more in terms of expressive values than in instrumental terms. Closeness to home, a recommendation by relatives or friends and the lack of other alternatives were the main motives of parents with children in worker cooperatives, which clearly express the more instrumental attitudes of these parents.

Many parents have previously had a child(ren) in municipal day care services, and their comparisons between cooperative and municipal services are clearly to the advantage of cooperatives in terms of the openness of the staff of all types of cooperatives. They also categorically feel that cooperative day care service, regardless of the type, is better than municipal services. Finally, given a free choice, they state a clear preference for the cooperative form, regardless of the type of social enterprise.

Our findings require a modification of the idea of a "service democracy", where parents prefer municipal services due to the burden of responsibility and few of them saw participation in the operation of their daughter's and/or son's day care center as a value in itself. The WECSS Parent Study clearly shows that parents with a child in a parent cooperative or voluntary organization valued highly the integrative aspects of the work obligation and the possibilities for participation provided by holding an elective or honorary office. Furthermore, most parents stated unequivocally that alternative or cooperative day care services were better than municipal services, and they provided several reasons to motivate their choice, including the deterioration of municipal services. A service democracy may be the ideal of many Swedes, but a growing number of them want to reduce the uncertainty in their relation to the providers of enduring services, as seen in the rapid growth of social enterprises providing day care services in recent decades.

Co-production is motivated by the degree of uncertainty in the exchange between the producer and consumer of goods and services and the potential benefit to the participants from eliminating such uncertainty. Social enterprises and cooperative social services with clear social goals and nonprofit motives help to generate trust between producers and consumers of such services, by minimizing or eliminating possibilities for opportunistic behavior. In the case of child care, some types of social enterprises eliminate uncertainty by promoting parental participation as co-producers, i.e. by the work obligation combined with their democratic procedures and parents holding honorary offices. The creation of benefits related to the values of the parents is made possible by some types of social enterprises. In particular the values of parent influence, participation in their child(ren)'s daily life, special pedagogics, feelings of belonging were important values to the parents of children in parent cooperative and voluntary organizations. Co-production eliminated the uncertainty related to interaction between producers and consumers of such services since it involves parents in the production, and their participation was the best guarantee of quality. Co-production both enabled the parents and empowered them in fulfilling their own values related to the institutional care of their children.

It is not as easy, if at all possible, to promote the same expressive values in worker cooperatives, nor for that matter in municipal or private day care services. But worker cooperative day care services nevertheless promote the instrumental values of the parents. In this respect it can be maintained that parent co-ops and voluntary organizations day care services are unique in promoting the creation of the values related to co-production. Without the existence of this form of day care for children and without the participation and involvement of parents in the production of the cooperative day care services such values would not be created for these parents. Thus, these special forms of day care service have created value for the parents by engaging them as co-producers. Both the lives and values of the parents with children in such day care services, and most likely of their children too, would not be enriched by the possibilities provided by co-production, if such alternatives no longer existed or were curtailed for political or financial reasons. None of these values associated with co-production are available in services provided by worker co-ops, municipal or private day care services, as parent participation and co-productions are not promoted by them. Without forms of day care services that were based on active parent participation, these parents would not be able to obtain such values. Thus, co-production promotes unique values for large groups of parents. It thereby enriches publicly financed personal social services and contributes to the renewal the welfare state by turning it into a more participatory welfare society.

11.C Vision for a New Millennium?

In the empirical part of the WECSS Project we saw that worker cooperatives were consistently rated higher by the staff. This should not be simply interpreted as worker cooperatives provide a superior model for worker empowerment. Rather the worker cooperative model is based on organizational structures that facilitate group processes that are positive for promoting the interest of workers/employees. This may, however, take place at the expense of parent involvement and engagement. Voluntary organizations appear often to function like mixed or multi-stakeholder cooperatives, with the big difference that they had a common ideology or pedagogical perspective which united the interests of various stakeholders. Parent cooperatives often demonstrated several clear signs of dysfunctional parent/staff relations, which detracted from their psychosocial work environment.

Taken as a group, however, all three types of cooperatives were rated much better in term of their psychosocial work environment than municipal day care services. Social enterprises providing day care services appear to turn high-stress jobs into active jobs by promoting structures and processes for providing more decision authority and control, more social support, and even more client involvement.

Taking into account client relations, we maintain both parent cooperatives and voluntary organizations turn clients into co-producers. Parents in all three types of social enterprises express a similar level of satisfaction with the running and administration of their child(ren)'s day care service. Thus, our materials suggest that no single type of cooperative nor organizational formula can meet the needs and requirements of all parents. Rather a greater welfare mix and welfare pluralism requires a greater diversity of forms for providing personal social services.

Voluntary organizations appear, in this context, to provide an alternative to both the worker and parent cooperatives. They were often evaluated more positively by their staff in terms of improving the work environment, than were parent cooperatives; but they were also rated more positively by the parents in terms of promoting the value of parent influence than by parents with children in worker co-ops. Voluntary organizations appear to be rudimentary form of multi-stakeholder organizations that are able to combine the interests of both groups in the pursuit of a common pedagogical program. Whether this is possible for other types of social services remains to be seen. More formal multi-stockholder institutions in other areas may provide the necessary basis for facilitating the trade-off between different and sometimes conflicting interest of various groups that contribute to the success of a social enterprise.

11.C.1 Different Paths to Privatization

Market failure and information asymmetries make personal social services well suited for provision by third sector and nonprofit organizations, since the latter mitigates some kinds of market failure and instills more trust in the relations between the consumers and providers of such services. The enduring nature of some personal social services renders them better suited for voice than exit. Moreover, the transaction costs of providing such services via markets are prohibitive for the consumers, producers and society. All these considerations argue for third sector alternatives to both markets and politics. Here citizens as co-producers and social enterprises can provide an alternative to markets and quasi-markets. They also contribute to the development of civil democracy and local cooperative self-management of social services.

Returning briefly to the question of the different paths to privatization and shifts in the welfare mix, we should contrast briefly the privatization of social services taking place in Sweden with that in Central and Eastern Europe. We can note that the following pattern at the micro-level for reforming social services in Central and Eastern Europe. The market, has thus, far proved highly uninterested in providing social services for the overwhelming majority of citizens in Central and Eastern European countries. Most citizens quite simply lack the purchasing power to make this a lucrative alternative and to attract firms to enter the "market" for personal social services. The third sector also falls short of the need for social services in Central and Eastern Europe. Moreover, it is highly dependent on public funding, and thus its possibilities of expanding to fill the vacuum left by the withdrawal of state are sharply curtailed by the lack of funds. Thus, privatization of the provision of social services in most CEE countries is mandated by the IMF and World Bank, and the "social safety net" recommended by them and other international actors will replace universally provided enterprise social services. This appears primarily to follow the path of pushing or dumping responsibility for providing social services on to the family and to women. This in turn means that women have to provide the overwhelming bulk of such services; but no longer in their professional roles as paid practitioners or professional providers of public social services, but rather as unemployed and unpaid housewives, single mothers and/or daughters. Thus, women are being de-franchised in mass from their previous working and human rights and forced to return to the fold of the "small world" of the household, with no escape in sight. For many it may seem like exchanging one type of tyranny for another, changing the tyranny of the communist system for that of the household, with all its unpaid responsibilities, but no rights what-so-ever.

By contrast, the path followed in Sweden promises to be much more positive for its citizens and for its women in particular, as it is primarily based on a democratization and cooperativization of the provision of personal social services. Only a small amount of the day care services are provided today by private commercial for-profit firms. The overwhelming proportion of day care services are provided by social enterprises of the three types examined above. Moreover, privatization in Sweden clearly results in numerous improvements of work life, work environment and co-determination, when any of the three types of social enterprise models are employed. Furthermore, women comprise 95-100 per cent of the staff of parent co-ops, voluntary organizations and worker co-ops providing day care services. Thus, the improvements in work life documented herein are by-and-large improvements experienced by professional paid women in Sweden.

It is, therefore, highly misleading, if not simply inaccurate, to argue that the privatization of personal social services in Sweden is merely a disguised or hidden marketization. Rather, opposition to privatization of the Swedish type implies support for maintaining a total public monopoly of production of personal social services, in the name of an even more illusive equality between groups. But, now it also means, intentionally or not, being opposed to concrete models for the enrichment and improvement of work life of Swedish women in the public sector, to citizen empowerment as co-producers, to promoting other social values enshrined by social enterprises, and/or to the rejuvenation of the welfare state by transforming it into a welfare society.

Many critics note that the time has come to rethink the welfare state in a fundamental way (Giddens, 1994 & 1996, Blair, 1998, Ministry for Welfare Reform, 1998). In many European countries socialist are currently concentrated on protecting the welfare state against attacks of the neo-liberals. The welfare state was founded on a "class compromise" nearly 50 years ago. But social conditions have changed radically in all European countries since then. Change is inevitable, not least due to globalization, European integration, the communications revolution, etc. The welfare state has been less than successful in keeping up with these changes, in alleviating poverty or in producing large scale income or wealth redistribution (*ibid.*). Moreover, it must be radically rejuvenated to meet the needs of today's citizens not yesterday's.

A new social contract for welfare is necessary today. It should not merely dispense funds and services to passive objects of various programs. It should aim at empowering both the workers and clients of these services, as citizens and co-producers. Moreover, it should pay attention to various social cleavages, like gender, age, work status, ethnic origin, etc.; and not only to class. In particular, it should focus much more on the position of the young, women, unemployed, the elderly and various minority or excluded groups. It must find ways to provide them with a stake in the rapidly changing societies of Europe and to involve them actively in improving their own future. All groups in European societies must be guaranteed a stake and active role in forming a welfare society in the New Millennium, not only those mobilized in previous decades. But in order to do so we must move beyond the market and state. We must develop social enterprises and civil democracy; we must encourage citizens to engage themselves actively as citizens and co-producers; we must facilitate multi-stakeholder organizations and social auditing. If we succeed we can rejuvenate the welfare state from within and transform it into a participatory welfare society in the New Millennium.

11.C.2 THE NEED FOR FURTHER RESEARCH

Our study of Swedish women's work environment in social enterprises focused on one clearly delimited segment of personal social services, i.e., day care services. We hope that it can contribute to a greater understanding and pluralism of potential models for enriching work life, empowering citizens as co-producers and rejuvenating the welfare state. No single model is universally applicable to *all* segments of work life nor *all* types of production, *all* types of services nor for *all* types of clients or consumers. Neither public, private nor cooperative models alone provide a panacea nor *the* model for producing all types of goods and services for everyone in modern societies. Solutions based simply on privatizing, on guaranteeing continued public provision or on running it as a social enterprise, all fall short of the mark. Thus, we do not intend to propose *the* solution to the problems facing the welfare state at the turn of the century, but rather to propose *one* solution to *one* type of problem for *one* type of service in *one* welfare European state. It may have some relevance for other types of problems or for social services in some other countries. But, were it to be interpreted as *the* solution, we would have clearly failed in our endeavor. However, in combination with other solutions to other problems facing the public sector, it can contribute to enriching working life, to empowering citizens as co-producers, and, thereby to rejuvenating the welfare state.

This study suggests that the distinctive social values promoted by social enterprises providing social services should be observable in other areas, like chronic long-term health care; elderly care, both domestic and institutional; handicap care, both domestic and institutional; education, etc. In all such areas social enterprises have developed in recent years in Sweden and in other European countries. These developments need to be studied closer in order to understand their unique contributions, to the enrichment of work life, to the improvement of the psychosocial work environment, to developing good jobs, to the empowerment of citizens as co-producers and to promoting civil democracy. There is no reason to believe that such benefits are restricted to day care services, nor to Sweden. Rather, we expect that many of the beneficial aspects of social enterprise providing social services noted here will also be found in other areas and other countries. They probably take somewhat different expressions, due to variations in laws, the organizational constraints and structural differences between various sectors of personal social service provision. Moreover, the interaction between the producers and consumers of these social services will also vary with differences in these organizational and sectoral constraints. The nature of this relationship is important for the development of good jobs and for empowering citizens as co-producers.

Such differences will need to be better understood before the contribution of social enterprises can be fully appreciated and evaluated in these other service sectors. We do not expect that social enterprises providing social services in these other areas will be identical with that found in day care services. Nor do we assume that the differences noted here between different types of social enterprises providing day care will always be the same in other areas of personal social service. But we do, however, expect that there will be many similarities. We also expect that these similarities will be greater than the differences between social enterprises, on the one hand, and the public and/or private for-profit provision of such services, on the other hand. Thus, we feel that there is a strong case for continuing the research started here, by extending it to other areas of personal social services in Sweden where social enterprises and cooperative social services have also taken root and to explore them in other countries.

We also feel that comparisons of Swedish social enterprises and cooperative social services with those found in other parts of Europe is well motivated, and perhaps also with those found in Japan and elsewhere. In particular in countries like Italy, Spain and France, where social enterprises have grown rapidly in recent decades; but also in countries like Germany and the Netherlands, where established voluntary organizations have traditionally played a more important, prominent and active role in providing personal social services; not to forget of course our Nordic neighbors, Denmark, Finland and Norway. In all these countries, it seems worthwhile to compare social enterprises providing social services with those found in Sweden, in particular in terms of being able to promote the social values associated with these social enterprises. But in order to do so we must strive to break the simple black/white, left/right ideological domination of the public vs. private perspective of providing social services. We must move beyond the market and state. We need to recognize the contribution of social enterprises providing social services for the unique social values they promote. We must stop trying to reduce the third sector and social enterprises to the lowest possible public or private denominator, and we must stop trying to perceive of their contribution in simple economic terms that are measures or aggregated solely in financial terms.

The main reason for recognizing social enterprises and cooperative social services in their own right are, of course, the enrichment of work life, the improvement of the psychosocial work environment, the development of good jobs, the empowerment of citizens as co-producers and the promotion of civil democracy. Persons who do not value such social goals will of course not be attracted by social enterprises. Others might argue that the same social goals could be promoted by public services of private firms. We however, strongly disagree with them. However, those who do value such goals and who feel that they are best promoted by social enterprises, will hopefully find food for thought in this book, and perhaps even encouragement to continue their study of this unique phenomenon and to promote such values and objectives.

This book might then contribute to helping to place these important social values on the research agenda of the social science in Sweden and perhaps also maybe to make a contribution to the public debate about the future of the welfare state, the renewal of the public sector and the transformation of the welfare state into a welfare society. If the social values promoted by social enterprises gain broader recognition in Swedish social science research and in the public debate, they may comprise a vision for the New Millennium. If the welfare state can not be rejuvenated from within, by expanding the room for citizen participation, by promoting social enterprises and civil democracy, then it may become a historical relic. It faces declining support by citizens who lost faith in its ability to provide the services they wanted, at the quality they expected, and at a price they were willing to pay. No social institution can survive without the support of its citizens, without renewing its legitimacy in the younger generation that are replacing the older citizens, who first built the existing social institutions. To earn and retain their support, the welfare state must grow and develop to fit the needs and values of today's population, not merely reflect those of yesterday's.

The rapid and unexpected collapse of communism in Central and Eastern Europe is perhaps an omen. Moreover, the minimal safety net promoted there by the IMF and World Bank for the "deserving poor", to replace the previous enterprise welfare state bears witness to what certain groups would like to replace the universal welfare state of Sweden and Europe with. Unless alternatives are actively developed for rejuvenating the welfare state from within, for providing more room for citizen participation as co-producers and for developing it into a welfare society, it too faces a real risk of loosing legitimacy and ultimately of collapsing under its own weight. In military strategy it is often said that the best defense is to take the offensive. Perhaps it is time for those who support the universal social values underpinning welfare state to ask whether there might not be something to learn from this. If offense is the best defense, then the uncompromising defense of the existing welfare state institutions in all the details that contributed to its original popularity and legitimacy might only speed the ultimate collapse of the existing institutions. Perhaps then the best way to prevent its collapse, and with it the loss of the universal values enshrined by it, is to rejuvenate it from within by the enrichment of work life, by the improvement of the work environment, by the development of good jobs, by the empowerment of citizens as co-producers and by the promotion of civil democracy.

Thus, the question whether social enterprises and civil democracy provide a vision for the New Millennium might be tentatively answered in the following fashion. Without a vision for developing and rejuvenating the welfare state into a welfare society and without the development of civil democracy, the welfare state of today will most likely collapse under its own weight and become a relic of the past. In addition to growing resistance to tax increases and to growing possibilities for capital to avoid high tax countries, the rapid internationalization of the economy will erode support for the welfare state of today. Internationalization of business not only facilitates social dumping, but the isomorphic tendencies promoted by global competition and multi-national companies often result in their outright rejection of the universal welfare state. The massive "roll-back" campaigns of organized business can only be met by an invigorating vision for the future rejuvenation of the welfare state in the New Millennium. Hopefully this book will make a small contribution to that vision.

References

Abrahamson, P., 1991; "Welfare and Poverty in the Europe of the 1990s: Social Progress or Social Dumping?", *International Journal of Health Services*, v. 21/2:237-64.

Ackoff, G., 1981; *Creating the Corporate Future: Plan or be Planned For*, New York: J. Wiley.

Ajzen, I., Fishbein, M., 1980; *Understanding Attitudes and Predicting Social Behavior*, Englewood Cliffs, NJ: Prentice Hall.

Aldrich, H. & R. Stern, 1983; "Resource Mobilization and the Creation of US Producer's Cooperatives, 1835-1935", *Economic and Industrial Democracy*, v. 4:371-406.

Alfredsson, B. & G. Cars, 1996; *De boende som medarbetare - Sjävförvaltning i Holma*, Stockholm: SABO, rap. nr. 61.

Ambjörnsson, R., 1988; *Den skötsamme arbetaren*, Stockholm: Carlssons.

Anderson, E., 1983; *Social Audit: a Key to Excellence*, Ann Arbor, MI: NASCO, No. American Students of Cooperation.

Anheier, H., 1997; "The Nonprofit Sector in Germany: a Brief Introduction", Baltimore & Stockholm: conference paper.

Anheier, H. & M. Knapp, 1990; "An editorial statement", *Voluntas*, v. 1/1:1-12.

Anheier, H. & Seibel, W., (eds), 1990; *The Third Sector: Comparative Studies of Nonprofit Organizations*, W. de Gruyter, Berlin & New York.

Antman, P., 1996; *Välfärdsprojektet: Barn och äldreomsorg, Sverigedelen*, Stockholm: Socialdept. Skriftserie: *Fakta/kunskap*, nr. 5.

Aronson, G., Lantz, A., Westlander, G., 1992; *Akademiker under 90-talet. En studie av SACO-medlemmarnas arbetsvillkor*, Undersökningsrapport 1992:11, Stockholm: Arbetsmiljöinstitutet.

ASS/SCB, 1994; *Arbetsmiljön 1989/93*, Stockholm & Örebro: *Statistiska meddelanden*, AM 68 SM 9401.

Babchuck, N. & A. Booth, 1969; "Voluntary Associational Membership: a Longitudinal Analysis", *American Sociological Review*, v. 34:31-45.

Babchuck, N. & J.N. Edwards, 1965; "Voluntary Associations and the Integration Hypothesis", *Social Inquiry*, v. 35.

Barry, B., 1971; "Exit, Voice & Loyalty. A Review Article", *British Journal of Political Science*, 4:79-107.

Bartlett, W., 1996; "Square Pegs in Round Holes: the Privatization of Guidance Services", Trento: conf. paper, 19pp.

Bartley, K. & S. Hanson, 1994; *Barnomsorg i tiden;* Gothenburg: Dept. of Sociology.

Belkaoui, A., 1984; *Socio-Economic Accounting*; Westport, CN & London: Quorum Books.

Bell, D., 1973; *The coming of the post-industrial society: a venture in social forecasting*, New York: Basic Books.

Ben-Nar, A., 1986; "Non-profit organizations: why do they exist in market economies?" in S. Rose-Ackerman (ed.), *the Economics of Nonprofit Institutions. Studies in Structure and Policy*, Oxford & NY: Oxford Univ. Press.

Ben-Nar, A. & T. v. Hoomissen, 1994; "The Governance of Nonprofit Organizations: Law & Policy", *Nonprofit Management & Leadership*, v.4; Twin-Cities: University of Minnesota Press.

Berg, E., 1987; "Det civila samhället", *Festskrift till prof. skytteanus Carl Arvid Hessler*, Uppsala: Acts Universitatus Upsaliensus, no. 103.

Berrefjord, O. & G. Hernes, 1989; "Storforetak, marked og burokrati" *Forhandlingsökonomi i Norden*, Nielsen, K. & O.K. Pedersen, (eds); Copenhagen & Oslo: DJÖF and Tano.

Berrefjord, O., 1981; *Norsk maktutrednings slutrapport* /Norwegian Power Investigation's Final Report; Oslo: NOU 1981:22.

Berrefjord, O., 1982; *Rafnes-saken forhandlingsökonomien i aksjon*, Olso: Universitets forlaget.

Blair, T., 1998; "Ny väg för Europa vänster"/New Way for the Left in Europe, *Dagens Nyheter & The Independent*, 9 April, 1998.

Blake, D.H., *et al.*, 1976; *Social Auditing: Evaluating the Impact of Corporate Programs*, New York: Praeger Publs.

Blomkvist, K., 1993; "Privata daghem och fritidshem—blir fler", Stockholm: Socialstyrelsen, BF-enheten.

Bogason, P., 1994; "Community Power Based on Institutional Change", Berlin: IPSA conf. paper.

Bold., J., 1991; "Accounting for Change: Co-ops and the Social Audit", Ch. 5 in Fairbairn, B. (ed.), *Co-operatives & Community Development - Economics in a Social Perspective*, Saskatoon: Center for Co-op. Studies, Univ. of Saskatchewan.

Borzaga, C., 1998; "Multi-Stakeholder Organizations, an e-mail message", Trento: University of Trento, Dept. of Economics, 21 April, 1998 at 14h37:27.

Borzaga, C., & L. Mittone, 1997; *The Multi-Stakeholder vs. The Nonprofit Organization*, Trento: Univ. of Trento, Dept. of Economics, Discussion Paper no. 7

Bowen, H.R., 1953; *Social Responsibility of the Businessmen*, New York: Harper.

Braverman, H., 1974 & 1975; *Labor and Monopoly Capitalism: the degradation of work in the twentieth century*, New York: Monthly Review Press.

Breton, G. & L. Côté, 1995; "Agency Relationship and Stakeholder Theory Revisited", Brussels: Workshop on Accounting in its Organizational and Social Context.

Brochorst, A., 1990; "Political Motherhood and Child Care Policies", *Gender and Caring: Work and Welfare in Britain & Scandinavia*, Ungerson, C. (ed.); NY & London: Harvester Wheatsheaf, pp. 160-178.

Campbell, J.P, 1990; "The Role of Theory in Industrial and Organizational Psychology", Dunnette M.D. and Hough L.M. (eds.) *Handbook of Industrial and Organizational* Psychology, Palo Alto, CA: Consulting Psychologists Press.

Carrol, A.B. & G.W. Beiler, 1975; "Landmarks in the Evolution of the Social Audit", *Academy of Management Journal*, 18/3:589-599.

Cars, G., 1994; "Utvärdering av utvecklingsinsatser i projektområdena Kroksbäck, Holma, Rosengård och Persborg", Stockholm: KTH rapport.

Castano, J., 1990; "The Health Co-operatives in Catalan", Barcelona: conference paper.

CGM, 1994; I *Rapporto sulla Cooperazione Sociale*, Milano.

CGM, 1997; II *Raporto sulla Cooperazione Sociale del Italia*, Torino.

Chandler, J.A., 1993; "The consumer, citizens and charters", The Waves of Change - Strategic Management in the Public Services, 5-6/4-93, Sheffield.

Christensen, T., 1996; "Inter- and Intra-Class Solidarity", Denmark: ISR conference paper.

Chubb, J. & T. Moe, 1990; "Market Forces in Education", *American Political Science Review*, v. 84/2:549-567.

Clarkson, M.B.A., 1995; "A Stakeholder Framework for Analyzing & Evaluating Corporate Social Performance", *Academy of Management Review*, v. 20/1:92-117.

Co-operative Union of Canada, 1985; *Social Auditing: a Manual for Co-operative Organizations*, Toronto: CUC, Social Audit Task Force.

Cooper, C. L., & M. Davidson, 1987; "Sources of stress at work and their relation to stressors in non- working environments", Kalimo, R., El-Batawi, M.A:, Cooper, C.L. (eds). *Psychosocial factors at work, and their Relation to Health*, England: World Health Organization.

Coser, L., 1956; *The Functions of Social Conflict*, London: Routledge and Kegan Paul.

Crouch, C., 1985; "Exit & Voice in the Future of the Welfare State", *Government and Opposition*, v. 20/3:407-421.

Cyert, R.M. & J.G. March, 1963; *A Behavioral Theory of the Firm*, Englewood Clifts: Prentice Hall.

Dagens Nyheter, 10/1-90, Claes Örtendahl; 18/1-90, "Missnöjd personal kartläggs"; 23/1-90, A. Christensen, "Barnomsorg i den svenska fabriken"; 29/1-90, D. Tarschys, "Barnomsorgens förlorade år"; R. Premfors, 17/11-94; H. Ben Habib & F. Andersson, 22/5-97;

Day, P., 1992; "Accountability", Birmingham: conference paper.

Deacon, B. 1992; *The New Eastern Europe. Social Policy Past, Present and Future*, London: Sage.

Deetz, S., 1994; *Transforming Communication, Transforming Business: Building Responsive and Responsible Workplace*, Cresskill, NJ: Hampton Press.

Defourney, J. & J.L. Munzon (eds), 1992; *Économie sociale: the Third Sector*, Bruxelles: De Boeck. London: Routledge & Kegan Paul.

Dehoog, R.H., 1990; "Competition, Negotiation or Cooperation: Three Models for Service Contraction", *Administration & Society*, v. 22/3:317-340.

Dellenbrant, J.Å., 1988; "The Changing Role of Co-operatives in Socialist Countries" Uppsala: conference paper.

Donaldson, T. & L. Preston, 1995; "The Stakeholder Theory of the Corporation: Concepts, Evidence & Implications", *Academy of Management Rev.*, v. 20/1:65-91.

Dunnette, M.D., 1990; "Blending the Science and Practice of Industrial and Organizational Psychology: Where are we and where are we going?", Dunnette M.D. & L.M. Hough (eds.) *Handbook of Industrial and Organizational Psychology*, Palo Alto, CA: Consulting Psychologists Press.

Elcock, H., 1993; "What price citizenship? Public management and the Citizen's Charter", *The Waves of Change - Strategic Management in the Public Services,* 5-6.4.93, Sheffield.

Elvander, N., 1989; "Inkomstpolitik i Norden" *Forhandlingsökonomi i Norden*, Nielsen, K. & O.K. Pedersen, (eds), Copenhagen & Oslo: DJÖF & Tano.

Enjolras, B., 1993; "La Structuration de L'Offre de Services de Proximité", Paris:UNIOPSS.

Enjolras, B., 1994; "Local Services and Public Policies: International Comparative Aspects", Paris: UNIOPSS.

Enjolras, B., 1995; *Le marché providence: Aide à domicile, politique sociale et création d'emploi*; Paris: Desclée de Brouwer.

Esping-Andersen, G., 1990; *The Three Worlds of welfare Capitalism*, Cambridge: B. Blackwell, Polity Press.

Esping-Andersson, G. (ed.), 1996; *Welfare States in Transition. National Adaptations in Global Economies*, London, Thousand Oaks & New Delhi: Sage.

Esping-Andersen, G. & W. Korpi; 1987; "From Poor Relief to Institutional Welfare State: the Development of Scandinavian Social Policy", *International Journal of Sociology*, v. 16/3-4.

Espriu, J., 1995; *Mrs. Life*, Barcelona: the Espriu Foundation.

Etzioni, A., 1961; *Modern Organizations*, Engelwood Cliffs: Prentice-Hall.

Etzioni, A., 1993; *The Spirit of Community Rights, Responsibilities and the Communitarian Agenda,* New York: Crown Publishers, 270pp.

European Communities, 1986; *The cooperative, mutual and non-profit sector and its organizations in the European Community*, Luxembourg, the European Community.

Evers, A., 1993; "The Welfare Mix Approach. Understanding the Pluralism of Welfare Systems", Barcelona: conference paper.

Evers, A., 1995; "Part of the welfare mix: the third sector as an intermediate area", *Voluntas*, v. 6/2:159-182.

Evers, A. and H. Wintersberger, (eds) 1990; *Shifts in the Welfare Mix: their Impact on Work, Social Services and Welfare Policies*, Frankfurt & Bolder: Campus Verlag & Westview Press.

Fairbairn, B., 1991; *Cooperatives & Community Development - Economics in a Social Perspective*, Saskatoon: Center for Cooperative Studies, Univ. of Saskatchewan, CAN

Ferris, J. & Graddy, E., 1989; "Fading distinctions among the nonprofit, governmental, and for-profit sectors", Hodgkinson, V.A., R.W. Lyman & Assocs (eds), *the Future of the Nonprofit Sector*; San Francisco: Josssey-Bass,

Filios, V., 1991; "Human Systems Management", *Accounting, Organization & Society*, v.10:267-80.

Firat, A.F., 1990; "The Consumer in Postmodernity", Holman, R.N. & M.R. Slomon (eds), *Advances in Consumer Research*, XVII, Provo, UT: Association for Consumer Research.

Firat, A.F., & A. Venkatesh, 1995; "Liberatory postmodernism and the reenchantment of consumption", *Journal of Consumer Research*, v.22:239-267.

Fletcher, J., *et al.*, "Competing for tots: operating objectives and characteristics of for-profit and nonprofit child care centers in the Pacific Northwest", *Voluntas*, v. 5, 1: 59-85.

Flynn, R., 1992; "Marketization in the public sector: implications for citizenship, professionalization and welfare", Limerick: ECPR paper.

Folkrörelseutredning, 1987; *Ju mer vi är tillsammans*, del 1 - 3, Stockholm: SOU 1987:33-35.

Folkrörelseutredning, 1989; *Mål och resultat*, Stockholm: SOU 1989:39.

FoU-rapport 1991:4; *Socialtjänsten*, Stockholm: FoU-byrån.

FoU-rapport 1993:2; *Socialtjänsten*, Stockholm: FoU-byrån.

FSE, 1995; *The Delivery of Public Services - A Social Economy Perspective*, London: Forum for the Social Economy.

Fölster, K., 1996; "Barn och äldreomsorg i Tyskland", Stockholm: Välfärdsprojektet, *Fakta/kunskaper*, nr. 4.

Gastere, L. & M. Taylor, 1993; *Learning from Consumers & Citizens*, Luton: Local Gov't Management Board.

Geddes, M., 1992; "The social audit movement", *Green Reporting: the challenge of the nineties*, Owen, D., (ed.), London: Chapman & Hall.

Giddens, A., 1994 & 1996; *Beyond Left and Right. The Future of Radical Politics*, Oxford: B. Blackwell, Polity Press.

Gidron, B. *et al.*, 1992; "Government & the Third Sector in Comparative Perspective: Allies or Adversaries?", pp. 1-30 in *Government & the Third Sector - Emerging Relationships in Welfare States*, Gidron, B. *et al.*, (eds), San Francisco: Jossey-Bass Publs.

Gramsci. A., 1971; *Selections from Prison Notebooks of Antonio Gramsci*, Hoare, Q. & G.N. Smith (eds), London: Lawrence & Wishart.

Gray, R., *et al.*, 1987; *Corporate social reporting - accounting and accountability*, Engelwood Cliffs, NJ, London, etc.: Prentice Hall International.

Gray, R., *et al.*, 1996; *Accounting & Accountability. Changes and challenges in social and environmental reporting*, London, New York, etc.: Prentice Hall.

Grindheim, J-E. & P. Sells, 1990; "The Role of Voluntary Social Welfare Organizations in Norway: a democratic alternative to a bureaucratic welfare state?", *Voluntas*, v. 1/1:62-76.

Gröjer, J-E., 1993; "Redovisa anställda på balansräkningen!", Stockholm: Labora Press.

Gröjer, J-E., 1995; "Employees on the Balance Sheet - a matter of cost allocation", Stockholm: Workshop in Human Resource Costing and Accounting.

Gröjer, J-E. & U. Johanson, 1991; *Human Resource Costing & Accounting*, Stockholm: Joint Industrial Safety Council.

Gröjer, J.E. & A. Stark, 1978; *Social Redovisning*/Social Accounting, Stockholm: SNS.

Grönroos, C., 1990; *Service Management and Marketing: Managing the Moments of Truth in service Competition*, Lexington, MA & Toronto: Lexington Books.

Guba, E.G. & Y.S. Lincoln, 1988; *Effective Evaluation: Improving the Usefulness of Evaluation Results through Responsive and Naturalistic Approaches*, San Francisco: Jossey-Bass Publs.

Gulliam, M. & C. Perrow, 1992; *The AIDS Disaster in New York and the Nation*, New Haven: Yale Univ. Press.

Gummesson, E., 1993b; *Quality Management in Service Organizations*, NY: Internat. Service Quality Org., ISQA.

Habermas, J., 1989; *Structural Transformation of the Public Sphere: an inquiry into a category of bourgeois society*, Cambridge: Polity Press.

Habermas, J., 1992; "Further Reflections on the Public Sphere", Calhoun C. (ed.), *Habermas and the Public Sphere*, Cambridge, MA: MIT Press.

Hall, P.D., 1987; "Abandoning the Rhetoric of Independence: Reflections on the Nonprofit Sector in the Post-Liberal Era", *Journal of Voluntary Action Research*, v. 16: 11-27.

Hall, P.D., 1992; *Inventing the Nonprofit Sector and other Essays on Philanthropy, Voluntarism and Nonprofit Organizations*, (Baltimore: Johns Hopkins University Press).

Hansen, H,., 1993; "Social Insurance Problems and Structural Reforms", pp. 89-115, *Social Security in Sweden and other European Countries - three Essays*, Olsson-Hort, S-E., *et al.*, (eds), Stockholm: Finansdept. & ESO, Ds 1993:51.

Hansmann, H., 1980; "The Role of Nonprofit Enterprise" in *Yale Law Journal*, v.89:835-850.

Hansmann, H, 1988; "Ownership of the Firm", in *Journal of Law, Economics and Organizations*, v.4, no. 2:276-304.

Hansmann, H., 1996; *The Ownership of Enterprise*; Cambridge, MA & Oxford: the Belknap Press of Harvard University Press.

Hansson, J., 1995; "Avtal och taxor för koopertiva daghem", Stockholm: WECSS project report.

Hausner, J., *et al.* (eds), 1993; *Institutional Frameworks of Market Economies - Scandinavian & Eastern European Perspectives,* Aldershot & Brookfield: Avebury.

Havel, V., 1978; "De maktlösas makt", *En dåre i Prag*, Stockholm/Stehag: Symposion bokförlag.

Hegel; G.W.F., 1911; *Grundlinier der Philosophie der Reichs- Sämtliche Werke*, Leipzig: Verlag von Felix Meiner.

Hellqvist, S.N., 1995a; *Förskolan i fokus - föräldrarnas och personalens upplevelse av barnomsorg i tre olika driftsformer*, Stockholm: FoU byrån, Stockholm socialtjänst.

Hellqvist, S.N., 1995b; "Det kommer mera! IKS-95. En studie av kvalitet, inflytande och samverkan i barnomsorg i socialdistrikt 5", Stockholm: FoU byrån, Stockholoms Socialtjänst.

Henriksen, L.S., 1993a; "The Voluntary or Third Sector in a Sociological Perspective", Leiden: ECPR paper.

Henriksen, L.S., 1993b; "Frivillige organisationer i en lokal kontekst et case studie", Oslo: conference paper.

Henriksen, L.S., 1994; "Det civile samfund: Tilbage til politisk filosofi", *Norsk Statsvitenskaplig Tidskrift*, v. 4:357-74.

Henrilsen, L.S., 1996; *Lokal frivillig organisering i nye* omgivelser, Aalborg: Forlaget ALFUFF

Henriksen, L.S., 1997; "Voluntary Organizations & Local Government - Lessons from a Danish Case Study", *Voluntas*, v.7/2.

Herman, R., & R. Heimovics, 1995; "Researching nonprofit organizational effectiveness: whose criteria? A rejoinder to Osborne & Tricker", *Voluntas*, v. 6/1:93-99.

Hernes, 1978; *Forhandlingsökonomi og blandningsadministrasjon*, Olso: Universitetsforlaget.

Hill, C.W. & T.M. Jones, 1992; "Stakeholder-Agency Theory", *Journal of Management Studies*, v. 29/2:131-154.

Hirschman, A.O., 1970; *Exit, Voice and Loyalty. Responses to Decline in the Performance of Firms, Organizations and States*, Harvard University Press, Cambridge, MA & London.

Hirschman, A.O., 1981; *Essays in Trespassing - Economics to politics and beyond*, Cambridge, MA & New York, NY, Harvard University Press.

Hirschman, A.O., 1982a; *Shifting Involvements - Private Interest and Public Action*, Princeton: Princeton University Press.

Hirschman, A.O., 1982b; "Rival Interpretations of Market Society: Civilizing, Destructive or Feeble?", *Journal of Economic Literature*, v. XX:1463-1484.

Hirsh, P., 1994; *Associative Democracy. New Forms of Economic and Social Governance*, Cambridge: Polity Press.

Hirsh, P. & G. Thompson, 1996; *Globalization in Question*, Cambridge: Polity Press.

Hobbes, T., 1651/1962; *Leviathan*, London: Collins.

Hoyes, L., *et al.*, 1992; *Made to Measure? Performance Measure & Community Care*, Bristol: School for Advanced Urban Studies.

Huber, E., & J. Stephens, 1996; "Reconsidering the Welfare State in Europe", Chapel Hill, NC: conference paper.

Hunt, M., (1993), "Accountability, openness and the Citizen's Charter", *The Waves of Change - Strategic Management in the Public Services*, 5-6/4-93, Sheffield.

Hutton, W., 1995; *The State We're In*, London: Random House, Vintage.

Häggström, H., 1994; "Personalkooperativ och arbetsrätt" Örebro: uppsats; Institutionen för samhällskunskap.

International Cooperative Alliance, 1995; *Making Membership Meaningful: Participatory Democracy in Co-operatives*, Saskatoon, CAN: Centre for the Study of Cooperatives. Univ. Of Saskatchewan.

Jessop, B., 1990; *State Theory: Putting Capitalist States in Their Place*, Cambridge: Polity Press.

Jessop, B., 1992; "Welfare and Workfare States - Theory and Practice", Chicago: paper.

Johnsson, N., 1989; "The Privatization of Welfare", *Social Policy & Administration*, v. 23: 17-29.

Jonsson, E, 1993, *Konkurrens inom sjukvård*, Stockholm: Spri.

Jordan, J., 1987 & 1989; "The Multi-Stakeholder Approach to Worker Ownership", Quarter, J. & G. Melnyk, (eds.), *Partners in Enterprise: the Worker Ownership Phenomenon*, Montreal: Black Rose Books, pp. 149-171 and in *Yearbook of Co-operative Enterprise*, 1989, Oxford: the Plunkett Foundation.

Jordan, J., 1995; fax to V. Pestoff, 27 July, 1995.

Juul, P, 1996; "Dumrkehim's View on Social Solidarity", Denmark: ISP conference paper.

Jönsson, S., *et al.*, 1997; *Decentraliserad välfärdsstat: Demokrati, effektivitet och service*, Stockholm: SNA förlag.

Kalimo, R.,1987; "Psychosocial factors and workers' health: an overview", Kalimo, R., El-Batawi, M.A:, Cooper, C.L. (eds). *Psychosocial factors at work, an their Relation to Health,*. England: World Health Organization.

Kallinikos, J., 1995; "Cognitive Foundations of Economic Institutions: Markets, Organizations and Networks Revisited", *Scandinavian Journal of Management*, v. 11, no. 2:119-137.

Karasek, R. & T. Theorell, 1990; *Healthy Work: Stress, Productivity, and the Reconstruction of Working Life*, NY: Basic Books, Inc., Publishers.

Kazenstein, P., 1985; *Small States in World Markets*, Ithaca & London: Cornell University Press.

Kenis, P., 1992; *The Social Construction of an Industry. A World of Chemical Fibers*, Frankfurt am Main & Bolder: Campus Verlag & Westview Press.

Klausen, K. K., 1989; "Den Tredje Sektor: Frivillige organisationer mellem stat og marked", i *Stat og Marked: Fra Leviathan og usynlig hånd till forhandlingsökonomi;* Klausen, K.K. & T. Hvid Nielsen (eds.), Köpenhamn: Jurisit- og Ökonomforbunders Forlag, DJÖF.

Knapp, M., 1984; *The Economics of Social Care*, London: Macmillian.

Kommunallagen, 1991; Stockholm: *SFS*, 1991:900.

Kooperativa Förbundet, 1974; *Konsumentägt*/Consumer Owned, Programkommitten, Stockholm: KF.

Kooperativa Förbundet, 1979a; *Svensk konsumentkooperation inför 1980-talet*/Swedish Consumer Cooperatives Facing the 1980s, Stockholm: KF.

Kooperativa Förbundet, 1979b; Internal report on "membership attendance at annual general meetings 1977-1979", Stockholm: KF.

Kooperativa Förbundet, 1983; Internal report on "membership attendance at annual general meetings 1980-1982", Stockholm: KF.

Kooperativa Förbundet, 1989; *Tjäna varandra i samverkan: verksamhetsidé, mål och riktlinjer för konsument- kooperationen*/Working together for Mutual Gain: business idea, goals and guidelines, Stockholm: KF.

Kooperativa Förbundet, 1990; "Det konsumentkooperativa medlemsengagemanget på 90-talet", Stockholm: KFs Medlemskommitténs rapport till förbundsstyrelsen.

Kooperativa Institutet, 1991; *Medikoop - Vård och omsorg i konsumentkooperativa former*, Stockholm: Kooperativa Institutet.

Kooperativt Utvecklingscentrum i Skåne ek. för. Rapport 2. *Personal- resp. föreningsdrivna daghem i Skåne.*

Kornhauser, W., 1960; *The Politics of Mass Society*, London: Routledge and Kegan Paul.

Kramer, R., 1981; *Voluntary Agencies in the Welfare State*, Berkeley: Univ. of California Press.

Kramer, R., 1990a; "Nonprofit Social Services and the Welfare State: Some Research Considerations" Anheier, H. & W. Seibel (eds), 1990; *The Third Sector: Comparative Studies of Nonprofit Organizations*, Berlin & New York: de Gruyter.

Kramer, R., 1990b; "Voluntary Organizations in the Welfare State on the Threshold of the '90s", London: paper presented 29.11.89 at the London School of Economics.

Kramer, R., 1992; "The Role of Voluntary Social Service Organizations in Four European States: Policies & Trends in England, the Netherlands, Italy & Norway", pp. 34-52 in *Governments & Voluntary Organizations*, Kuhnle, S. & P. Selle (eds),

Kreps, T., 1940; *Measurement of the Social Performance of Business*, Washington, DC: An Investigation of Concentration of Economic Power for the Temporary Economic Committee.

Kuhnle, S., 1991; "Government and the Voluntary Sector in Norway in the Post War Period", Vienna: EGOS paper.

Kuhnle, S. & P. Selle, 1992; "Government & Voluntary Organizations: a relational perspective", in *Government & Voluntary Organizations*, Kuhnle, S. & P. Selle (eds), Aldershot, Brookfield, USA: Avebury.

Kumar, K., 1993; "Civil society: an inquiry into the usefulness of an historical term", *Brit. Journal of Sociology*, v. 42:375-95.

Kumar, K, 1994; "Civil society again: a reply to C. Bryant's 'Self-organization, civility and sociology'", *British Journal of Sociology*, v. 45/1.

Lantz, A., & B. Pingel, 1988; *Att gestalta en organization -perspektiv på offentlig barnomsorg*, Stockholm: Akademitryck.

Laville, J.L., 1992; *Les Services de Proximité en Europe*, Paris: Syros Alternative.

Laville, J-L., 1994; *L'économie solidaire. Une perspective internationale*, Paris: Desclée de Brouwer.

Laycock, D., 1994; "Can co-operatives make a difference? Political culture, state institutions and civil society in the development of economic democracy in Canada", Berlin: IPSA World Congress, paper.

Le Grand, 1990; *Quasi-Markets & Social Policy*, Bristol: SAUS, Studies in Decentralization & Quasi-Markets.

Le Grand, J. & W. Bartlett, 1993; *Quasi-Markets and Social Policy*, London: Macmillan.

Leibfried, S., 1991; "Towards an European welfare state?: on integrating poverty regimes in the European Community", Bremen: Zentrum für Sozialpolitik, 1991:2.

Leira, A., 1990; "Coping with Care", *Gender and Caring: Work and Welfare in Britain & Scandinavia*, Ungerson, C. (ed.), NY & London: Harvester Wheatsheaf, pp. 133-159.

Lennerlöf, L., 1981; *Arbetsmiljön ur psykologisk och sociologisk synvinkel. En introduktion i beteendevetenskaplig arbetsmiljöforskning*,. Stockholm: Liber Förlag.

Levi, L., 1987; "Definitions and the Conceptual Aspects of Health in Relation to Work", Kalimo, R., El-Batawi, M.A:, Cooper, C.L. (Eds). *Psychosocial Factors at Work and their Relation to Health*, England: World Health Organization.

Lewis, H., 1989; "Ethics and the private nonprofit human service organizations", *Administration in Social Work*, v. 13:2, 1-14.

Likert, R., 1959; *New Patterns of Management*, New York: Mc Graw-Hill.

Lindblom, C., 1959; *Politics and Markets: the world's political economic system*, New York: Basic Books.

Lindkvist, L., 1990; *Arbetskooperation*, Stockholm: Nordiskt Ministerråd & Kooperativa institutet.

Lindkvist, L., & A. Westenholz (eds.) 1987; *Medarbetarägda företag i Norden*, Stockholm : Nordiskt Ministerråd.

Lipset, S.M., 1960 & 1963; *Political Man*, New York; Doubleday & Co.

Ljungdahl, S. & M. Mörner-Walter, 1993; *Vägledning i barnomsorg*, Stockholm: Föräldra-kooperativens Riksförening - Våart Dagis & Folksam.

Locke, E. A., 1984; "Job satisfaction", Gruneberg M. and Wall T. (eds.) *Social Psychology and Organizational Behavior*, New York: John Wiley & Sons.

Locke, J., 1946; *Second Treatise of Civil Government and a Letter Concerning Toleration*, J.W. Gough, (ed.); Oxford: B. Blackwell.

Lundström, T. & F. Wijkström, 1994; "The Swedish Nonprofit Sector", Stockholm: School of Economics, EFI.

Mabon, H., 1977 & 1992; *Organisationslära - struktur och beteende*, Stockholm: Psykologiförlaget.

Manfield, R., 1984; "Formal and Informal Structure", Gruneberg M. & Wall T. (eds.) *Social Psychology and Organizational Behavior*, New York: John Wiley & Sons.

Marin, B. & P. Kenis, 1997; *Managing AIDS: Organizational Responses in Six European Countries*, Aldershot & Brookfield: Ashgate.

Marshall, T.H., 1973; *Class, Citizenship and Social Development*, Westpoint, CT: Greenwood Press.

Marshall, T.H., 1975 & 1977; *Social Policy*, London: Hutchinson.

Marshall, T.H., 1981; *The Right to Welfare*, London: Heinemann Educational.

Mellbourn, A., 1986; *Bortom det starka samhället. Socialdemokratiska förvaltningspolitik*, Stockholm: Carlssons.

Meyer, M. & L. Zucker, 1989; *Permanently Failing Organizations*, Newbury Park, CA, London & New Delhi: Sage.

Michels, R., 1911 & 1962; *Political Parties*, New York & London: the Free Press.

Minister for Welfare Reforms, 1998; *A New Contract for Welfare*, the Green Paper, 26 March, 1998; http://www.dss.gov.uk/hq/wreform/.

Möller, T., 1996; *Brukare och klienter i välfärdsstaten: om missnöje och påverkans möjligheter inom barn- och äldreomsorg*, Stockholm: Publica, Nordstedts juridik.

Nielsen, K., 1989; "Flexible adjustments and political stability: the terms of the debate", *Scandinavian Political Studies*, v. 12:297-313.

Nielsen, K. & O.K. Pedersen, 1988; "The Negotiated Economy: Ideal and History", *Scan. Political Studies*, v. 11, no. 2: 79-101.

Nielsen, K. & O.K. Pedersen, 1989a; "Is Small Still Flexible? - an Evaluation of Recent Trends in Danish Politics", *Scandinavian Political Studies*, v.12, No. 4: 343-372.

Nielsen, K. & O.K. Pedersen, (eds), 1989b; *Forhandlingsökonomi i Norden*, Copenhagen & Oslo: DJÖF and Tano.

Nisbet, R .A., 1966; *The Sociological Tradition*, New York: Basic Books.

North, D., 1990; *Institutions, Institutional Change and Economic Performance*, Cambridge University Press, Cambridge and New York.

North, D., 1993; "Economic Performance through Time", Stockholm: Nobel Prize Lecture.

Official Statistics of Sweden, 1992a; *Den psykosociala arbetsmiljön. Information om arbetsmarknaden*, 1992:4, Stockholm: Statistiska Centralbyrån.

Official Statistics of Sweden, 1992b; *Statistiska Meddelanden. Arbetsmiljön 1989/91*. Stockholm: Statistiska Centralbyrån.

Olson, M., 1965 & 1971; *The Logic of Collective Action*, Harvard University Press, Cambridge, MA & London.

Olsson Hort, S-E., 1993; "Models and Countries - the Swedish Social Policy Model in Perspective", *Social Security in Sweden and Other European Countries -*

Three Essays, Olsson-Hort, S-E., *et al.*, (eds), Stockholm: Finansdept. & ESO, Ds1993:51.

Onn, G., 1995; "Kooperativdaghem och deras ekonomi", Stockholm: WECSS project report.

Onn, G., 1995; "Effectiveness, Co-Production and Swedish Child-Care Co-operatives", Stockholm: School of Business, Ph.D. seminar paper.

Osborne, S. & M. Tricker, 1995; "Researching nonprofit organizational effectiveness: a comment on Herman & Heimovics", *Voluntas*, v. 6:1:85-92.

Parry, R., 1993; "The Political and Financial Basis of the New Welfare Mix in Britain", Leiden: ECPR conference paper.

Palme, J., 1990; *Pension Rights in Welfare Capitalism - the Development of Old-Age Pensions in 18 OECD Countries 1930 to 1985*, Stockholm: SOFI no. 14.

Pedersen, O.K., 1992; "The Social Responsibility of the Firm", Copenhagen: paper.

Perrow, C., 1986 (3rd edit.); *Complex Organizations: A Critical Essay*, New York: Random House & McGraw-Hill.

Perrow, C., 1988; "A Society of Organizations", New Haven: paper.

Pestoff, V., 1977; *Voluntary Associations and Nordic Party Systems, A study of overlapping memberships and cross-pressures in Finland, Norway and Sweden*, Stockholm: Studies in Politics: 10.

Pestoff, V., 1978; "Soviet Non-Governmental Organizations - Limits of Empirical Studies", *Politikki*,

Pestoff, V., 1984; *Konsumentinflytande och konsumentorganisering - den svenska modellen*/Consumer Influence & Consumer Organization - the Swedish Model, Stockholm: Min. of Finance, Ds Fi 1984:15.

Pestoff, V., 1988 & 1989; *Näringslivsorganisationerna och politiken i Sverige*/Business Interest Associations and Politics in Sweden; Stockholm: TCO.

Pestoff, V., 1989; "Organisationernas medverkan och förhandlingar i svensk konsumentpolitik"/Organizational Participation and Negotiations in Swedish Consumer Policy, *Forhandlingsökonomi i Norden*/The Negotiated Economy in the Nordic Countries, Nielsen K. & O.K. Pedersen (eds) Copenhagen & Oslo: DJÖF & Tano; reprinted in *Tidskrift för rättssociologi*, v.6, nr.3/4, 1989: 150-203.

Pestoff, V., 1990; "Joint Regulation, Meso-Games and Political Exchange in Swedish Industrial Relations", in *Governance & Generalized Exchange. Self-Organizing Policy Networks in Action*, Marin, B. (ed.), Frankfurt & Bolder: Campus Verlag & Westview Press.

Pestoff, V., 1991 & 1996; *Between Markets and Politics - Co-operatives in Sweden*, Frankfurt, Bolder & Tokyo: Campus Verlag, Westview & English Books.

Pestoff, V., 1992; "Cooperative Social Services - an Alternative to Privatization", *Journal of Consumer Policy*, v 15:21-45.

Pestoff, V., 1994a; "Beyond Exit and Voice in Social Services - Citizens as Co-producers", in 6, P. & I. Vidal (eds), *Delivering Welfare - repositioning non-profit and co-operative action in western European welfare states*, Barcelona: CIES.

Pestoff, V., 1994b; "Employer Organizations: their Changing Structures and Strategies in Nine OECD Countries", *Changing Structures and Strategies of the Employers' and Employees' Organizations*, Helsinki: Proceedings from the IIRA 4th European Regional Congress.

Pestoff, V., (ed.) 1995a; *Reforming Social Services in Central and Eastern Europe - an Eleven Nation Overview*, Cracow: Cracow Academy Press.

Pestoff, V., 1995b; "Towards a New Swedish Model of Collective Bargaining", *Employer Organizations and Trade Unions in Changing Industrial Relations*, Crouch, C. & F. Traxler (eds) London & Newbury Park: Sage Publs.

Pestoff, V., 1995c; "Local Economic Democracy and Multi-Stakeholder Cooperatives", *Journal of Rural Cooperatives*, v.XXIII, no.2:152-167.

Pestoff, V., 1996a; "Social Enterprises and Civil Democracy: Enriching Working-Life & Empowering Consumers as Co-Producers in Sweden", Stockholm: School of Business.

Pestoff, V., 1996b; "Reforming Social Services in Central and Eastern Europe: Shifts in the Welfare Mix and Meso-Level Institutional Change", in *Legacies of Change - Transformations of Postcommunist European Economies*, Campbell, J. & O.K. Pedersen (eds), New York: A. De Gruyter

Pestoff, V., 1998a; "Enriching Swedish Women's Work Environment - the Case of Social Enterprises in Day Care", *Advances in the Economic Analysis of Participation and labor-Managed Firms*, v. 6:233-256.

Pestoff, V., 1998b; "Social Enterprises and Civil Democracy in Sweden: Developing a Participative Welfare Society in the 21st Century", *21st Century Economics: Perspectives of Political Economy for a Changing World*, Halal, W. & K. Taylor (eds), New York: St. Martins Press.

Pestoff, V., 1998c; "Civil Democracy and Trust", Tokyo & Vienna, JCCU, SASE conference paper.

Pestoff, V., forthcoming; *Social Enterprises in Sweden: Enriching Work Life, Empowering Citizens as Co-Producers and Transforming the Welfare State*, Stockholm: Södertörns Acta series, no. 1.

Pestoff, V. & L. Gullström, 1994; "Social service i kooperativ regi: dess population, mätinstrument och urval av daghem samt annan social service", Stockholm: WECSS Project paper.

Peters, B. Guy, 1994; "Alternative Models of Governance: the Changing State and Public Service", Berlin: IPSA World Congress, paper RC 27.

Petersen, J., 1989; "Pensionsfonde som aktieejere" i *Forhandlingsökonomi i Norden*, Nielsen, K. & O.K. Pedersen, (eds), Copenhagen & Oslo: DJÖF and Tano.

Pierre, J., 1995; "The Marketization of the State: Citizen, Customer and the Emergence of the Public Market", pp. 55-81 in Savoie, D. &. B.G. Peters (eds.), *Governance in a Changing Society* ,Montreal: McGill/Queens Univ. Press.

Polanyi, K., 1944 & 1957; *The Great Transformation*, New York: H. Holt & Co.

Pontusson, O. & E Åkerlund, 1993; *Daghemsverksamhet - kostnader och konkurrens - förutsättningar*, Stockholm: Konkurrensverket.

Porter, M., 1985; *Competitive Advantage Creating*, New York: Free Press.

Porter, M., 1992; "Capital Choices: Changing the Way America Invests in Industry", Boston: Harvard Business School.

Porter, M. *et al.*, 1991; *Advantage Sweden*, Stockholm: Nordstedts.

Prior, C. & M.J. Sabel, 1984; *The second industrial divide,* New York: Basic Books.

Prop. 1993/94/11; Utvidgad lagreglering av barnomsorgsområdet, mm., Stockholm: Riksdagstryckeri.

Prop. 1994/95:100; *Budget propsitionen 1994/95*/ The Swedish National Budget, 1994/95, Stockholm: Riksdagens tryckeri.

Putnam, R. D., 1993; *Making Democracy Work - Civil Traditions in Modern Italy*, Princeton, NJ: Princeton Univ. Press.

Putnam, R., 1995; "Tuning In, Tuning Out: the Strange Disappearance of Social Capital in America", *PS: Political Science & Politics*/APSA, pp. 664-683.

Ramanthan, K.V., 1976; "Towards a theory of corporate social accounting", *The Accounting Review*, 516-528.

Rehnman, E., 1967; "Företagsdemokrati och företagsorganisation", Stockholm: Dept. of Business Administration, RR 1967:3.

Riesman, D., 1950 & 1969; *The Lonely Crowd*, New Haven, CN: Yale University Press.

Rose-Ackerman, S., 1990; "Competition between non-profits and for-profits: entry and growth", *Voluntas*, 1/1:13-25.

Rose-Ackerman, S., 1989; "Altruistic Nonprofit firms in competitive markets: the case of day-care centers in the US", *Journal of Consumer Policy*, v. 9:291-310.

Rosseau, J.J., 1919; *Om samhällsfördraget eller Statsrättens grundsatser*, Stockholm: Bonniers Förlag.

Rovira, J., 1990; "The Role of Nonprofit Organizations in the Spanish Health Care Market", *The Third Sector: Comparative Studies of Nonprofit Organizations*, H. Anheier & W. Seibel (eds.), Berlin & New York: de Gruyter.

Sackett, P.R., Larson, J.R., 1990; "Research Strategies and Tactics in Industrial and Organizational Psychology", Dunnette M.D. and Hough L.M. (eds.) *Handbook of Industrial and Organizational Psychology*, Palo Alto, CA: Consulting Psychologists Press.

Salamon, L., 1987; "On Market Failure, Voluntary Failure, and Third Party Government: Towards a Theory of Government-Nonprofit Relations in the Modern Welfare State" *Journal of Voluntary Action Research*, v. 16: 29-49.

Salmon, L., & H. Anheier, 1996; "The Third Route: Government - Nonprofit Collaboration in Germany and the United States", Baltimore, ML: Johns Hopkins Univ., Occasional Paper, No. 9.

Saltman, R. & C. v. Otter, 1992; *Planned Markets and Public Competition: Strategic Reform in Northern European Health Systems*, Buckingham & Philadelphia: Open Univ. Press.

Scarpello, V. & H. Theeke, 1989; "Human Resource Accounting: a Measurement Critique", *Journal of Accounting Literature*, v. 8:265-280.

Schmitter, P., 1974; "Still the Century of Corporatism?", Pike, F. & T. Stritch (eds.), *The New Corporatism: Socio-Political Structures in the Iberian World*, Notre Dam & London: University of Notre Dam Press.

Seibel, W., 1990; "Government/third sector relationship in a comparative perspective: the cases of France and W. Germany", *Voluntas*, v.1/1:42-60.

Seidler, L.J. & L.L. Seidler (eds), 1975; *Social Accounting*, Los Angeles: Melville Press.

Siim, B., 1990; "Women & the welfare state: between private and public dependence. A comparative approach to care work in Denmark and Britain", *Gender and Caring: Work and Welfare in Britain & Scandinavia*, Ungerson, C. (ed.), NY & London: Harvester Wheatsheaf, pp. 80-109.

Simmel, G., 1912; *Melangees de philosophie relativiste*, Paris: F. Alcan.

Simon, H.A., 1957; *Administrative Behavior*, New York: Macmillian.

Sjöstrand, S-E., 1992; "On the Rationale behind Irrational Institutions", *Journal of Economic Issues*, v.XXVI, no. 4:1007-1040.

Sjöstrand, S-E., 1993; *Om företagsformer*, Stockholm: Stockholm School of Economics, EFI.

Socialstyrelsen, 1992/93; *Privata daghem och fritidshem*, Stockholm: Socialstyrelsen.

Socialstyrelsen, 1994; *Privata daghem och fritidshem*, Stockholm: Socialstyrelsen.

Socialstyrelsens statistik, 1995; *Barnomsorg 1994*, Stockholm: Socialtjänst 1995:9.

Sommer, R., *et al.*, 1989; "Cost and program availability in co-operative pre-schools", *Journal of Consumer Studies & Home Economics*, v. 13:285-91.

SoS & SCB, 1997; *Jämförelsetal för socialtjänsten, 1996*, Stockholm: Socialstyrelsen, Svenska Kommunförb. o. Statistiska centralbryrån.

SOU 1972:26 & 27, *Förskolan*, Stockholm: 1968 års Barnstugautredning, Liber/allmänna förlaget.

SOU 1981: 25, *Bra daghem för små barn*, Stockholm: Familjstödsutredningen, Liber/Allmänna förlaget.

SOU 1990:80 *Förskola åt alla 1991 - Hur blir det?*, Stockholm: Liber/Allmänna förlaget.

SOU 1993:82; *Frivilligt socialt arbete*, Stockholm: Social Service Committee, Liber/Allmänna förlaget.

SOU 1996:162; *På medborgarnas villkor - en demokratisk infrastruktur*, Stockholm: betänkande av Demokratiutvecklingskommittén, Liber/Allmänna förlaget.

Steen, A., 1989; "Velferdsstat, korporatisme og selvreglering" i *Forhandlingsökonomi i Norden*, Nielsen, K. & O.K. Pedersen, (eds), Copenhagen & Oslo: DJÖF and Tano.

Steinberg, R., 1987; "Nonprofit organizations and the market", in W. Powell (ed.), *the Nonprofit Sector: a Research Handbook*, New Haven, CT: Yale Univ. Press.

Stephens, J.D., 1996; "The Scandinavian Welfare States: Achievements, Crisis and Prospects", in Esping-Andersen, G., (ed.), *Welfare States in Transition. National Adaptations in Global Economies*; London, Thousand Oaks: Sage Publs.

Stiglitz, J.E., 1988, 2nd edit.; *Economics of the Public Sector*, New York: Norton.

Stockholms finanskontor, 1995; "Likvärdiga villkor: för enskilt driven barnomsorg och skolbarnomsorg", Stockholm: Stockholmstads finanskontor.

Streeck, W., 1989; "The Social Dimension of the European Firm", Florence: paper.

Streeck, W., 1991; "Industrial Relations in a Changing Western Europe", Bari: IIRA keynote speech.

Streeck, W. & P. Schmitter, 1985; "Community, Market, State - and Associations?" in *Private Interest Government - Beyond Market and State*, Beverly Hills and London: Sage.

Stryjan, Y., 1989a; "Why Does Established Cooperation Need New Cooperation?", Uppsala: conference paper.

Stryjan, Y., 1989b; *Impossible Organizations. Self-management and Organizational Reproduction*, Greenwood Press, Westport, CT.

Stryjan, Y., 1990; "Co-operatives in a Changing World: Membership, Organizational Strategies and Adaptation", Madrid: conference paper.

Stryjan, Y., 1994; "Cooperatives in the welfare market: the Swedish Case", in *Delivering Welfare: repositioning non-profit and cooperative action in western European welfare states*, Perri 6 & I. Vidal (eds), Barcelona: CIES.

Stryjan, Y., 1995; "Kooperativa dagis - de första åren"/Cooperative day care - the first years, *Kooperation & välfärd*/Cooperatives & Welfare, Stockholm: Föreningen Kooperativa Studier.

Stryjan, Y., 1996; "Systemskiftets irrgångar", Stockholm, School of Business, Research Report No. 1.

Stryjan, Y., 1997; "Personalkooperativ - bättre än sitt rykte?"/Worker Co-ops - Better than their Reputation?, *Förändring och förnyelse*/Change & Renewal; Stockholm: Föreningen Kooperativa Studier.

Stryjan, Y. & F. Wickström, 1996; "Cooperatives and Nonprofits in Swedish Social Welfare", *annals of Public and Cooperative Economy*, v. 67/1.

Ståle, Y., 1995; *Insyn eller medverkan? Hur huvudmannaskapet påverkar föräldrars val av barnomsorg, trivsel och föräldrarmedverkan*, Stockholm: Socialtjänstens FoU.

Svenska Dagbladet, 1990; 05.11, interview with Ulf Laurin, SAF's Chairman; Selander, 17/5-97, NL, p.1.

Svensson, L., 1986; *Grupper och kollektiv- en undersökning av hemtjänstens organisation i två kommuner*. Utredningsrapport nr 2,.Göteborg: Graphic Systems.

Sweden, Ministry of Civil Affairs, 1992; "Kommittédirektiv: en konsumentpolitisk översyn", Ministry of Civil Affairs, 1992:63, Stockholm.

Széman, Z., 1995; "The Role of Non-Governmental Organizations in the Transformation of Hungary", Pestoff, V. (ed.), *Reforming Basic Social Services in*

Central and East Europe - an Eleven Nation Overview, Cracow: Cracow Academy of Economics.

Szulkin, R., 1989; *Privat eller offentlig? Organisationsstruktur och arbetsförhållanden under olika ägandeformer.* Stockholm: Institutet för social forskning.

Szulkin, R., & M. Tåhlin, 1994; "Arbetets utveckling", Fritzell, J. & O. Lundberg (eds), *Vardagens villkor. Levnadsförhållanden i Sverige under tre decennier*, Stockholm: Blombergs, pp. 87-116.

Taylor, M., *et al.*, 1992; *Using empowerment in community care: unraveling the issues*, Bristol: School for Advanced Urban Studies, University of Bristol, Studies in Decentralization and Quasi-Markets, no. 11.

Thullberg, P. & K. Östberg, 1995; *Den svenska modellen*/the Swedish Model; Stockholm: Raben & Sjögrens förlag.

Titmuss, R.M., 1958; *Essays on the "Welfare State"*, London: Allen & Unwin.

Titmuss, R.M., 1970; *The Gift Relationship* , London: Allen & Unwin.

Titmuss, R.M., 1974; *Social Policy. An introduction*, London: Allen & Unwin.

Truman, D., 1951 & 1971; *The Governmental Process*, New York: Knopf.

Turner, B.S., 1986; *Citizenship and capitalism: the debate over reformism*, London: Allen & Unwin.

Turner, B.S., 1994; "Citizenship", *Citizenship: critical concepts*, Turner, B.T. & P. Hamilton, (eds), vol. 1 & 2, London: Routledge.

Turner, G., 1995; "Human Resource Financial Accounting - Whim or Wisdom?", Stockholm. Workshop in Human Resource Costing and Accounting.

Tåhlin, M., 1989; *Psykosociala arbetsvilkor och nedsatt hälsa i olika yrkesgrupper i Sverige - en analys på grund av levnadsnivåundersökningen 1981*, Stockholm: Dept. of Sociology.

Tåhlin, M, 1995; "Psykosociala faktorer i arbetet", *Arbetsliv och hälsa*, Järvholm, B. (ed.), Stockholm: ASS, ALI & RALF, pp. 34-41.

United Kingdom, Home Office, (1992), *The citizen's charter: first report 1992*, Her Majesty's Stationary Office, London, Cm 2101.

Viviani, M., 1995; "Tools of co-operative identity - Fixing values in turbulent conditions: the case of Lega delle Cooperative", Manchester: ICA conference paper.

Wagner, J.A., 1994; "Participation's Effects on Performance & Satisfaction: a Reconsideration of Research Evidence", *Academy of Management Review*, v. 19, no. 2: 312-30.

Wahlgren, I., 1996; *Vem tröstar Ruth? En studie av alternativa driftsformer i hemtjänsten*/Who Comforts Ruth? A Study of Alternative Providers of Home Help Services for the Elderly, Stockholm: Stockholm University, School of Business.

Walden Laing, D. & V. Pestoff, 1997; "The Role of Nonprofit Organizations in Managing HIV/AIDS in Sweden", in Marin, B. & P. Kenis, 1997; *Managing AIDS: Organizational Responses in Six European Countries*, Aldershot & Brookfield: Ashgate.

Walsh, K., 1995; *Public Services and Market Mechanisms: Competition, Contracting and the New Public Management*, London: Macmillan.

Walzer, M., 1990; "The Civil Society", Stockholm: Gunnar Myrdal Lecture.

Weisbrod, B.T., 1988; *The Nonprofit Economy*, Cambridge, MA & London: Harvard University Press.

Wells, M., 1981; "Success in Whose Terms? Evaluations of a Cooperative Farm", *Human Organizations*, v. 40, no. 3:239-246.

Westerberg, L., 1992; *Föreställningar på Arenan - ett utvecklingsarbete kring eget budgetansvar på kommunala barnstugor*, Stockholm: Akademitryck.

Wikman, A., 1989; *Att beskriva arbetsmiljön med hjälp av surveyfrågor - slutrapport från arbetsmiljöprojektet*, Stockholm: Statistiska Centralbyrån.

Wikman, A., 1991; *Att utveckla sociala indikatorer - en surveyansats belyst med exemplet arbetsmiljö*/Developing Social Indicators - A Survey Approach Exemplified by the Working Environment, Stockholm & Örebro: SCB, *Urval 21*.

Wikström, S., 1993; "The Customer as Co-Producer", *Studies in Action and Enterprise*, Stockholm: Dept. of Business Administration, PP1993:1.

Wikström, S., 1996; "Value Creation by Company-Consumer Interaction", *Journal of Marketing Management*, v. 12:359-374.

William-Olsson, I., 1988; *Vilka tar ansvar inom barnomsorgen*, Stockholm: Lärarhögskolan.

Williamson, O., 1985, *The Economic Institutions of Capitalism: Firms, Markets and Relational Contracting*, New York: the Free Press.

Williamson, O., 1992, "Institutional Aspects of Economic Reform: the Transaction Cost Economic Perspective", *Transformation Processes in Eastern Europe - Challenges for Socio-economic Theory*, Sem. paper, no. 19, Cracow Academy of Economics.

Wistow, G. & M. Barnes, 1993; "User Involvement in Community Care: Origins, Purposes and Applications", in *Journal of Public Administration*, v.71/3.

Young, D.R., 1989; "Beyond tax exemption: a focus on organizational performance vs. legal status", in V. A. Hodgkinson, R.W. Lyman & Assocs (eds), *the Future of the Nonprofit Sector*; San Francisco: Josssey-Bass.

Zadek, S. & R. Evans, 1993; *Auditing the Market: A practical approach to Social Auditing*, London: New Economics Foundation.

Zadek, S., 1993; "Socializing the Accounting Process", *Social & Environmental Accounting*, v. 13/2.

Zan, S., 1982; *La Cooperazione in Italia* (Bari: De Donato coop).

Zan, S., 1988; "The Social Responsibility of Consumer Co-operatives", Stockholm: speech delivered at the ICA World Congress.

6, Perri, & V. Pestoff, 1994; "La recherche sur la troisième secteur en Europe: directions et perspectives", *Revue des Études Coopératives, Mutualistes et Associatives*, no. 47:142-57.

Appendix

Exhibit 1 Work Environment and Cooperative Social Services, Project Sample

Type of org.:	Parent Co-ops	Vol. Org	Worker Co-ops	Total
Gothenburg no. orgs. no. Staff Qs. no. Par.Qs.	G2, G4, G5, G6 & G7 5 (17) (34)	G1, G3, G8 & G9* 4 (18) (33)	G10 &G11 2 (8) (18)	11 (43) (85)
Jämtl. & V.bot **no. orgs.** no. Staff Qs. no.Par. Qs.	J1, J2 & J3/ V1 & V2 5 (J=9,V=6)=15 (17 + 20=37)	none	V3 1 (3) (10)	3+3 (18) (47)
Malmö no. orgs. no. Staff Qs. no. Par. Qs..	M2, M3 & M4 3 (12) (27)	M1*, M5 & M6 3 (12) (28)	M7 to M11 5 (22) (64)	11 (46) (119)
Sockholm no. orgs. no. Staff Qs. no. Par. Qs.	S3, S4, S5, S6, S8, S9, S10, S15, S16 & (S19) 9 + 1 (37) (81)	S1*, S2*, S7*, S11*, S12*, S13 &S14 7 (25) (83)	S21 to S27 7 (57) (101)	24 (119) (265)
Uppsala no. orgs. no. Staff Qs. no. Par. Qs.	U1 1 (7) (11)	U2* & U3* 2 (4) (45)	U4 & U5 2 (7) (8)	5 (18) (64)
Total orgs. no. Staff Qs. no. Par. Qs.	23+1 (88) (190)	16 (59) (189)	17 (97) (201)	57 (244) (580)

* = voluntary organizations which became economic associations.

Exhibit 2 Staff Comments to General Comparisons with Municipal Day Care Services[1]

-Parent cooperatives: half of the staff provided comments, the overwhelming majority of which were positive or neutral.
-Voluntary organizations: nearly half of the staff provided comments, the overwhelming majority of which were positive.
-Worker cooperatives: nearly three fourths of the staff provided comments, the overwhelming majority of which were positive.

A. Positive Comments (Q. 66):
-PCs: "you can influence the board, which makes all decisions about our activities" (G72);
-or "you have more responsibility, but at the same time more freedom" (J31);
-or "contacts between the staff and parents means very much especially for the children" (J34);
-or "(there are) near and quick decisions and involvement in everything, no decisions without everybody's participation"(M23);
-or "in the co-op. everybody is very involved in everything, together with the parents, which leads to common decisions, being closer to decisions and everybody being involved in the day care home" (M34);
-or "families care and are concerned about each other in a fashion that favors child care service" (M41);
-or "more parent involvement, and with so many parents you learn so much new and the work requirement means that there are more men in the children's groups, i.e., fathers!" (M43);
-and "(there are) more possibilities to influence and quicker decisions, you have direct contact with your employer, you can explain and show directly what you want, which leads to a quicker result, you increase the demands placed on yourself and you get more work enjoyment" (S153).
-VOs: "more of your own responsibility, more insights into the future of the school and its present economy, more freedom, quicker decisions from idea to action, better unity among teachers, more resources to distribute, better economy (now the main municipal preoccupation is what can we decreased), better salaries, more flexible solutions to working hours, more encouragement to work overtime, the children's best is put before our economy, since it may cost a little (more)" (G84);
-or "the distance to decisions is short, you get much more encouragement, there are greater possibilities for co-determination, we've got a better economy, better

---

[1] Note that the figures here indicate the type of co-op day care service, i.e., PC, VO or WC and the number of the organization and respondent. Thus, VO, U26 stands for voluntary organization, Uppsala 2, respondent no. 6.

salaries, more engaged parents and more trust from our employers, who listen to us" (G94);
-or "much greater possibilities to influence the content, since you get closer to the decision-maker and receive praise and criticism eye to eye" (G97);
-or "better contact with my employer due to almost daily contact" (S111);
-or "parent influence in the activities isn't so big when there is a special pedagogical content to follow. But parents help in making material things, Spring & Fall cleaning, washing and other jobs at the school according to needs" (S134);
-and "you avoid having to deal with the municipality (more than economically) and can devote yourself to your work. You're much freer and more responsibility....my reflection is that the co-op. form for child care is better for families than municipal day care. Parents gain a whole lot of insights in the children's daily life and become involved. I would absolutely choose a parental co-op. for my own eventual children. This form also gives the personnel greater feeling of responsibility for their work. There is a risk, however, in taking too much responsibility, since the dividing lines are so unclear. An employer should have the main responsibility, but it is also a question of the personnel must set limits for how much responsibility to take. It is positive to have a lot of responsibility and the staff at our co-op. is very positive, ambitious and effective" (M12).
-WCs: "increased responsibility and decision rights increases your engagement. Your professional role is strengthened and you feel more motivated to work. I work with colleagues with the same basic ideology and goal, which is reflected both by the private individual and the way they work" (G112);
-or "possibilities to influence most things concerning your work have increased 100%" (M112);
-or "increased influence and increased responsibility, more ambitious, a more generous attitude towards parents, more flexibility and more enjoyable" (S211);
-or "greater pleasure of work, all your strength goes to solve problems instead of bottling up your frustration. Often we can resolve the economic limits we face with solutions we believe in, rather than unrealistic solutions given us from above" (S212);
-or "greater participation and influence over your work and more pleasure of work" (S214);
-or "we decide ourselves how we want to plan all of it" (S216);
-or "we are independent and know how things are in the children's groups and can devote resources where they're most needed, without waiting for answers from higher up. It's more flexible, we decide everything at the annual general meeting and board" (S217);
-or "we have much greater influence over things like employing new personnel, the composition of children's groups and in general important decisions concerning the day care home. It's more pleasant to work when you control all aspects of the work, not just your own unit" (S255);
-or "I have complete insight in everything concerning our worker co-op. The staff

takes care of and plans our activities together" (S241); and "it's so good, that I couldn't think of going back to work for the municipal sector again. A great job means work pleasure" (U52);
-and "democracy, self-governing, overview, long term planning and peace of work...uneasiness exists when you loose your work security as a municipal employee after 18 years, as in my case. Although there's an uncertain future, but there's an even greater chance to influence things. It depends more on us how things develop, not on someone higher up in the hierarchy to solve different problems. I have a lot of negative experience with incompetent management in municipal day care, with poor planning and idiotic reorganizations that help the managers, but not the front-line staff" (S231).

B. Neutral Comments (Q. 66):
-PCs: "smaller children's groups with fewer social problems in the groups and better contacts with the parents and better working times; otherwise most things are worse" (G22)/...."the day care center is our work place, but there is nobody with sufficient responsibility to make it a good work place, and we don't have sufficient authority, but rather must rely on the parents capability and good will. We have 20 'employers' and they change every fifth year. We have no possibility to transfer to another place of work, no access to work-site health care, much poorer access to psychologists, speech therapists, etc. Extra resources are sometimes needed for the children, but there is no one to consult in such situations. The parents have little knowledge in employer question and in meeting techniques. Their mandate period is too short and co-op child care means segregation. We can't take more than a few children to single parents, while admitting families with social problems is unthinkable. Children with problems are sent to larger municipal groups with more children with 'special needs'" (G22);
-or "working close to/together with the parents makes this job special. You have to be able to collaborate. You must be able to combine the role of employer, staff, colleague, friend, etc. (even foreman at times). When it works well its excellent and gives our activities very much, but the parent part that can be very difficult" (G23);
-or "I support the cooperative form with its short distance decision and greater possibilities to influence, but I think its very tiring and my work enjoyment disappears with so many and frequent confrontations between the personnel. I think it would work better with two units, as four staff members is too small a work group, especially if some are away (sick) since we have no reserves and it feels isolated to work in such a small work group when you are used to more colleagues around you" (G151);
-and "disadvantages are due to the incompatibility of parents being both employers and 'consumers', which are opposite roles. Worker co-ops with an active parent group would probably be better. Advantages are parents become strong when they together create a good environment which favors their own children. The small format, one unit is a pleasant work place both for children and adults" (M41).

-VOs: "the advantages is that this form provides access to the parents' experience, which is available through an open exchange in this form, letting you participate in life outside all the time. The disadvantage is trying at the same time to find someone to take responsible for the heavy administration" (G12);
-or "you're more involved in decisions, have more freedom of choice about how to do you work. I feel that the staff is more engaged in a co-op. On the negative side there is the future of the firm and the possibility of bankruptcy" (M67).
-WCs: (none)

C. Negative Comments (Q. 66):
-PCs: "worse working hours, we work some days without a pause, a lot of nagging from parents when they have to contribute if someone in the staff is sick. Even the economy of the co-op. is given priority over the interests of the children, like more children enrolled without more staff, just like in the municipal services. In spite of all the over enrollment in the municipal services employment felt more secure there" (S91);
-or "we can't influence our situation very much, since everything depends on the number of children. Every child is worth a certain sum of money. To make the budget function we have to have a certain number of children enrolled! The politicians cut back our support every year, so there will be more children in every group. We recently faced bankruptcy, but are able to continue for the time being. But we had to lay off some of the staff, and the remainder had to accept a reduction of 2,000 kr./month, plus we do the cleaning now. We're looking for new premises. Support for the children decreases the older they become." (S163).
-VOs: (none)
-WCs: "personally I feel that parent co-ops are a better model than worker co-ops. There are few persons who are capable of working in a worker co-op. You have to be willing to commit a whole lot of time and money" (X43)
-or "increased responsibilities, increased freedom, more congenial atmosphere between the staff, plus not the same anxiety for (budget) reductions" .... "the staff composition is very important and functions very good now, since we can influence it, something not always possible in municipal day care services. I think that this makes things much worse in the municipal child care service activities, since it implies discomfort and unnecessary conflicts. What I find negative with co-ops is that you avoid/sort out children with 'priority', mostly 'social priority'. It is a shame, since I think that our positive spirit, the excellent atmosphere here and very good parent collaboration would have a very positive on one or more such families. I feel that it is good to mix different social classes a bit" (G101);
-or "in our worker co-op. the manager decides everything and is very dominant and driving, which renders more difficult the idea of everybody's involvement and co-determination. It also means that cooperation as an idea seem very thin/weak, under such circumstances" (X42)
-and "at the same salary as a civil servant, I have a higher work tempo, with many

more work chores, which due to a lack of time aren't done well, and someone who erodes the general comfort for several of us" (X44).

Exhibit 3 Staff Comments on their Personal Engagement in the Social Enterprise's Work[2]

-Parent cooperatives: more than two fifths of the staff provided comments, many of which were negative.
-Voluntary organizations: more than half of the staff provided comments, most of which were positive.
-Worker cooperatives: more than one quarter of the staff provided comments, mostly positive.

A. Positive Comments (Q. 74):
-PCs: "I feel happy with my work, and we have good parents and employers and wonderful children" (S63b);
-or "it feels if it is our (the staff's) day care facility, and we want to show that we love our work" (S8); or "I learn something new every day, and it's very exciting" (S152);
-and "in the beginning I was so occupied with everything new, participating in the new system, which I've done now and that increases my engagement" (S195).
-VOs: "I enjoy my work very much, which depends on the open and democratic decision-making process we have achieved (G96);
-or "in connection with defining our goals we have the opportunity to express our feelings about our activities. This makes work more fun and challenging" (G97);
-or "it took a long time to get started, which depended a lot on the personnel we had then. Today we work for the same goals and have the same pedagogical ideas" (M1);
-and "It took time to get into it, but the more time that passes the greater the engagement" (S7).
-WCs: "since the staff all have the same basic idea about how to work, it's always rewarding to meet the children with enthusiasm in what you do together with them. This creates a good atmosphere (most of the time) at work" (G111);
-or "it's different now, we are independent and work for ourselves (S216);
-or "we avoid the heavy bureaucracy and decide more ourselves" (S217);
-or "you are more motivated since you run it yourself. Everything depends on how you run it" (S2211);
-or "you learn, which increases your engagement" (S235);
-or "I was uninformed in the beginning about worker co-ops. Now I know more

---

[2] See the footnote to Exhibit 2 above.

about them and that gives security and more engagement. It's nice and fun to be able to influence" (S24);
-and "in the beginning we weren't a co-op, since the chairwoman took all the responsibility and work duties. When she quit we've divided the responsibilities, so it functions very good now, and I enjoy it and have lots of fun" (S255).

B. Neutral Comments (Q. 74):
-PCs: "the new 'interest' cools down with time, which doesn't mean that I don't like my job" (S31); or "I've got two children of my own now, which meant that there isn't enough time for the same engagement" (M41);
-and "I have the same degree of engagement as at the start, but we've realized how difficult it is to implement all the planning" (S62b).
-VOs: "administrative work took too much time in the beginning, but now I can concentrate on more important things (G8);
-or "too big an engagement takes a personal costs, *lagom är bäst*" (S2).
-and "there have been changes in the staff and I've been away for two child-births" (J1).
-WCs: (none)

C. Negative Comments (Q. 74):
-PCs: "but we've gotten tired because of the lack of recognition by parents and working free of charge" (G43);
-or "when you work to develop the activities, but get no response, you become passive, but hopefully only for a short time" (S43);
-or "all the benefits are reduced or taken away, while the work load increases and possibilities decrease" (S61b);
-or "there are staff reductions, more children and fewer engaged parents than before" (U11);
-or "the poor division of responsibilities, unclear management and a bad atmosphere among the staff" (S151);
- or "unfortunately, it has become a 'revolving-door' day care home" (S9);
-or "due to the uncertain future of whether our place of work will survive. Many voices want to decide and make changes, largely because of ignorance about what day care means" (S63a);
-or "due to uncertain employment" (S62a), or another who laments: "we've had a tough Fall, 'shall we go bankrupt or survive with less money?', so my energy hasn't been sufficient for the same engagement as in the beginning" (S16).
-VOs: Negative comments from the staff of voluntary organizations mention things like changed work responsibilities and problems with employers.
-WCs: "increased work has resulted in the loss of will and all the enthusiasm I had at the start" (G103);
-or "the work load is too big and the salary too small"(G114);
-or "the work is physically demanding and your engagement decreases therefore

with your capability. Full time is too much" (S239);
-or "it wasn't what I expected, and I feel a bit 'burnt out'. Perhaps I had too many expectations. It's hard to get acceptance for co-op ideas and to get an engagement for them" (S26);
-and "a certain person" who is always right and [feels that] those who don't want to work under such conditions should look for a new job" (U44).

Exhibit 4 Parent Comments on the Work Obligation and Holding an Elective Office

A. Two Descriptions of Work Obligation.
The work obligation varies from one cooperative day care center to another. A good description of it from parents in two voluntary organizations is given here: -"the work obligation is limited, only weekly-cleaning and a spring cleaning per family...It keeps the costs down and the parents get to know each other, and it's interesting to get an insight into the children's daily environment and materials. However, I feel that parental participation and influence via the parental groups is important. For example, the our-doors environment group, the traffic group, the party committee, the premises group. Many common activities helps the parents to get know each other, and many participate" (VO; U26), while another says: -"there is a work obligation for all parents, except for the chairperson and treasurer: making food twice in six weeks, cleaning two weeks per term, and everybody has a particular responsibility: i.e., one parent is responsible for scheduling the cleaning and another for planning the purchase of food for meals, one is responsible for repairs and others for books and reading materials, a preparations committee is responsible for the applications, plus the board, someone is responsible for the personnel, a treasurer who is responsible for salaries, fees, the post- and bank-giros, plus a secretary" (VO, U31).

B. Comments on Work Obligation.
The positive comments on the work obligation include: -"it is through this that I'm able to get to know my child's playmates and their parents plus the teachers" (PC, G67)/ -"it provides a good start and security for the children" (PC, M45)// -"it's nice being together with the children on their terms and seeing your own child in a group" (VO, M61). The neutral comments state: -"{it} comprises cleaning, maintenance, administration and purchases, which are a condition for our economic survival" (PC, M32); - "since this is Montessori day care, the staff provide the pedagogical knowledge and we provide common sense and labor for cleaning" (VO, S1305). The critical comments say: -"{it} is very positive, but of course it's not free from conflicts, in part in relation to my own work situation, where I must be absent from important things and in part since it's not so easy to suddenly go in the staff's "world" their work place and be an equal. It's exciting, but not always

easy" (VO, S123); "the work obligation gives good insights, even if it feels too demanding at times (PC, M22); -"it's OK with a work obligation, but if you have two other children at home it's rather tough" (PC, U14).

C. Comments on holding an elective or honorary office.
The positive comments on honorary and elected offices include: "one in every family has an ordinary position on the board, the other is a replacement. In this fashion everybody participates in what happens and can discus what they feel is important (PC, M43); while negative comments state: "at times it feels tough with board meetings, general meetings, etc., since we both work and also have school children" (PC, J23); -"parents who accept an elective office have a rather unwelcome post and a lot of work at times" (PC, U17)// -"the staff sometimes lacks an understanding of how much work the board does and what a big responsibility it bears" (VO, S115).

D. General Comments of the Cooperative Form.
More general comments on the cooperative form, work obligation and elective offices, etc. include: -"a co-op gives a feeling of belonging and participation, while municipal day care is a place to park your child and you don't have any idea of what happens there" (PC, G77)// -"that's the meaning of parent co-op, it's fun and I wouldn't change it for municipal day care" (VO, U31); -"one parent participates everyday in day care activities, this is why it works so well, and all families are in the board (VO, S104)/ -"it should be both a right and responsibility in all activities - municipal as well as alternative (services), even in school" (VO, S23).

Exhibit 5 Parent Comments on their Relations with the Staff

A. Collaboration with the Staff of Cooperative Day Care Services.
Several parents comment on their good relations with the staff in the following fashion: -"the staff is opened to the parents' thoughts and ideas, and moreover they are respectful in their treatment of both the parents and children" (PC, U13)// -"the staff is concerned about good parent contacts, they tell you what happened during the day and follow up problems" (VO, M610)// -"there is daily contact with the staff when I leave or get my child, (so) if problems occur or if there is something positive we're informed about it. Parent discussions every three months (kvartssamtal) is a good compliment for parents to make deeper contacts with the staff, which makes for cooperation" (WC, S2115); or -"(it's) 'the children's other home' (that) certainly says everything" (WC, S2229).

Other parents speak of the necessary of a clear division of labor between the staff and parents: -"from the outset the staff indicated its independence and that they didn't want the parents to interfere in the activities" (PC, S81)/ -"rather good, because cooperation - in our case means to understand the pedagogics and work in the same direction/have the same basic view of the children and their development. That can cause conflicts sometimes in our otherwise stressful lives" (VO, S1305)//-

"I can't influence much since it's a Montessori with a special pedagogical profile in their activities, but that is why I choose it in the first place" (WC, M72).

Difficulties combining their roles as a parent with those of an employer are experienced by some parents: -"it's difficult to influence and cooperate with the staff due to the situation of being a parent and employer. The chairperson should be someone from outside and the staff shouldn't be on the board." (PC, G47); -"I think it's a problem being both an employer and parent, for example setting salaries or giving criticism, you're always afraid it may have consequences for the children." (PC, S63). Others combine both roles as a parent and staff member: "I work at the co-op. and I'm a parent" (PC, G75); -"since you're both employer, staff and parent it can lead to conflicts occasionally" (PC, M45); -"very good, I work at the co-op myself" (PC, V12)// -"my wife works at the co-op" (WC, G1104). Finally, we note some shifting problems: - "very good now, but earlier so-so. It's important for this kind of child care to have a clear division of responsibility and not to change it subjectively depending on the composition of parents" (VO, U34).

B. Staff Openness and Willingness to Discuss with Parents.

The staff listens and is open to suggestions by parents for changes is the most frequent comment received. Some examples read: -"we have monthly meetings between all the staff and parents, when we discuss the activities in general and reasonable suggestions are implemented" (PC, S62)// -"since we all work twice a month, it's natural to discuss things" (VO; S76); -"that is a precondition for a co-op" (VO; S1301)// -"now, but not always before" (VO, S1309)// -"(there are) regular parent meetings with information and discussion of suggestions" (WC, G1001); -"suggestions are channeled through a parent association, but even individual wishes are taken in to account" (WC; S2210). Several parents note, however, that the co-ops' pedagogics can't be questioned. They read: -"that's taken for granted at our co-op day care, but the staff has the pedagogical responsibility" (PC; G67)// -"they have an open and engaged attitude, but are unconditional when it comes to pedagogics, which I think is good" (VO, U26)// -"since this is Montessori day care with special pedagogical rules that can't be changed it feels heavy and a little stiff" (WC, M74). Some parents lament that the staff won't or can't take their suggestions to heart. They argue: -"the staff finds it difficult to listen to changes coming from the parents. It is more difficult for them with a co-op since new parents with (new) opinions and ideas come each year" (PC; G47)// -"unwilling to make the changes we suggest" (VO, S116)// -"No, I (mamma) think that the staff had shown clearly that the parents aren't welcome to interfere, that feels sad" (WC, G1108); or -"due to the economy the staff is rather restricted as to what changes they can make, in particular when it comes to the time outdoors" (WC, S243).

C. Examples of Parents' Suggestions Adopted by Cooperative Day Care Services.
Between one third and two-fifths of the parents with children in different types of cooperative day care services provided examples of changes initiated by their own or other parents' suggestions. Their examples span a wide range of topics, including opening hours, vacations & holidays, work routines, food & drink, material & equipment, the activities, pedagogics and other things. A few of their examples concerning hours, etc. read: increased opening hours; sleep time for the children, the timing and content of meals, brushing teeth, etc.; sick-relief replacement schedule and cleaning schedule; the length of vacations, opening times and holidays, planning days on week-ends/holidays, and opened during the summer. Suggestions concerning food include milk for lunch, sandwich as an afternoon snack, not just yogurt; or even changing the lunch supplier from the local school to another; while those concerning activities mention: more outdoors activities, excursions, etc., swimming, cooking food, more music, opening an afternoon section, help with baby-sitting and cloths exchange days; and material and equipment suggestions name: equipment for outdoors activities, and gravel in the yard. Discussion of pedagogics concern: the pedagogical goals/profile, transition to Montessori and a Montessori night course for parents, while other matters include: the age composition of the children's groups, more liberal implementation of the 3-hour rule, parent participation in excursions, changed parent fees, taking into account parents' views when hiring new staff (WC), and non-smoking staff. Few of these changes can be considered marginal, and even fewer would seem likely if suggested by parents to children in municipal or private day care services.

Exhibit 6 Parent Comparisons with Municipal Day Care Services

A. Openness of Staff in Cooperative and Municipal Day Care Services.
Some parents praised cooperative day care by saying: -"(there is) a big difference, this organization is for the parents and the children are primary" (PC, S41); -"as a parent at a co-op. day care center you have possibility to influence the section, the staff is more open" (PC, S46)// -"the staff is more concerned both about the parents' and children's wishes, they are more opened and are willing to make changes" (VO, M66); -"here you're involved, at the municipal you're not" (VO, S105); -"the answer is self-evident, since at our daughter's previous municipal day care faculty there were 96 children and here there are 14. Moreover, since we parents have responsibility as employers, its natural that the staff is more concerned and open" (VO, S79)// -"the staff owns the day care and must be more open and concerned in order to keep their 'customers', but when they took over responsibility of this day care center their engagement became considerably greater" (WC, S2115); or -"it's a lot easier to communicate and discuss, much less bureaucracy than before" (WC, V310).

Other parents claim that staff openness and concern is the same in both forms of day care: -"our child has had problems at both places" (PC; J14); -"we have the same good contacts with the staff of the co-op. as at the municipal (facility)" (PC,

M21); -"the staff's willingness to collaborate has nothing to do with if it's cooperative or municipal child care" (PC, V14)// -"at the municipal day care they were also open, but they had limited possibility to make changes" (VO, U236)// -"very hard to say since it's the same day care/staff" (WC, S2238); -"there was no noticeable difference when the (municipal) day care transformed to a worker co-op." (WC, S253); -"I was just as satisfied with municipal day care services" (WC, U48).

Many parents who could compare both forms expressed their dissatisfaction with municipal day care services, saying that: -"at the municipal day care you always felt like a stranger and unwelcome, as if you were disturbing and the staff didn't know how to behave among the children if a parents was there" (PC, G22)// -"routines in the municipal (day care) leave no room of parent collaboration" (PC, V203)// -" municipal day care was a night-mare, both for me and my son" (VO, M63); -"the comparison isn't quite fair for the staff at municipal day care, since they work under such great stress" (VO, U26)// -"we couldn't rely on municipal day care services, we were often nervous and stressed, for example we left our crying child to a complete stranger (who was a) substitute" (WC, G1002); -"the staff and co-op are much more service orientated and more interested of the children. At the municipal day care facility there was no dialogue among the staff, nor between the staff and parents, besides the staff (there was) mean" (WC, S2147).

B. Which form is Better?

The advantages of different types of cooperative day care centers are: -"it probably depends on the greater engagement, we are the employers and due to that we can influence more" (PC; M43); -"it's family like, the parents are concerned about each others children, the staff has more fantasy and are more unconventional, it's very positive for me and my child that I as a parent can participate in the activities" (PC, S53)// -"as a parent I can be more involved, the staff listens more to my opinion as a parent and I feel that I have more to say" (VO; M66); -"better since I can influence 'everything' at the co-op. The municipal day care was good if you didn't want to or have the energy to devote your work after work" (VO; S106); however another parents notes "for those of us who choose from a pedagogical profile, the cooperative form is a must, something forced on us. Without that form there is no Waldorf pre-school. We would prefer that all municipal pre-schools had Waldorf pedagogics as their base." (VO; G13)// -"the staff is more secure in their employment and position, they decide how to allocate resources, they feel good, all of which influences the children in a positive sense" (WC, G1006); -"the staff feels better now, they're more flexible and service minded" (WC, S202); -"this was a municipal day care facility before and we were happy then, but now it feels like we can participate and influence our child's day care more directly" (WC, S244); -"our staff has chosen to work together, they feel good together, is catches" (WC, V305); -"it feels more secure with a worker co-op, you're less exposed to the municipal reductions made in all the municipal day care services" (WC, S241); and finally -

"the biggest advantage is small children's groups, sibling groups the environment is nice, more like home (small, few children, quite) no personnel turnover" (WC, S243).

Criticism of municipal services reads: -"in the municipal day care a dramatic decline took place in connection with (financial) reductions" (VO; U26)// - "compared with municipal service where the children went before, this is pure heaven" (WC, G1004); -"before the children and parents existed for the day care center, now it exists to help us. We have good direct contacts with the present staff" (WC, S2147); -"the staff at this day care center try to bring up the children, but the municipal day care facility was just a storage space for the children" (WC, V304). However, parents seeing no difference between cooperative and municipal day care services said: -"no big difference, just as good or better" (PC, G76)// -"no big difference, except for the pedagogics" (VO; U210)// -"we're very satisfied with both types of child care" (WC, S257). Parents expressing preferences in relation to pedagogics state: -"my preference for this day care center is due to the Wandorf pedagogics, not that it's cooperative" (VO; G16)// -"(I prefer) Montessori pedagogics, if there was a Montessori pre-school under municipal guidance I would probably have taken it" (WC, M72).

C. If you could choose again, which form would you choose?

Parents expressed their preference for cooperative day care services in the following fashion: -"possibilities for insights and involvement in this children's daily life is terribly important!, so too the social network the co-op comprises" (PC, G63); -"I'm satisfied and would never change to municipal day care services" (PC, S811); -"possibilities for self-governance and influence and perhaps the best, being able to participate in the child's day at the day care center through daily contact with the staff and other parents" (PC, S101); -"with the involvement in and possibilities for influencing our child's daily life plus the friendship with the staff and other parents that a co-op gives (and that municipal don't give), it's evident that I'd choose the co-op alternative." (PC, V203)// -"I want to be able to be a part of and influence the place where my child spends a large part of the day, through the work obligation you get to know the other children and even the staff better" (VO; S24); -"an invaluable feeling of belonging here, it's 'our' day care service" (VO; S71); -"I want to influence and be a part of (things), parent work = effective quality control" (VO; S710)// -"Yes, the staff is very engaged in making the day care center work well, the parents are satisfied and the atmosphere is good" (WC; S2102); -"Yes, you have more possibility to influence your child's daily life, since a worker co-op must listen more to the wishes of parents too keep the children" (WC; S2106); -"the staff's engagement is considerable greater, the staff ratio is better and the children are at the center of activities" (WC, S2115).

Parents once again expressed criticism of municipal day care services: - "compared with municipal day care facilities, where the children's groups are big, with few staff and no possibility for creative or different activities than staying in the same yard five days a week, the time you 'must' be involved (here) worth every minute" (PC, S84); -"I'd never put my child in municipal day care, primarily due to the large children's groups" (PC; S86); -"I'd definitely choose the same alternative. Moreover, I believe that municipal services should make the space for greater parental involvement" (PC, U13)// -"Yes, everything is being reduced in municipal day care, where you don't have a voice of your own in the activities" (VO; S74); -"Yes, but if municipal day care permitted parental involvement/participation and wasn't subject to reductions we wouldn't have anything against municipal day care service" (VO; U236). However, some parents were also critical of one type of co-op day care service: -"No, we even have school-aged children with parent meetings, lessons, etc., which have been hard to keep up with. It has been a trying but an instructive time, which at times has consumed large part of our free-time, but now we see the end of our day-care period" (PC; J23)// -"No, this co-op is for parents with little need for child care, parents with 'normal' working hours and work find it difficult" (VO; S1324); -"No, too many rules, poor opening hours, long vacations/holidays and intolerance against other opinions" (VO; U229). A clear preference for special pedagogics was once again expressed by some parents. -"our choice was entirely based on pedagogics, thus the co-op form is irrelevant" (VO, G13); -"Yes, Waldorf pedagogics aren't found in municipal day care services" (VO; G14); -"a co-op with this pedagogical profile" (VO; G18).

Some parents with children in worker cooperatives could also compare them with parent co-ops, as they had children in both forms. They expressed a preference for worker co-ops for the following reasons. -"earlier we had our child in a parent co-op day care center. The difference between worker and parent co-ops, according to us, is that it's difficult having the double role as parent and employer in parent co-ops." (WC, S2106); or -"several of us have consciously chosen worker co-op rather than parent co-op day care, just in order to avoid having to sit on the board, responsibility for the staff, being both a parent and manager, etc. It's important that the staff is free towards the parents in situations when the children aren't taken care of well, need support. It's nice not to have to go in as a temporary relief person when one of the staff is sick. We can make greater demands when we don't sit on the board" (WC, S2202).

Exhibit 7 Swedish - English Definitions

barnomsorg: institutionalized child care for children between 0 - 12 years old
barnskötare: pre-school assistant
daghem: a day care center, which provides institutionalized pedagogical activities for children between the age of 0 - 6 years old to parents who work or are studying
daghemsavdelning: day care center section or unit
dagmamma: day care mother, an approved provider of small scale day care services at her home, also referred to as *familjedaghem*
enskild daghem: private or non-municipal day care center
familjedaghem: family day care, institutionalized pre-school activities for children between the ages of 0-6 years old in the home of the provider of the services
fritidshem: recreation center or "after-school home" for children between the ages of six/seven to 12 years old, in practice children seldom go beyond the age of 10 years old or the third grade
fritidspedagog: recreation instructor or youth teacher
förskola: pre-school activities comprised of institutionalized child care; i.e., day care, part-time groups and family day care for children under six years old, i.e., a pre school
förskollärare: pre-school teacher
förskolebarn: pre-school children six years old or less
huvudman: responsible agency
icke-kommunl barnomsorg: child care run by other than the municipal authorities
sexårs verksamhet: pre-school activities for six year olds, a newly established form of pre-school activities for children who are six year old, sometimes called a "zero class" or a *fritidshem*
Socialstyrelsen: the National Board of Health and Welfare
verksamhet: activities or a facility
verksamhetsform: type of day care